Camilo José Cela Revisited: The Later Novels

Twayne's World Authors Series

Arthur Kinney, Editor

University of Massachusetts, Amherst

TWAS 891

CAMILO JOSÉ CELA
CORBIS/Colita

Camilo José Cela Revisited: The Later Novels

Janet Pérez

Texas Tech University

Twayne Publishers
New York

Twayne's World Authors Series No. 891

Camilo José Cela Revisited: The Later Novels
Janet Pérez

Twayne Publishers
1633 Broadway
New York, NY 10019

Library of Congress Cataloging-in-Publication Data

Pérez, Janet.
     Camilo José Cela revisited : the later novels / Janet Pérez.
        p.   cm.—(Twayne's world authors series ; TWAS 891)
     Includes bibliographical references and index.
     ISBN 0-8057-1640-8 (alk. paper)
     1. Cela, Camilo José, 1916—Criticism and interpretation. I. Series.

  PQ6605.E44 Z783 2000
  863'.64—dc21   00-030268

This paper meets the requirements of ANSI/NISO Z3948-1992 (Permanence of Paper).

10 9 8 7 6 5 4 3 2 1

Printed in the United States of America

For Kevin

Contents

Preface   *ix*
Acknowledgments   *xiii*
Chronology   *xv*

Chapter One
Cela's Life and Works   1

Chapter Two
Memoir, Self-Portrait, Autobiographical Novel   19

Chapter Three
Antecedents and Echoes   37

Chapter Four
One Week in July: *San Camilo, 1936*   51

Chapter Five
Midnight Mass: *Oficio de tinieblas*   69

Chapter Six
Dance of Death: *Mazurca para dos muertos*   86

Chapter Seven
A Trip to Arizona: *Cristo versus Arizona*   104

Chapter Eight
The Return of Pascual Duarte: *El asesinato del perdedor*   123

Chapter Nine
Death and Disintegration in Galicia: *La cruz de San Andrés*   140

Chapter Ten
Summary and Conclusions   154

Notes and References   *161*
Selected Bibliography   *173*
Index   *179*

Preface

This volume's title, suggested by the publishers, implies both an antecedent (D. W. McPheeters's 1969 Twayne book, *Camilo José Cela*) and a focus: those novels not included in the earlier study, which—in common with most monographs dedicated to Cela—concentrated on his first two decades as a writer (1942–1962), emphasizing the first half-dozen novels. Many early studies cover only through *La Catira* (1955; The Redhead), and McPheeters paid relatively less attention to *Tobogán de hambrientos* (1962; Toboggan of the Starving), a curious variant of the antinovel, which many scholars have failed or refused to recognize as belonging to the novel genre. Published in fairly rapid succession and covering a scant decade—three in the 1940s, three between 1950 and 1955—the first six novels exhibit significant common aesthetic features despite formal differences and possess a constantly reiterated nucleus of obsessive themes. After *La Catira*'s negative reception, Cela's focus changed from the novel to lesser genres, with much of his writing directed to the collectors' market. For several years, he produced high-priced nonfiction (plus some brief fiction) in limited editions, along with varied works of erudition.

With *San Camilo, 1936* (1969), Cela's long-anticipated novel about the Spanish civil war, the novelist enters a second phase of "serious" novelistic production that (in comparison with his first quarter century) has received comparatively little scrutiny. The 14-year hiatus between *La Catira* and *San Camilo* (in which Cela published no long fiction excepting *Tobogán*) constitutes a de facto division of his novels into two periods. During the interim, literary scholars began to treat his novelistic career as having ended or at least defined itself with the half-dozen early titles; consequently, de facto divisions also occur in the critical corpus.

Cela's chronological pattern of publication naturally demarcates "early" and "later" periods in his novelistic production, with *Tobogán* standing between two approximately equal halves. The first half was covered by McPheeters, whose 1969 study coincided with the publication of *San Camilo, 1936* (which initiates Cela's second period). Partial reform of censorship with Spain's new "Press Law" in the late 1960s allowed writers more freedom, possibly accounting for some "increased license" perceived in *San Camilo* and characterizing the second period as a whole. Meanwhile a major aesthetic change began during the 1960s with the decline of "social literature," the essentially neorealist and neo-naturalist mode of most of Cela's early novels. The so-called New Novel succeeding the "social novel" fits an eclectic model, reviving not only surrealism and Vanguardist experimentalism but also lexical and syntactic aspects of the baroque. Novels of the Latin American "boom" provide important input, as do imported techniques and structures from influential novelists of European and American modernism (visible in *San Camilo*). Neo-baroque, neo-surrealist, neo-Vanguardist, Spain's New Novel becomes increasingly postmodern, the same trajectory traced in Cela's evolution. Thus aesthetic as well as chronological distance separates Cela's later novels from their predecessors. Constant themes and motifs notwithstanding, and despite aspects of style and technique characterizing both periods, sufficient historical and aesthetic reasons exist to justify separate treatment of Cela's later period and for comparing the two halves of his novelistic production.

Between 1969 and 1999, Cela published six long novels, some 15 collections of short fiction, numerous essays, several dramatic works, various volumes of erudition, and miscellany. Much has transpired in the last three decades of the century, bringing major changes to Spain—and to Cela. The death of long-term dictator Francisco Franco in November 1975 and Spain's return to a constitutional monarchy began the transition to democracy, with the first national elections in 40 years held in 1978. That year's final day saw the official abolition of governmental censorship. Cela was named a senator by King Juan Carlos in 1977 and, in addition to new political activities, increased his participation in Galician cultural affairs. Under the monarchy, long-suppressed regional cultures and literatures have flowered, with publishing explosions in the vernacular languages (especially Catalan, Galician, and Basque). With Galicia's cultural revival, Cela was inducted into the Royal Galician Academy (1980), strengthening ties to his native region—and also impacting later novels.

Cela's ambiguous relationship with the Franco regime, its censorship, and its cultural establishment resulted in long denial of official recognition. That, too, has changed, and in 1984 he received the National Prize for Literature, followed in 1987 by the Prince of Asturias Literary Prize. Two years later, international fame came with his receipt of the 1989 Nobel Prize for literature, and in 1993, the Andrés Bello Medal from Venezuela. Last but by no means least is the prestigious Cervantes Prize, awarded by consensus of the Association of Academies of the Spanish Language in 21 Spanish-speaking countries (including the United States, where Spanish is the second language). The Cervantes Prize, won by Cela in 1995, recognizes a writer's lifetime work and is the highest literary honor available to those writing in Spanish. These significant developments since 1969 constitute further justification for studying Cela's life and work during the three decades thereafter.

The present study briefly surveys Cela's life and works, examining recent autobiographical and biographical publications in more detail than earlier ones. The early novels, seen from today's vantage point, are revisited as antecedents for his later period, with relevance to Cela's poetics noted. Excepting *Madera de boj* (Boxwood), published when the present volume was already in press, later novels are studied individually and in relation to the writer's corpus as a whole, in the context of antecedents and of relevant developments in the contemporary Spanish novel. Certain of Cela's nonfiction works receive comment when they shed light on his personal beliefs, loyalties, or aesthetic practices. My goal is to read Cela's difficult, complex postmodern later novels in relation to his total novelistic development and experimentation, his personal idiosyncrasies, and relevant statements of values, drawing on overall context for illumination.

Acknowledgments

I gratefully acknowledge assistance from the Office of the Provost of Texas Tech University via the Horn Professor Fund, and from the Inter-library Loan staff of Texas Tech University Library.

Very special thanks are due to my husband for his long-suffering patience during the completion of this project.

Chronology

1916   May 11: Camilo José Cela born at Iria Flavia (La Coruña), Galicia, Spain.

1921–1924   Primary schools in Vigo, with various religious orders.

1925   Family moves to Madrid.

1933   Completes secondary studies.

1934   First hospitalization for tuberculosis. Attends classes at Central University of Madrid; befriended by Pedro Salinas.

1935   First poems appear in *El Argentino* (daily of La Plata, Argentina).

1936   Spanish civil war begins 18 July. Writes poems later published as *Pisando la dudosa luz del día.*

1937   Escapes from besieged Madrid to join Nationalist army, serving in infantry regiment of Bailén (Logroño).

1938   Wounded; hospitalized in Logroño. Upon discharge, goes to Galicia.

1939   Discharged from army and returns to Madrid. Begins to study law.

1940   First articles appear; begins writing *La familia de Pascual Duarte.*

1941   First short stories published; second hospitalization for tuberculosis.

1942   First novel, *La familia de Pascual Duarte,* appears.

1943   Second edition of *La familia de Pascual Duarte* confiscated by censors. *Pabellón de reposo* (novel) published.

1944   Marries María del Rosaro Conde Picavea on 12 March. Publishes *Nuevas andanzas y desventuras de Lazarillo de Tormes* (novel).

1945   Publishes *Esas nubes que pasan* (stories), *Mesa revuelta* (essays), and *Pisando la dudosa luz del día* (poetry).

1946   Only son, Camilo José Cela Conde, born 17 January. Summer walking tour of La Alcarria region.

1947   Publishes *El bonito crimen del carabinero y otras invenciones* (stories).

1948   *Viaje a la Alcarria* (travel literature) and *Cancionero de la Alcarria* (poems) appear.

1949   *El gallego y su cuadrilla y otros apuntes carpetovetónicos* (stories) published.

1951   *La colmena* (novel) prohibited in Spain, appears in Buenos Aires.

1952   Travels to Argentina and Chile. Publishes *Del Miño al Bidasoa* and *Avila* (travel); *Timoteo el incomprendido* and *Santa Balbina 37, gas en cada piso* (novelettes).

1953   *Baraja de invenciones* (stories), *Café de artistas* (novelette), and *Mrs. Caldwell habla con su hijo* (novel) appear.

1954   Begins residence in Palma, Majorca. Lectures in England. Publishes *Ensueños y figuraciones.*

1955   *La Catira* (novel) appears; third trip to Latin America.

1956   Publishes *Judíos, moros y cristianos* (travel), *El molino de viento y otras novelas cortas* (novelettes), and *Mis páginas preferidas* (anthology). Begins publishing monthly, *Papeles de Son Armadans,* in Palma.

1957   Initiated into Royal Academy of the Spanish Language 26 May. Publishes *Cajón de sastre* (miscellany), *Recuerdo de Don Pío Baroja* and *La obra literaria del pintor Solana* (criticism), *Nuevo retablo de don Cristobita* (stories), *La rueda de los ocios* (travel), and *Historias de España: Los ciegos, los tontos* (vignettes).

1958   Two trips to France; begins friendship with Picasso.

1959   Publishes *Primer viaje andaluz* (travel), and *La rosa,* first volume of *La cucaña* (memoirs).

1960   *Los viejos amigos,* first series (vignettes), *Cuaderno del Guadarrama* (travel), and *Cuatro figuras del '98* (criticism) appear.

1961   *Los viejos amigos,* second series.

1962 *Tobogán de hambrientos* (antinovel), *Gavilla de fábulas sin amor* (illustrated by Picasso), and first volume of *Obras completas* appear. Spanish publication of *La colmena* authorized.

1963 *Garito de hospicianos, Las compañías convenientes, El solitario y los sueños de Rafael Zabaleta, Toreo de salón,* and *Once cuentos de fútbol* (miscellany) appear.

1964 Lectures in United States, receiving honorary doctorate from Syracuse University in June. *Izas, rabizas y colipoterras* (photography and social commentary), and *Obras completas,* volume 2, published.

1965 Visits Havana. *Viaje al Pirineo de Lérida* and *Páginas de geografía errabunda* (travel), *El ciudadano Iscariote Reclús, A la pata de palo* (miscellany), and *María Sabina* (first drama). *Nuevas escenas matritenses,* volumes 1 and 2 (photographic commentary), and *Obras completas,* volumes 3 and 4, appear.

1966 *Nuevas escenas matritenses,* volumes 3–7, and *Obras completas,* volume 5, published.

1967 *Viaje a USA* (festive verse). Commemorates 25th anniversary of *Pascual Duarte.*

1968 *Diccionario secreto,* volume 1 (erudition) and *El carro de heno o el inventor de la guillotina* (play). *Obras completas,* volume 6.

1969 Publishes *San Camilo, 1936,* initiating "later novels." *La bandada de palomas* and *Al servicio de algo* (essays). McPheeters publishes *Camilo José Cela.*

1970 *María Sabina* performed in Carnegie Hall. *Barcelona* appears.

1971 Cela publishes *Diccionario secreto,* volume 2; *Cinco glosas a otras tantas verdades de la silueta que un hombre trazó a sí mismo* and *La Mancha en el corazón y en los ojos.*

1972 *La bola del mundo* (articles) appears.

1973 Publishes *Oficio de tinieblas, 5* (second of "later novels"), *A vueltas con España* (essays), *El tacatá oxidado* (miscellany), and *Balada del vagabundo sin suerte y otros papeles volanderos* (reedited stories).

1974   *Cuentos para leer después del baño* (stories).

1976   Begins publication of *Enciclopedia del erotismo;* publishes *Rol de cornudos.*

1977   Cela named senator by King Juan Carlos I; works on text of Constitution and campaigns for democratic government.

1979   *Los sueños vanos, los ángeles curiosos.*

1980   Royal Galician Academy inducts Cela, strengthening ties with Galicia.

1981   *Vuelta de hoja* (articles) and *Los vasos comunicantes* (essays) published.

1983   *Mazurca para dos muertos* (novel) and *El juego de los tres madroños* (essays). Announces work on projected novel, *Madera de boj.*

1984   *Mazurca* receives National Prize for Literature.

1987   Prince of Asturias Literary Prize awarded to Cela.

1989   Receives Nobel Prize for literature.

1993   *Memorias, entendimientos y voluntades* (autobiography) appears; *El huevo del juicio* (essays). Receives Andrés Bello Medal from Venezuelan president.

1994   *El asesinato del perdedor* and *La cruz de San Andrés* (novels) published. *La dama pájara* (stories). *La cruz* receives Planeta Prize.

1995   Cela wins the Cervantes Prize.

1998   *¡A bote pronto!* (essays) published.

1999   *Madera de boj* (novel) published.

Chapter One
Cela's Life and Works

Camilo José Cela Trulock (whose full name is Camilo José Manuel Juan Ramón Francisco Santiago de Cela)[1] was born on 11 May 1916 in the village of Iria Flavia del Padrón in the northwest coastal province of La Coruña, part of the now autonomous region of Galicia. Galicia was colonized in prehistoric times by a series of Celtic migrations, supposedly from North Africa. Celtic settlers mixed with indigenous Iberians without losing many peculiar cultural and physical traits marking the Celts' present-day descendants in Ireland and Scotland, including their huge monoliths associated with heliocentric cults, the characteristic bagpipes, and numerous similar legends, superstitions, and witchcraft. Unlike the residents of other parts of Spain, and differing from stereotypes of "Spaniards" widely held abroad, many Galicians are tall, large boned, and fair skinned, with green or gray eyes and reddish hair. Seacoast areas typically suffer successive waves of occupation and conquest, and Galicia came under Roman control before the Christian Era (Iria Flavia still preserves its Roman name unchanged). Roman bridges dot the countryside, a large number of them still in use today, and near the port of La Coruña stands a legendary Roman lighthouse known as the Tower of Hercules. Various relevant details appear in several of Cela's short stories, in his most recent novel, *La cruz de San Andrés* (1994; St. Andrew's Cross), and in another major novel set in Galicia, *Mazurca para dos muertos* (1983; *Mazurka for Two Dead Men,* 1992).[2]

Cela's Family and Youth

Curiously, Cela and his parents all share the same first name. His maternal grandparents were of English and Italian origin, and his mother, Camila Emanuela Trulock y Bertorini, held English nationality until her marriage. One Italian great-grandfather was allegedly governor of Parma, Italy. D. W. McPheeters affirms that the Trulock British forebears were of Cornish origin,[3] another Celtic strain; he compares Cela's physical type and blunt outspokenness to a Welsh acquaintance (16). Both Cela's maternal grandfather, John Trulock, and great-grandfather

Bertorini were associated with the West Galician Railway, and Cela's grandmother's home, where he spent much of his childhood, stands close by the railroad track. The second volume of Cela's memoirs, *Memorias, entendimientos y voluntades* (1993; Memories, Understandings, and Wills) mentions his desire to build a museum celebrating railways and his grandfathers.[4] His father, Camilo Cela y Fernández, was a customs officer then assigned in Galicia; his career necessitated various moves, but the paternal family had strong roots in Galicia, to which he returned whenever possible. Another paternal relative (the exact nature of the relationship is vague), Juan Jacobo Fernández, reportedly beatified in the Catholic Church by Pope Pius XI, figures repeatedly in Cela's memoirs, *La rosa* (1959; The Rose), and in *Mazurca*.

The future writer was the eldest of a numerous family, of which at least seven children lived to adulthood and two or more died in infancy. In childhood Cela's health was delicate, and this apparently abetted his poetic sensitivity. He received a traditional Catholic education in private schools, first in Galicia, then in Madrid, where his family moved in 1925. He was not merely an indifferent student but, by his own account, prone to tantrums, heavy-handed pranks, and fighting, as a result of which he was expelled from one school after another (*Memorias,* 18, 37, 55, 56). Among those he lists as having requested that he not return are a primary school in Vigo run by the Sisters of St. Joseph de Cluny, a Jesuit elementary school in Vigo, and a Marist school in Madrid where he began his *bachillerato* (high school equivalency), attending from 1927 to 1932. McPheeters states that Cela graduated from "the Instituto de San Isidro of the Marist fathers" (16), but there is some confusion here: the *Instituto* is typically public; furthermore, Cela recounts in *Memorias* that he was "unfairly" expelled by the Marists for another prank around the end of his fourth year (55), being blacklisted by the friars, with the result that "they wouldn't take me anywhere. My father, not knowing what else to do, hired a tutor for me" (56). Cela's father was then running a preparatory academy for young men planning careers in the Customs Service; unable to enroll his son elsewhere, he began accepting secondary school students so that the future writer could finish his diploma equivalency. Both Charlebois (2) and McPheeters (chronology) state that Cela graduated from high school in 1933 and suffered his first serious bout of tuberculosis in 1934, being hospitalized in a sanatorium in the Guadarrama Mountains, north of Madrid. This experience, together with two or more subsequent hospitalizations for tuberculosis, prompted the later genesis of his second novel, *Pabellón de reposo* (1943; *Rest Home*, 1961).

Various legends exist concerning Cela's early life, perhaps the earliest alleging childhood visits to, and stays in, England (cited in numerous biographical sketches, and repeated by McPheeters {17} and Charlebois {2}). Other family members dispute these stories, including his brother Jorge, and "[a]necdotes about his life—apocryphal or otherwise—are innumerable, and require being sorted out by an attentive biographer. . . . a good deal of Cela's work involves confusion . . . between the real and imaginary biography of Cela himself."[5] One example appears in *La rosa,* where Cela describes visiting an aunt in England, although his later, more definitive *Memorias* mentions no such trips, and the biography by his son, Cela Conde, recounts anecdotes illustrating his father's total lack of familiarity with even the most elementary English.[6] Among Cela's immediate Galician literary forebears was Ramón del Valle-Inclán—a writer Cela much admired—who created various fanciful autobiographical legends about himself. Similarly, Vanguard writers and artists (e.g., Ramón Gómez de la Serna and Salvador Dalí) created colorful public images cloaking their true selves, and Cela apparently did likewise. Further confusion exists concerning Cela the man, his personality, his values, and the thrust of his work, making it important to read more than his often hermetic fiction, especially the dark, cruel, and violent novels. Cela has an unexpected comic side, best illustrated by his own *Memorias* and numerous anecdotes recounted by Cela Conde; his sensitive, humane, and ethical aspects are seldom revealed or even suggested in his "creative" writings, although essays and newspaper articles are sometimes more open concerning feelings and beliefs. Not all should be taken literally, but several other sources of biographical information exist.[7]

Young Adulthood

Around his 18th birthday, while convalescing after his release from the first tuberculosis sanatorium, Cela read the 70-volume classical collection *Biblioteca de Autores Españoles* from *A* to *Z,* acquiring exceptional education concerning early Spanish authors. He also perused major contemporary Spanish and foreign writers, and henceforth, names of writers proliferate in his memoirs, alongside those of young women. Cela relates that before finishing high school, he wanted to be a poet, but his parents insisted he study a profession to keep from starving. By 1934 he was obsessed with the uncertain, bohemian lifestyle, dreaming of becoming a writer, viewing security as boredom and monotony. McPheeters mentions "trips to England and France" (19) before Cela's beginning to study medicine, but *Memorias*—which is extraordinarily detailed, including minutiae, daily headlines, current entertainment, and obituaries—omits all mention of foreign travel—as well as medical school. Cela entered Madrid's Central University (1934–1935), hoping to study literature, but had officially to enroll in law, given paternal insistence. Disinterest notwithstanding, he acquired a respectable understanding of the Civil Code (a background bearing on aspects of *El asesinato del perdedor* (1994; Murder of the Loser). He associated with other aspiring writers, befriending others who were already becoming established: Miguel Hernández, María Zambrano, Julián Marías, to name a few. Most significantly, Cela came under the influence of the philosophy and writings of José Ortega y Gasset (Spain's intellectual leader of the day) and attended literature classes taught by Pedro Salinas (1891–1951)—already a well-known poet—who became his mentor. Cela considers Salinas decisive in his commitment to a writing career. Several chapters of Cela's *Memorias* depict the excitement of Madrid under the Second Republic, its intellectual ferment, rich cultural environment, theatrical events, new books, writers, and political figures, evoked against the ominous background of growing political undercurrents and social unrest. Cela began writing during this period, initially poetry, and on 30 September 1935, his first poems were published in *El Argentino* (daily of La Plata, Argentina).

Desirous of studying literature ("Filosofía y Letras"), then deemed a "major for young ladies," Cela eventually compromised with his parents, agreeing to attend his father's Customs Academy and prepare for the professional examinations while also attending literature classes (without formal university enrollment). Major thinkers whose classes he attended included Ortega y Gasset, Xavier Zubiri, García Morente, plus eminent intellectuals and critics Américo Castro, Ramón Menéndez Pidal, José Montesinos, and others. Dozens of the great and near-great of Ortega's generation populate Cela's *Memorias,* together with poets of the younger "Generation of 1927," including Federico García Lorca, Rafael Alberti, and 1978 Nobel Prize winner Vicente Aleixandre. At this time, Cela became enthralled with surrealism, as evinced in his first poetry collection, *Pisando la dudosa luz del día* (Treading Doubtful Daylight), composed partially during bombardments of Madrid in the early months of the civil war (1936–1939) but unpublished until 1945. The title (an intertextual allusion to baroque poet Góngora) reveals another influence, and Cela records his contemporaneous discovery of works by Pablo Neruda, then attached to the Chilean consulate in Madrid.

Zamora Vicente, an eminent present-day critic and Cela's longtime friend (then part of his circle of aspiring writers), recalls that

> our generation read [James] Joyce before the English themselves, who had prohibited him. Dámaso Alonso's translation of *Portrait of the Artist as a Young Man* was totally familiar to all of us. And *Ulysses* we read in French translation . . . we read it as we walked to campus in the same way that we became acquainted with Proust and Valéry. And my year-book that year reflects contact with Sartre.[8]

Zamora Vicente cites Dos Passos, Faulkner, and French writers Gide, Maritain, Mauriac, and Bernanos among important readings for their group (1997, 30–31). Spain's "Vanguard years" (late 1920s and early 1930s) thus had more lasting impact on Cela than usually recognized. Echoes of these readings appear in such major works as *La colmena* (1951; *The Hive,* 1953), reflecting Dos Passos, and *San Camilo, 1936* (1969), echoing Joyce and Faulkner, and so on. Perhaps the most profound and enduring impact, however, was that of surrealism. Numerous anecdotes concerning "scandalous" behavior throughout the writer's career attest to his identification with the surrealists' delight in paradox and the unconventional, their mocking of rational thought and conformity, and the movement's desire to shock the bourgeoisie. The most surrealist of Cela's mature works is *Oficio de tinieblas, 5* (1973; *Office of Darkness*), with its suppression of rational connections, but surrealist traces already pervade his early poetry, fill the pages of *Mrs. Caldwell habla con su hijo* (1953; *Mrs. Caldwell Speaks to Her Son,* 1968), and dominate several novels of the 1980s and 1990s.

Like various writers from romanticism hence, Cela deliberately contributed to creating a mythified persona blending the apocryphal and playful, and his controversial public image sometimes challenged conservative values, surrounding him with polemics. The cover blurb of *Cela, mi padre* cites difficulties in separating the "real Cela" from his public image:

> This prolific and gifted author has surrounded himself with an aura of *casticismo* [ultra-Spanishness], originality, and sometimes uncontrolled humor, befitting a being [who is] as fascinating as he is difficult to clas-

sify. None of that, however, has helped us understand much of the life and work of this still unknown protagonist of our best literature. (Cela Conde, n.p.)

Nowhere are misunderstanding and controversy more evident than in the area of Cela's ideological development and related activities during the war and early postwar period (he remained largely silent until telling his still-cryptic version in the 1993 *Memorias*). As Cela Conde observes, Cela's ideological position is "one of the mysteries best guarded by the writer. Some keys are as evident as they are banal: his scorn for politics . . . his extreme individualism, his conversion to Monarchist. But that, with varying shades, is the standard portrait of practically any Spaniard today" (211).

The War Years

The date the civil war erupted, 18 July, was ironically the day of St. Camillus of Lelis, the saint's day for Cela, his mother, and father. This saint, as Cela reminds readers in the front matter of *San Camilo, 1936*, his first major work about the civil war, is the "celestial patron of hospitals." Cela had just turned 20, but his tuberculosis initially disqualified him for military service. The country was quickly split into two zones, with the rebels under General Franco (who had crossed the border from Portugal) occupying the western portion. Madrid and areas to the east remained under the Republic. In many ways, the Spanish civil war of 1936 to 1939 continued a struggle begun more than a century before between liberals and conservatives, between those anxious for change and reforms and those wanting to preserve the status quo. Supporting Franco were some enormously powerful groups: the church hierarchy (which before the Republic began its land reforms was the country's largest landowner, possessing nearly one-third of the land), most of the military establishment, the hereditary aristocracy, and Spain's major capitalists. The country's small middle class (including most intellectuals) joined with the working class in supporting the Republic, making the Loyalists numerically superior, although they lacked military training and technology. Spain's civil war, deemed a "dress rehearsal for World War II," ultimately pitted the Fascist troops of Germany and Italy against leftists and Russian Communists on Spanish soil. The war—which gained unenviable distinction as the first in which aerial bombings were used against civilian populations—divided families, son against father and brother against brother, creating deep rifts still unhealed four decades later. A major literary event of this or any century, the Spanish civil war inspired more than 12,000 works (in all genres) in Spain alone and left traces on many of Cela's writings. During the war's final weeks, he was with Franco's Nationalist troops in Torremejía, the town where—as Cela relates in *Memorias*—he "met" the protagonist of his first novel, *La familia de Pascual Duarte* (1942; *Pascual Duarte and His Family,* 1965). War's immediate aftermath appears in *La colmena,* Cela's second most celebrated novel. Besides the war's first days, depicted in *San Camilo, 1936,* Cela presents a mythic version of the war in Galicia in *Mazurca* and portrays its lasting psychological damage and fragmentation in *Oficio de tinieblas.*

Regarding Cela's wartime experiences, McPheeters says laconically that the future writer was "[e]vacuated through Valencia on the British relief ship 'Maine,' [and] accepted for duty by the Nationalist forces after his health improved" (19), adding that he was wounded in 1938. Cela, who devotes nearly 200 pages of *Memorias* (121–299) to the period between 18 July 1936 and 1 April 1939, provides another version amid personal recollections of the war's effect on his family, friends, relatives, and acquaintances. He remembers 18 July especially in relation to his lover, "Toisha" Vargas, whom he planned to "marry" that day in a semiserious nude ceremony invented by his friend Ibarra. Their erotically intense relationship ended when she was killed during a bombardment on 1 November 1936, when the Franco forces had already reached Madrid's outskirts. Cela re-creates their final encounter, with the two young lovers descending opposite sides of a small stream, when an *obus* (mortar) shell landed on Toisha, blowing her to bits. He found one of her eyes and kept it for a few days in a flask before disposing of it in the kitchen stove (*Memorias,* 140–41). A poem expressing his grief at Toisha's death appears in *Pisando la dudosa luz del día,* identified by her initials.

Cela recounts that his parents' home was searched 33 times between September and December 1936 as Leftist extremists sought Franco sympathizers (*Memorias,* 139). He describes events affecting residents of their apartment building at Claudio Coello, 91 (including incidents involving servants and relatives of neighbors), with various descriptive passages strongly resembling his antinovel *Tobogán de hambrientos.* He evokes political assassinations and reprisals (150–56), mentioning fugitives taking refuge in foreign embassies, and offering a surrealist description of terror (151). Early published references to Cela's wartime activities stated that he was "mobilized" into the Franco forces (language usually meaning that draft-age men in conquered areas could "choose" between joining the Nationalists and being shot). *Memorias* describes how in July 1937 Cela attempted to escape Madrid's hunger, bombings, and terrorism, obtaining a pass to Valencia, where he intended to board a British ship for Marseilles, but was detained. Escaping amid confusion the following day, he returned to Madrid, hitching a ride in an ambulance (154–61). Two months later, on 1 October 1937, his second attempt succeeded; he reached Marseilles and boarded a train for Hendaye on the French-Spanish border, where he entered the Nationalist zone (161–71), declared that he had come to join Franco, and was sent to the Logroño barracks.[9]

Subsequent pages portray his progressive disillusionment with military life while detailing special treatment he received at successive posts thanks to officials acquainted with his grandparents, parents, or relatives. Of his ideological position, he remarks:

> I had nothing to do with anybody, maybe I was mistaken, but I wanted to save my life . . . the two sides were more or less equally likable, these less distasteful for one reason, those for another. I felt intellectually left-ist—you couldn't say that in the Nationalist zone—and socially conservative—you couldn't say that in the "Red" zone—and politically liberal (and that you couldn't say on either side). (*Memorias,* 190)

That same month, Cela was wounded by bomb fragments while resting beside a truck, and he was hospitalized in Logroño (an episode echoed in *Mazurca*). Upon his release, he traveled to León, where an uncle placed him in an inn serving abundant meals (203–9), and in February 1938 he went to his grandmother's house in Iria. "In Galicia, except for mourning the dead . . . everything was abundance and comfort" (212). He spent the rest of 1938 in Galicia, mostly in the luxurious home of cousins in La Coruña (corresponding pages of *Memorias* {215–24] shed light on characters and incidents in *Mazurca*). In January 1939, he traveled via Zaragoza to Extremadura; firsthand experiences there were literarily transformed in *Pascual Duarte*. After resting in Torremejía, Cela's group was ordered to Levante, where he nearly drowned in a swimming accident (*Memorias,* 290), initiating another hospitalization in Castellón during the war's final chaotic days (Charlebois's chronology confuses and combines this with the hospitalization in Logroño). "We learned about the fall of Madrid from prisoners, we never had much information about happenings. I asked the captain's permission to go find my family" (*Memorias*, 295).

The Early Postwar Years

Cela attained legal maturity on his 23d birthday, according to statutes of the day, and was also released from military status. Recalling his saint's day in July 1939, he associates it with the Nationalists' burning of libraries in Madrid, noting that books by philosopher María Zambrano, plus others by Pablo Neruda that Cela had loaned to Zambrano, were burned outside her home (where he had frequently attended prewar gatherings). The Cela family went to Galicia to recuperate from wartime privations. Return to normalcy found them with many debts, and Cela was again hospitalized for tuberculosis, this time in Hoyo de Manzanares. McPheeters affirms that Cela "immediately began the study of law, only to abandon it after three years and some courses of the fourth and fifth years" (20); Cela omits details but mentions "vegetating in the huge old [former university] building on San Bernardo while studying law" (*Memorias*, 327) and working thereafter as a clerk in the National Textile Syndicate—a job he describes as "second from the bottom, after the doorman." Today that position is memorable only because Cela began writing *La familia de Pascual Duarte* to combat boredom in the office. He also wrote for newspapers and took a position with the censorship: "I didn't go to the censors' office much . . . around midmorning, and not every day. I'd smoke a cigarette, put seals on the galleys placed before me, and then leave for the editorial offices of *El Español* or *La Estafeta* [literary periodicals]" (333). In a 1989 interview, Cela explains that the publications that were most censored were newspapers or periodicals with a possible political bent. Allowed to choose the publications for which he would be responsible, he selected clearly apolitical ones: *Farmacia Nueva* (New Pharmacy), *Boletín del Colegio de Huérfanos de Ferroviarios* (Bulletin of the School for Orphans of Railroad Workers), and *El mensajero del Corazón de Jesús* (Messenger of the Sacred Heart of Jesus).[10]

Cela skips rather quickly over 1940, 1941, and 1942, suggesting that these were the least-happy years of his life, although he was thankful to be alive. The relevant chapter "My First Article, First Lecture, First Story" emphasizes his literary beginnings. His first article, "Photographs of Countess [Emilia] Pardo Bazán," appeared in February

1940, and his first short story, "Don Anselmo," was published in *Medina* (a weekly of the women's section of the Falange) on 24 April 1941 (interview 1989), although McPheeters, Charlebois, and others say that Cela's first published story was "Marcelo Brito." *Memorias* (335) indicates that he received PTA 75 for "Don Anselmo"—PTA 68.25 after withholding—hardly a princely sum, but remuneration nonetheless. Other stories, published in succeeding months, were eventually anthologized.

Cela became seriously ill in late 1941, and believing that he had little time to live, on 6 January 1942, "I asked my mother for the notebooks where I was writing [*Pascual Duarte*]; I couldn't even get out of bed" (*Memorias,* 336). He quickly drafted the letters with which the novel ends, not wishing to leave it incomplete if he died, and soon afterward found himself hospitalized again, this time in the tuberculosis sanatorium of Dr. Valdés Lambea. *Pascual Duarte* achieved considerable notoriety, despite censorial prohibition ordering that the work be withdrawn from circulation a few months later. Pascual's neo-naturalistic "confession," the autobiography of a convicted murderer awaiting execution, abounds in shocking violence. It spawned numerous would-be imitators, a "movement" termed *tremendismo* because of the "tremendous" impact on readers (Cela steadfastly refused to be associated with either the term or the vogue). Around February 1943, he began writing *Pabellón de reposo,* a very different, almost lyric second novel, painting the monotonous solitude of tubercular patients forgotten and left to die. His accumulation of materials for what would eventually become *La colmena* also commenced at this time. Cela's health improved, and his life became more settled following his marriage on 12 March 1944 to his longtime fiancée, María del Rosario Conde Picavea, "Charo," who for some four decades rendered indispensable service as Cela's secretary. Also in 1944, he published his third novel, *Nuevas andanzas y desventuras de Lazarillo de Tormes* (New Adventures and Misfortunes of Lazarillo de Tormes), an updated spin-off of Hurtado de Mendoza's sixteenth-century picaresque classic, *La vida de Lazarillo de Tormes.* Critics began taking Cela more seriously; his visibility increased, and with growing demand, story anthologies and article collections were published in 1945 (*Esas nubes que pasan* [Those Passing Clouds] and *Mesa revuelta* [Messy Desk]).

His only child, Camilo José, was born on 17 January 1946, and during the following summer Cela began a series of walking tours that would produce several travel books. The first, *Viaje a la Alcarria* (1947;

Journey to the Alcarria), is still considered one of his best contributions to the travel genre, which—like the picaresque—he modified, adding his own idiosyncratic perspective and already unmistakable style. Like other postwar writers (e.g., Armando López-Salinas, Antonio Ferres, and Juan Goytisolo in the following decade), Cela made subversive use of the travel genre, visiting not famous monuments or tourist sites but some of the country's most forsaken areas, thereby covertly indicting governmental policies that relegated poorer regions to oblivion. From 1947 through 1950, the family began spending summers in the village of Cebreros, a hot, dry region in the lower part of Avila province, where Cela initiated his "carpetovetonic sketches," a variant of the narrative genre that he invented, comprising wry chronicles of minutiae, insepara-bly linked with scenes of these arid lands (the name alludes to one of Spain's five central mountain ranges). Initially published in newspapers, these vignettes were not collected until the 1965 edition of Cela's *Obras completas* (Complete Works, vol. 3), although some appeared in *El gallego y su cuadrilla y otros apuntes carpetovetónicos* (1951; The Galician and His Troupe and Other Carpetovetonic Sketches), which reprinted stories from prior anthologies, adding previously uncollected tales. Summer stays in Cebreros are noteworthy also because there in 1948 Cela wrote one of the five drafts of *La colmena* at a borrowed, marble-topped café table. In this humble, backward, impoverished environment, Cela's social conscience developed, and he identified profoundly with the vil-lagers and peasants. Also during summer 1948, the Madrid daily *Pueblo* commissioned him to tour the provinces and report on hostels for vaca-tioning workers, resulting in a book detailing Cela's foot travels in Gali-cia, *Del Miño al Bidasoa* (1952; From the Miño [River] to the Bidasoa).

Having decided to live entirely from his writing—a difficult under-taking in Spain—Cela sometimes endured the penury his father had foreseen. Both Cela's memoirs and his son's biography recount anec-dotes of financial hardship before fame and success arrived. A turning point came with the publication of *La colmena* in 1951, seen by many critics as Cela's masterpiece and a novel that cost him five years. Cen-sored in Spain, *La colmena* appeared in Argentina, consolidating Cela's international reputation and resulting in a trip to South America in 1952 for Argentinean and Chilean editions of his other works. McPheeters relates that en route from Buenos Aires to Santiago, Cela met the Italian writer Curzio Malaparte, and the two later suffered an automobile accident, generating considerable publicity in Spain. Later in 1952, Cela finished *Mrs. Caldwell habla con su hijo,* an obsessive, surrealistic monologue also requiring nearly five years. On his second trip to South America in 1953, Cela visited Colombia, Ecuador, and Venezuela, and in 1957 he published *La rueda de los ocios* (Wheel of Idleness), combining his two journeys to the Southern Hemisphere. Cela was honored by the Venezuelan government and contracted to write a novel about Venezuela, published in 1955, entitled *La Catira.*

Success and Recognition

Royalties from the English translation of *La colmena* increased Cela's income; he bought a home in Palma, Majorca, and undertook a lecture tour of England, revisited South America (1956), and began publishing the literary monthly, *Papeles de Son Armadans* (1956–1978; Papers from Son Armadans), named for the neighborhood of his first home in Palma. This independent literary review attracted contributions from leading Spanish and international writers and produced special issues devoted to major artists, including Cela's friend Picasso and his neighbor, the painter Joan Miró. Cela devoted considerable time and energy to this handsome periodical, printed on heavy vellum by an antique press where he later published other volumes as well. *Papeles de Son Armadans* ceased publication in 1978, when many veteran serials failed during the political transition's economic crises. Perhaps disappointed by critical coolness toward *Mrs. Caldwell* and *La Catira,* Cela moved away from the novel, devoting his energies to other genres. He published a third book of his travels on foot, *Judíos, moros y cristianos* (1956; Jews, Moors, and Christians), and, following a clever campaign described in detail by Cela Conde, was elected in 1957 to the Royal Academy of the Spanish Language. Cela's acceptance speech treated the literary works of the painter Solana, whose popular themes and types Cela greatly admired. According to McPheeters, Cela's "Rightist family did not consider him a successful writer until the Catholic daily *ABC* published his photograph reading his paper to the Academy with a minister, bishop, general, and [Academy] president Don Ramón Menéndez Pidal in the background" (27). Be that as it may, nothing published by Cela indicates estrangement from his family. That same year, he published a volume of miscellany, *Cajón de sastre* (Tailor's Box), and the bittersweet caricaturesque narratives entitled *Historias de España: Los ciegos, los tontos* (Tales of Spain: The Blind, the Idiots).

Official acceptance by the Royal Academy facilitated diffusion of Cela's works, establishing him as a leader among contemporary Spanish novelists. He continued to reside in Majorca for many years, hosting a stream of prominent international intellectuals (many are listed by McPheeters [27–29], and others are cited by Cela Conde, who includes numerous photographs). Notable among them are some of the founding figures of surrealism, indicating Cela's ongoing involvement with the movement. The writer maintained his apartment in Madrid, commuting to weekly meetings of the academy, and as an academician began compiling works of erudition. Beginning in 1958, he made various trips to France, meeting and deepening his friendship with Pablo Picasso, and later producing collaborations with him. Another travel book, *Primer viaje andaluz* (1959; First Andalusian Trip), depicts a visit to the south of Spain. In 1959 Cela also published the first volume of his memoirs, *La rosa*, initiating a series entitled *La cucaña* (suspended for more than three decades). *Los viejos amigos* (Old Friends) appeared in two "series," or volumes, in 1960 and 1961, comprising expanded portraits of minor, skeletal character sketches from earlier works: *La colmena*, various short stories, and the *Apuntes carpetovetónicos*. *Cuaderno del Guadarrama* (Guadarrama [Mountain] Notebook), another travel volume, appeared in 1960, when academician Cela also published his first volume of literary criticism, *Cuatro figuras del '98: Unamuno, Valle-Inclán, Baroja, Azorín* (Four Leaders of [the Generation of] '98). The first three of these offer significant antecedents for Cela's own fiction.

Beginning with *La colmena*, a discontinuous, open-ended work employing mosaic techniques, Cela had experimented with increasingly fragmentary narrative. His popularity waned during the next two decades, and some critics and literary historians began to define him in terms of the early novels, considering his creativity exhausted. The *Apuntes carpetovetónicos*, *Historias de España*, and *Viejos amigos* vignettes involve pictorial more than narrative elements, and *Mrs. Caldwell* uses fragmented divisions—some 200 "chapters"—including poems, letters, snatches of conversation, dreams, and reminiscences. These experiments cumulatively reduced "story" elements and minimized action, a process increasingly evident in *Tobogán de hambrientos*. Cela told interviewers of the 1950s and 1960s that he had previously collected some 300 definitions of the novel, after which he decided to write his own: "Novel is anything that says beneath the title, 'novel.' " This may well be the only definition that can accommodate all of Cela's works so labeled. *Tobogán* constitutes a still more radical experiment than *Mrs. Caldwell*, as discontinuity is not offset by a unifying protagonist-narrator. Also in 1962, Cela published *Gavilla de fábulas sin amor* (Knapsack of Loveless Fables), printed by *Papeles de Son Armadans* with original engravings by Picasso illustrating the brief texts, marking Cela's entry into another phase of literary production.

Subsequent similar works feature lavish photographs, with minimal texts. Examples include *El solitario y los sueños de Quesada de Rafael Zabaleta* (1963; The Recluse and Quesada's Dreams, by Raphael Zabaleta), *Toreo de salón* (1963; Drawing-Room Bullfighting), and *Izas, rabizas y colipoterras* (1964; Bawds, Harlots, and Whores), with stark black-and-white photos of Barcelona prostitutes at work in the red-light district. In these volumes, Cela experimented with the communicative impact of thematically unified visual images, drastically reducing dependence on the printed word. Variants appear in *Once cuentos de fútbol* (1963; Eleven Stories about Soccer), with brightly colored illustrations by an eight-year-old friend. Between 1965 and 1966, Cela published the seven-volume series *Nuevas escenas matritenses* (New Scenes of Madrid), comprising photographs of the capital accompanied by short texts. Other collections of sketches, tongue-in-cheek portraits of social inequity, bridge the boundary between fiction and documentary: *Garito de hospicianos* (1963; Gambling Den for Hospice Residents), and *Las compañías convenientes* (1963; Socially Acceptable Company). Sometimes Cela's apparently pitiless realism combines with humor, as in *La familia del héroe* (1965; The Hero's Family), *El ciudadano Iscariote Reclús* (1965; Citizen Iscariot Reclus), and *A la pata de palo* (1965; To the Wooden Leg). He continued contributing to the travel genre with *Viaje al Pirineo de Lérida* (1965; Journey to the Pyrenees of Lérida), and *Páginas de geografía errabunda* (1965; Pages of Vagabond Geography).

Although no edition of Cela's complete works yet exists, a first attempt was initiated in 1962, a lavish series suspended following volume 6 (1968). Cela meticulously established definitive texts for these editions, providing valuable prologues and often extensive notes. Darío Villanueva details Cela's preservation of variant manuscripts, annotated to provide a complete record of the genesis of his works.[11] From January to June 1964, Cela lectured at several U.S. universities (McPheeters, 28–29), receiving an honorary doctor of letters from Syracuse University, the first of many *honoris causa* degrees. His somewhat satiric reaction to that trip is commemorated in the burlesque poems of *Viaje a USA* (1967). In 1965 he served with other literary luminaries on the jury awarding the Casa de las Américas literary prize in Havana, and in 1966 he was featured at the International Writers' Conference at Long Island University. Also during the mid-1960s, Cela began experimenting with the theater, publishing his first play, *María Sabina* (1965), later performed as an operatic oratorio at New York's Carnegie Hall in 1970. The surrealism of *María Sabina* is echoed in his experimental play *El carro de heno o el inventor de la guillotina* (1968; The Haywagon, or The Inventor of the Guillotine), reportedly inspired by paintings of Hieronymous Bosch.

Cela's increasing fame and fortune in the late 1960s resulted in the design and construction of a much larger home in the fashionable area of La Bonanova, overlooking the Bay of Palma (to which the family moved in 1966). He participated in founding the publishing house Alfaguara, for which he reportedly provided his name and fame while others supplied the capital. Alfaguara, managed by two of Cela's brothers, has enjoyed long prosperity thanks to publishing his works, including some best-sellers. Cela Conde indicates that Alfaguara was responsible for Cela's finally deciding to write the oft-postponed war novel *San Camilo, 1936* (206). The 25th anniversary of *Pascual Duarte* was celebrated in 1967 in Madrid, and Cela published the first volume of his *Diccionario secreto* (1967; Secret Dictionary), a startlingly successful work of academic erudition and impeccable scholarship tracing the etimology, evolution, and connotation of obscenities. Although the series was indefinitely suspended after the letter *C*, the research enhanced Cela's already rich and varied lexicon. Cela Conde states that Alfaguara's greatest publishing success was unquestionably the *Diccionario secreto* (220). Over the next few years, Cela accumulated honorary degrees from SUNY/Binghamton, John Fitzgerald Kennedy University in Buenos Aires, the universities of Palma de Majorca and Santiago de Compostela, Interamericana (Puerto Rico), and Hebrew University in Jerusalem. Several others have since joined the list.

Cela's "Second Period"

For a quarter century following the 1942 publication of *Pascual Duarte,* Spain's predominant literary mode was "social literature," neorealist or neo-naturalist works of covert sociopolitical criticism targeting economic inequities and social injustice. Various critics and literary historians considered Cela a founder of this "movement," author of Spain's first neorealist novel. Indeed, his early fiction often exhibits elements of realism and naturalism, notwithstanding his continual experimentation and clear expressionist and surrealist affiliations. By the mid-1960s, however, the restrictive pseudo-Marxist tenets of "social literature" (essentially prohibiting any goals for writers other than those contributing to social reform) had begun producing defection and revolt: a major aesthetic change was occurring. Although aspects of Cela's next novel, *San Camilo, 1936,* were clearly anticipated by *Mrs. Caldwell* and even *María Sabina,* his increased subjectivity and experimentalism were hailed as "renovation" reflecting innovations already under way among Spanish novelists. Because the civil war was still a painful subject in Spain, however, Cela's treatment of it proved controversial, and *San Camilo,* initiating his "second period," was less well received in Spain than abroad. Another story collection, *La bandada de Palomas* (Flock of Pigeons) and an essay volume treating the writer's social responsibilities, *Al servicio de algo* (In service of Something) appeared in 1969, followed in 1970 by *Barcelona.* During this period, Cela also dabbled in cinema (the *Lenny* dialogues), finished an adaptation of Bertolt Brecht's *Arturo Ui,* and completed a modernization of the Spanish Renaissance classic *La Celestina.*

Despite Cela's personal fondness for *Mrs. Caldwell* and its obvious significance within his innovative experimentation with form, neither this novel nor *La Catira* had been well received, and *Tobogán* was so radical an antinovel that few recognized it as a novel at all. Cela had not had a major novelistic success since *La colmena,* and reception of *San Camilo* also proved disappointing. He continued producing genre-bridging works of difficult classification, largely nonfiction: in 1971, *Cinco glosas a otras tantas verdades de la silueta que un hombre trazó a sí mismo* (Five Glosses of Five Truths concerning the Silhouette a Man Drew of Himself), *La Mancha en el corazón y en los ojos* (La Mancha in One's Heart and Eyes), and volume 2 of the *Diccionario secreto. La bola del mundo: Escenas cotidianas* (The Terrestrial Globe: Everyday Scenes) appeared in 1972, and the following year, the essays *A vueltas con España* (Again about Spain), *El tacatá oxidado* (The Rusted Walking-Frame {reprinting several volumes of miscellaneous short narratives]), and *Balada del vagabundo sin suerte* (Ballad of the Luckless Vagabond). Another series of "complete works" was initiated, with nine volumes appearing before this series too was suspended. Cela's most significant publication of 1973, however, was *Oficio de tinieblas, 5,* a radically fragmented, abstract, surrealistic experiment classified as a novel, although Cela stated at a press conference marking the work's release, "This is not a novel, but a purging of my heart, and the death certificate for my expertise, which I hereby abdicate."

Another decade would pass before Cela returned to the novel. These were years of change for Spain: longtime dictator Francisco Franco died in 1975, and in 1977, King Juan Carlos I named Cela a senator; he took part in drafting the 1978 Constitution and campaigned for democratic government. Thanks to a decree from Spain's Ministry of Education allowing "persons of exceptional merit" to be named to university faculties, Cela for several years taught doctoral courses at the University of Palma de Majorca, where he held a "Chair of Literature and Popular Geography" while his friend Antonio Roig was rector. This appointment ended when Cela reached retirement age and the new rector would not reappoint him, possibly spurring Cela's return to Galicia. Meanwhile he published *Cuentos para leer después del baño* (1974; Stories to Read after Bathing) and *Rol de cornudos* (1976; Catalog of Cuckolds), and he began publication of his *Enciclopedia del erotismo* (1977; Encyclopedia of Eroticism). *Los sueños vanos, los ángeles curiosos* (1979; Futile Dreams, Strange Angels), a volume of miscellany, preceded his induction in 1980 into the Royal Galician Academy, and in 1981, three essay collections appeared: *Vuelta de hoja* (Turning the Page), *Album de taller* (Workshop Album), and *Los vasos comunicantes* (Communicating Vessels). The latter title comes from an early surrealist manifesto, again evincing Cela's ongoing interest in surrealism. During the 1980s, strengthened ties with Galicia heighten the region's visibility in his fiction. He reestablished residence in his native province and devoted his energies to creating the Camilo José Cela Foundation (initiated in the late 1980s in Iria Flavia), as Cela Conde relates.

Although Cela had achieved financial success, official recognition had eluded him: he had won no literary prizes. But this was about to change. Between 1983 and 1993, Cela published only two works but garnered numerous awards. *Mazurca para dos muertos,* his second novel about the Spanish civil war—a mythical, lyric portrait of war's echoes in Galicia— won the National Prize for Literature in 1984, and in 1987 he received the Prince of Asturias Prize for Literature. In 1988 he published *Cristo versus Arizona* (Christ toward Arizona), and in 1989 he claimed the Nobel Prize for literature. Published reports in the press affirmed that he had published "more than one hundred volumes"; Cela's output then greatly exceeded the works written about him (subsequently critical studies have multiplied). Around the time of the Nobel Prize, Cela divorced his wife of some four decades and married a much younger woman. Although he had reportedly been working since 1983 on a novel to be entitled *Madera de boj* (Boxwood), he published little but *Cristo versus Arizona* between 1983 and 1993. The latter year of that period witnessed publication of the second part of the memoir series *La cucaña,* entitled *Memorias, entendimientos y voluntades,* plus *El huevo del juicio* (The Egg of Judgment), essays. In 1994 two novels appeared, *El asesinato del perdedor* and *La cruz de San Andrés,* with the latter apparently produced in haste to compete for Spain's best-endowed commercial literary award, the Planeta Prize, which Cela won. His participation in the contest was predictably controversial, but the writer had lived with criticism for half a century and responded in characteristically sardonic fashion. The best was still to come: in December 1995, Cela won the Cervantes Prize—the most prestigious literary award of all for writers in the Spanish language, recognizing lifetime achievement and given by consensus of the language academies in the 21 countries where Spanish is spoken.

Cela turned 80 in 1996, and his novelistic production has slowed; the oft-promised *Madera de boj* appeared in September 1999, unfortunately too late for inclusion in this volume. Cela continues his newspaper contributions, remains active as an academician, and devotes his energies to the Camilo José Cela Foundation. Through the foundation, in 1995, he established another literary quarterly, *El Extramundi,* which in 1997 devoted two issues (nos. 9 and 12) to Cela and his work. The present slower rate of production need not be seen as ushering in his retirement, for even in his youth, Cela was deliberate and patient in composing his novels, polishing and retouching successive drafts of *La colmena* and *Mrs. Caldwell* over five-year periods. Cela's fans may still expect the unexpected, therefore, from this dean of Spanish letters who has never ceased to surprise, to experiment, and (gleefully) to shock. Besides proffering the now-fulfilled promise to complete *Madera de boj,* a section at the end of *Memorias* suggests a future continuation:

> Without the least mercy and with full details and real names and faces I'll attempt to clarify happenings in the muddy waters of the deceptive swamps, the dark and treacherous backwaters in which some of my contemporaries would have liked to see me drown. It didn't happen, and I must apologize for being so inconsiderate. (347)

One so meticulous as Cela in establishing the definitive texts of his literary works is unlikely to leave the "definitive version" of his autobiography with so much still untold, unless fate intervenes.

Chapter Two

Memoir, Self-Portrait, Autobiographical Novel

In 1993, some three and a half decades after *La rosa* (1959), Cela returned to his truncated memoirs, which he had completed only through early childhood. Textual evidence suggests he wished to set the record straight on questions raised concerning his relationship with the Franco regime.[1] Cela had initially planned *La cucaña* (The Tightrope) as a series of several autobiographical volumes (the series name has several meanings, two of them relevant: one refers to a greased pole that contenders must climb, a symbolic attainment of manhood; the other involves watching others walk a tightrope, risking a fatal plunge, an apt metaphor for the country's political situation in those years). *La rosa,* spanning Cela's early childhood, was to initiate an ambitious cycle beginning in 1916 and ending with his saint's day in 1936, his ceremonial 20th "birthday" on 18 July, when the Spanish civil war erupted (evoked by the title of *San Camilo, 1936*). *Memorias, entendimientos y voluntades* enlarges the time frame initially projected to comprise 1936 to 1942 (the war and early postwar period, including publication of *Pascual Duarte*). *Memorias,* billed by the publishers as an autobiography, covers a scant two decades, qualifying more properly as memoir. The novelist's version of controversial events holds special interest. *Memorias* presents a self-portrait, possibly retouched and certainly projecting Cela's own self-image, but nonetheless more extensive and revealing than anything preceding it. Accompanied by statements about his ideology—often a subject of conjecture and debate—*Memorias* is potentially valuable for interpretation and explication, even when read as autobiographical fiction. *Memorias* illuminates formerly obscure areas of Cela's life, ideas, and personality. The following discussion examines the memoir interchangeably as autobiography and possibly autobiographical fiction, stressing passages that clarify Cela's beliefs, character, and literary practice.

The Autobiographical Genre

Nineteenth-century liberal crusader in politics and literature Antonio Alcalá Galiano notes in his own autobiographical recollections the scarcity of the memoir as genre in Spain, a commentary echoed by others including distinguished philosopher José Ortega y Gasset and the contemporary novelist Juan Goytisolo. Recent critics suggest that autobiography is a modern genre appearing with romanticism; obvious antecedents aside, little doubt remains that significant increases in autobiographical activity have occurred in modern times, especially following major national crises such as Napoleon's 1808 invasion of Spain and the Spanish civil war. French autobiographical theorist Phillipe Lejeune, attempting to distinguish between autobiography proper (with its privileged status as "fact" or history) and the autobiographical novel, developed the concept of *le pacte autobiographique,* an implied contract between author and reader whereby the autobiographer sincerely strives to understand his or her own life.[2] Lejeune soon realized, however, that sincerity carries no guarantee of historical exactitude (which not even history can claim, according to contemporary postmodern critics and New Historicists). Lejeune's next discovery was the key role of the signature, de facto authorial acknowledgment of identity with the narrator and protagonist (who share the author's name). For Lejeune, the proper name's reference to a "real person" became temporarily decisive, denoting an individual whose existence is legally verifiable (see "Autobiographie, roman et nom propre," in Lejeune 1986, 37–72). He eventually recognized that autobiography is necessarily a fiction whose factual basis cannot change essential fictionality: autobiography employs fiction's narrative techniques, being similarly subjective and selective in the reality it presents, the characters it creates, the themes it emphasizes.

One cannot expect objectivity of life writings, therefore, and scholars of autobiography (Lejeune, Olney, Fernández) distinguish two major groupings, either largely self-justifying or masochistically self-condemning (as in many confessions). Memory is fallible, not merely selective but forgetful. Lejeune eventually derived a paradoxical formulation: "Telling the truth about the self, constituting the self as complete subject—it is a fantasy. In spite of the fact that autobiography is impossible, this in no way prevents it from existing" (Lejeune 1986, 30–31). Cela avoided terming his text an autobiography; the publisher's designation notwithstanding, the academician considered "memoir" the accurate term. *Webster's Encyclopedic Unabridged Dictionary of the English Language* defines memoirs as "records of facts or events in connection with a particular subject, historical period, etc., known to the writer or gathered from special sources" (in Spanish, *memorias* denotes both memoir and memory). The most significant meanings listed by the Royal Spanish Academy's dictionary include an exposition of facts or motives referring to a given subject, and a description of certain private events, written to illustrate history.

"Objective autobiography" is an oxymoron, and if Lejeune and the New Historicists are correct that (complete and objective) autobiography and history are impossible, biography is also an endangered species. Yet all three genres exist (even if impossible), and Cela Conde is a privileged autobiographer. Other partial biographies are not demonstrably more "objective" than the information provided by Cela and his son, and these offer firsthand advantages; despite presumptions of bias, readers may reasonably deduce that bias. Autobiography, history, and novel coincide in being subjective and intentional in selection and presentation of material, and all construct narratives wherein characterization and motivation play key roles. Contemporary theory affirms the interchangeability of fictional and documentary techniques; boundaries are further blurred by twentieth-century novelistic experimentation with "factual subjects" (e.g., Truman Capote's *In Cold Blood* [1966]).

The twentieth century has challenged traditional distinctions between biography and personal history (journal, diary, letters, confession) and has disputed concepts of genre. For recent writers, notes Roger Fowler, autobiographical art is "a means of defining identity"—a definition most emphatically applicable to *Memorias* and Cela's expressed intent.[3] Distinctions between novel and autobiography are rendered moot by such definitions, with both genres "united beyond their different forms in a single gesture of passionate self-exposure" (Fowler, 24). Practitioners of the New Journalism likewise obscure demarcations between "fact" and "fiction," "history" and inventive narration. Theoretical grounding thus exists for considering *Memorias* as an autobiographical novel, given numerous examples of Cela's fictional techniques—including authorial comments and asides, some illuminating his personal beliefs and values—conversations, collages, and cinematographic sections, as well as self-reflective and metaliterary passages. Cela declares that he will not seek pardon for situations into which he was forced in the civil war, or as a result of the "dirty spectacle of politicians' games, which is worse than war" (*Memorias,* 8). He thus refuses to address specific allegations while offering his own recollection, personal "understanding," and "will" concerning "interpretation" of those years and events. Cela obliquely proclaims his veracity, noting that in his maternal grandparents' home, where he was taught how to behave, "lying was strictly prohibited, considered always shameful, and telling the truth was rewarded" (8). *La rosa* had covered Cela's first four or five years; *Memorias* resumes approximately where its predecessor was suspended. The following discussion examines especially how the novelist constructs himself as a character, subsequently amplifying the self-portrait with additional coloration provided by Cela Conde.

Childhood Years

Around 1925, when the family moved to Madrid, the approximately nine-year-old future writer had already been expelled by two private boarding schools *(colegios)* in Vigo. Cela "wasn't happy in school, what I liked was being in Iria with my grandmother, or home with my mother, and I cried and hit the other kids, because I wanted to leave" (*Memorias*, 17). He gleefully recounts a tantrum during recess when he bit a nun in the leg, being expelled from this school as well and sent to a Jesuit school at Bellas Vistas. Cela fondly recalls his blue blazer—with baronial crowns—from the Royal Yacht Club of Villagarcía (which his grandfather John Trulock had founded). "The Trulocks were, or had been, Barons of Greenock, a title soon lost, along with practically everything else" (19). Cela relates that he was expelled from the Jesuit school soon after loosing a herd of swine into the garden. Such incidents serve to characterize him as an incorrigible prankster. Alongside occasional conservative nostalgia for things past, Cela's memoirs contain *tremendista* events;[4] for example, one day his friend Trinidad found a fetus—or perhaps a newborn infant—wrapped in a newspaper and called the gang to see it, so horrifying the future writer that "I became dizzy and terribly ill from the spectacle, threw up my guts, became incontinent, and had to run for home" (27). This candid confession characterizes Cela as unexpectedly vulnerable, as do incidents reflecting his fondness for animals.

Cela simultaneously characterizes himself as sexually precocious. Given the abundance of prostitutes in his novels, it is unsurprising to learn that his curiosity about the world's oldest profession dates from somewhere around the onset of puberty when his first attempted visit to a brothel ended as the madam slammed the door when he inquired "how much it cost to screw for half an hour" (37). Near the family's first home in Madrid, many expensive downtown dwellings "were whorehouses, in my novel *San Camilo 1936* I talk about those chalets and their residents and clients" (37). Francisco Umbral's study of prostitution in Cela's works affirms that "Cela is interested by the prostitute's singular humanity. . . . [His] treatment of prostitution in general and prostitutes in particular presupposes an implicit sociology [plus] the consequent denunciation of an entire society and its morality which postulates the institution of 'mercenary love.'"[5] Umbral examines different types and ages of prostitutes and corresponding locales portrayed by Cela, noting that the novelist treats some "with admiration and respect, others with tenderness, some with flattery, but for all he shows some final consideration (tenderness disguised as cruelty)" (54). Further illuminating Cela's attitude toward the real cruelty suffered by prostitutes and other defenseless creatures is his remembered discovery of several abandoned kittens. He wanted one, but "some maid put them on the trolley track, and the next car, number 32, flattened their heads or cut them in two. The maid was dying of laughter. . . . There are some really bestial people in the world, who don't deserve mercy or charity, the majority of adults are inconsiderate animals" (*Memorias,* 39). Umbral notes that "children, prostitutes and animals, in that order, are three helpless and exploited species that Cela always treats with sober, masculine empathy and compassion" (51). As the cruelty, deviance, and criminal violence of Cela's early period intensifies in the later novels, readers should remember that his sympathies are with the victims, his seeming impassivity notwithstanding.

Another private school attended during the "dictatorship" (of Primo de Rivera, 1927–1932) is evoked amid techniques abounding in *San Camilo, 1936.* One involves the collage technique: *San Camilo* bristles with references to sporting events, excerpts from literary publications of the day, obituaries, announcements of events in the lives of public figures, reports of births of persons who would become future entertainers, writers, and celebrities, accounts of the reorganization of the Royal Academy of the Spanish Language, and so on. *Memorias* similarly combines economic details; cultural obituaries; national news; ads for jobs wanted, boarding houses, contraceptives, tailors, public baths, typewriters, and furnished rooms; and "personal" announcements (cf. 124). Echoes of *San Camilo* also sound as Cela evokes his adolescence with lists of trolley routes, stops, and fares, interpolated among anecdotes involving schoolmates and pranks resulting in being sent home, suspended, or expelled. Youthful pranks included his participation in a group throwing dirt and sand through the window of an aristocratic kitchen. Gleefully he recalls hiding in stairways until elderly ladies arrived from the market loaded with bags of produce, then rushing downstairs screaming and knocking the victims over, spilling potatoes and onions everywhere, and trampling the unfortunate shoppers. He evokes with equal glee swimming nude in the Canal of Isabel II (which carries water from the reservoir to Madrid). Caught and stoned by the watchman, he escaped minus his clothes, surrounded by companions who concealed his indecent exposure until he arrived home.

Many pages of *Memorias* resemble the adventures of Huckleberry Finn and Tom Sawyer; others suggest the historical novel, whose subject matter typically encompasses both public and private happenings. Historical novels are, by definition, concerned with large-scale social change. *Memorias* centers on the Second Republic and Spanish civil war, providing as much basis for viewing it as a historical novel as an autobiographical one. "The protagonist [of historical novels] was often a man of mixed loyalties, and the diverse pressures which focused upon him mirrored in individual struggle the interplay of wider social forces," observes Fowler in words fully applicable to *Memorias*. "Historicism most often denotes an approach to literature which sets it in the context of the ideas, conventions, and attitudes of the period in which given works were written, the writer's social and intellectual climate" (88). This, *Memorias* also does. Ideas and attitudes change, even in an author's lifetime; thus mature writers reevaluate, reinterpret, or repudiate youthful works. Cela uses tools of literary historicism, obliquely demonstrating influences of the world in which he was raised and people with whom he associated—including his parents' generation. The title proclaims his memoir as the product of memory (notoriously fallible), understanding (i.e., subjective interpretation), and will (believing things were, in fact, as he wanted to remember them). The title itself is a disclaimer of objectivity.

Cela, raised in an open-minded atmosphere, recalls his father's readings of (Pérez) Galdós and members of the "Generation of 1898" (including Valle-Inclán, Baroja, Azorín, and Unamuno), as well as Ortega. Both liberal *(El Sol)* and monarchical *(ABC)* newspapers were routinely read in his home, as was the centrist *La Epoca*. Cela's father operated a preparatory academy for the Customs Service; being unable to enroll his son elsewhere, he began accepting secondary school students so that the future writer could finish his high school equivalency. Cela repeatedly characterizes himself as a born iconoclast, the despair of his well-meaning parents, a rebel from earliest childhood, determined to challenge, mock, and circumvent authority (a model often found in autobiographies). Pleasurable memories include freedoms under the Republic, the writer's infatuations and amorous skirmishes. Personal and familial reminiscences, interspersed with cultural and political references (many culled from newspapers of the period), exemplify the historical novel's mixture of public and private happenings; however, Cela also includes many typically postmodern passages of self-referential commentary and metaliterary critique, some humorous, some self-mocking, and others merely absurd. Recalling the new home to which his family moved after seven years in Madrid (where his first works were written), Cela includes complacent dialogues between narrator and putative reader as he reflects that nearly 50 years later, a commemorative plaque was erected there by Enrique Tierno Galván during his term as mayor of Madrid in 1984. This exchange resembles numerous Cela "auto-dialogues" between author or narrator and characters or reader in his later fictions (e.g., *El asesinato del perdedor*):

> "But for this part I'm telling you now, several years must pass in this true chronicle."
> "Wouldn't it have been better for you to wait and put them in the right order, when their turn came?"
> "Perhaps so, madam, but in these things, one never knows, you may believe me." (*Memorias*, 96)

Another reminiscence evoking literary resonances identifies the real-life originals for the tubercular sisters who cater to the narrator's erotic appetite in *San Camilo, 1936:*

> Around 1933 or 1934, I started going out with the sisters Nieves and Encarnita, both were tubercular and I think they pushed me over the edge. . . . We used to walk around Retiro Park while it was getting dark, and then I'd make love to one while the other stood watch to warn us of the approach of a guard. . . . Nieves and Encarnita were very pretty but also real sluts, very determined and really hot. (*Memorias*, 98)

Cela's first bout with tuberculosis and internment in the Royal Sanatorium in the Guadarrama Mountains north of Madrid is recalled amid memories of his first night alone as he burst into tears (illuminating the genesis of *Pabellón de reposo*). Convalescent readings of the Spanish classics were amplified by works of leading modern Spanish and foreign intellectuals, including Ortega, Baroja, Valle-Inclán, Dickens, Dostoyevsky, and Stendhal. Cela began associating with as many aspiring writers as possible: "My friends of that period tended to the Left, which is neither good nor bad, but related to the times and fashions and people you live with, more than moral character or temperament" (*Memorias,* 112). Delicate health notwithstanding, he preferred the uncertain, bohemian lifestyle; by 1934 he was obsessed with becoming a writer and imbued with surrealist scorn for the bourgeois life. Although unwilling or unable to defy parental insistence that he learn how to make a living, he avoided obtaining the necessary credentials. Upon taking the oral public examinations *(oposiciones)* for Customs, he did so well on the early questions that he realized the tribunal—friends of his father—intended to pass him. "I was horrified at the prospect of finding myself wearing white gloves in Port-Bou [on the Spanish-French border], opening French luggage, because what I wanted was to be a poet, so I walked out of the second half [of the exam]" (117).

The years before 1936 occupy one-third of *Memorias,* 120 of 375 pages of smallish print; the years from 1936 to 1942 fill the remaining two-thirds. These years historically saw the Spanish civil war and difficult early postwar period (treated in *San Camilo, 1936* and *La colmena*). The war years, not originally scheduled for inclusion in *La cucaña,* thus receive dominant emphasis. Incidents recounted from circa 1920 to 1936 insistently characterize the future writer as impish, somewhat spoiled and strong willed, struggling against the conservative values of loving, indulgent, but severe parents. His love of poetry—and, by extension, of literature and the writer's craft—attracted him to literary stars of the "Vanguard years" (approximately 1927–1936). His poetry during that period reflects dadaist contacts and the aegis of surrealism, and in his biography, Cela Conde includes numerous photographs, one showing his father with dada's founder, Tristan Tzara (apparently during the late 1950s). *Memorias* confirms the Vanguard's significance for Cela's formation, and tenets from that period inform his mature works. Zamora Vicente notes muffled lyric echoes of Cela's apprenticeship as a surrealist poet throughout his work (see Zamora Vicente 1997).[6] Youthful espousal of the bohemian surrealist tenet, *epater le bourgeois,* and Cela's never-outgrown impishness explain numerous episodes depicting the mature writer's "shocking" disregard for social conventions, polite manners, and "respectable people." Cela Conde's introduction hints obliquely at the difficulty of separating authentic, inner reality from external appearance when he questions who the "real" Cela is:

> The cruel, violent author of *Pascual Duarte?* Or the royal senator, who carefully polished the text of the constitution? The movie actor? Or bud-

ding immortal, photographed nude the day he was to read his entry speech to the Royal Spanish Academy? The apprentice bull-fighter, or punctilious, erudite annotator of obscenities. . . . or *enfant terrible* of post-war literature? (Cela Conde, 17)

The War Years

Several chapters that treat 1936 offer insights into Cela's values and associates on the eve of the civil war. Poet Enrique Azcoaga invited Cela and other aspiring Republican writers for a poetry reading. Cela appeared with three bottles of champagne "liberated" from his father's cellar, and "Azcoaga, Serrano Plaja, and Sánchez Barbudo all said they couldn't touch such a bourgeois beverage, so Miguel [Hernández] and I drank it . . . got stinking drunk . . . and upon leaving, stopped and pissed in a basketful of clean, starched laundry just ironed by the lady of the house [Azcoaga's mother, a laundress]" (*Memorias,* 121). This thoroughly surrealist anecdote illustrates enduring aspects of Cela's character as well as Vanguard mockery of rational behavior and delight in paradox, the rejection of customary norms in favor of artistic anarchy, and subversion of control to instinctive behavior. The other attendees, all professed leftists, suffered exile or imprisonment, with Hernández dying in prison. Cela's escape from the fate of many Republicans and his subsequent ambiguous relationship with the Franco regime have provoked repeated accusations of collaboration with the Fascists, and criticism of his apparent betrayal of Republican principles. Since penning the dedication prefacing his wartime poetry collection *Pisando la dudosa luz del día* (1945; 1963, Treading doubtful daylight), Cela has stressed his lack of ideological commitment to either side, affirming his identification with victims on both sides. The dedicatory epigraph, reiterated and expanded in the dedication to *San Camilo, 1936,* again rejecting both extremes, appears in the first three lines cited hereafter, after which Cela comments on the difficulties of not taking sides:

> To the boys drafted in '37, all of whom lost something—life, liberty, illusions, hope, decency. And not the foreign adventurers, Fascists and Marxists alike, who had their fill of killing Spaniards like rabbits . . . Nobody liked it, I remember that well; and everyone attacked me, but I continue thinking what I thought and said then, in 1969, referring to 1936, I don't add or take away so much as a comma. Time has shown me to be right, and today the Fascists and Marxists, naive Romantics with magical solutions . . . have disappeared, perhaps for the good of all. (*Memorias,* 122)

Cela's own vision of his ideological position and evolution is clearly that of an independent, whom time has vindicated.

"La moneda al aire" (A Flipped Coin) (*Memorias,* 128–34), examines the literary and cultural scene during the week re-created in *San Camilo.* Cela discusses various major contemporary periodicals and his acquisition of complete collections (132); many provided source materials for re-creating 1936 Madrid. He metaphorically presents the civil war, with the lyrical language emphasizing speculation, betrayal, vengeance, and self-interest, exemplifying the literary (as opposed to historical) nature of his memoirs:

> On the Madrid pavement, there began to slither the lizard of personal ventures, the toad of betrayal, the musty bird of filth, the viper of blood, all very confused, perhaps also exciting and numbing. When it's open season on your neighbor, everybody loses direction, feels disoriented, some more than others, but not the hunted doe more than the hunter, and it all begins with forgetting and despising the laws, in civil wars, neither grief nor valor are respected, but people pay homage to hatred, establishing an atrocious battle of cruelty . . . the important thing is saving your life, no matter what. (135)

Important textual coincidences exist between this text and Cela's wartime poem "El lagarto del miedo" (The Lizard of Fear). Also noteworthy is the number of times Cela mentions the idea of (the things one will do for the sake of) saving one's life.

Cela's recollections of his wartime (October 1937) hospitalization in Logroño (*Memorias,* 188–95) illuminate another fictional re-creation of the war: "I believe I talk about the prostitutes of Logroño in *Mazurca para dos muertos.* . . . I'd like to greet Conchita la Merondona, if she's still alive . . . and recall old times, because sometimes I'm very sentimental. Do you remember, Conchita, that you washed my clothes, sewed the buttons on my jacket, and made me herbal teas good for bronchitis?" (194). One section of *Memorias* corresponding to his stay in Galicia (215–24) also relates to *Mazurca.* The city's social and cultural life and local bordellos appear in "Memory of La Coruña" (216–24). Cela reminisces about throwing a piano off the balcony of a local bawdy house, linking this to a corresponding incident in *Mazurca.* Late in 1938, Cela decided to return to the front, instead reaching Zaragoza, where "I spent three or four days, I'm not sure if memorable, but certainly happy, and discovered the Royalty Cabaret, one of few in the National Zone . . . and also the sport of throwing Italians from the boxes {in the theater}"

(240). These and similar anecdotes underscore the writer's irrepressible youthful prankishness (and perhaps brawling) even in the face of wartime tragedy and atrocities. Unlike the prototypical historical novel, neither Cela's memoirs nor literary depictions treat the civil war as militarily significant:

> It isn't true that we Nationalists won the war, we didn't know how, nor did we have the wherewithal, the Spanish civil war was a shameful scuffle among amateurs, which the Reds limited themselves to losing, as they were even less skilled than we . . . heroic literature is merely grandiloquent fallacy, and antimilitarist literature—the apology for equally conventional antivalues—is the same, but from the opposite side, one and the other are two sides of the same coin. (*Memorias,* 248)

Such statements illuminate the seeming impassivity of many passages in *San Camilo.* Most literature published in Spain in the immediate postwar years exemplifies what is now called *triunfalismo*—an orgy of self-glorification by the victorious Falange (Fascist political arm of Franco's revolt and only legal party in Spain for forty years). *Triunfalismo* unfailingly portrayed the victors as heroes, the "Reds" (Republican Loyalists) as villains. Cela's recollections obviously differ. Descriptions of torrential winter rains, deep mud, lack of precise information, loss of some equipment and defects in the remainder, plus disorder and lack of planning (*Memorias,* 250–56) buttress his attributions of "amateurism" on both sides.

The war chapters parallel parts of later novels whose narrators are limited, self-contradictory, and confused. For example, Cela writes of the last winter campaign:

> From those days I remember—not too precisely—a few curious events; in this business of literature what you must have is memory. One day when we had to advance, we found that a hundred paces upstream, in the Arroyo of la Marina, or del Tolote, or la Patuda, I don't know, it could have been another, there were two dead mules and two dead militiamen, all rotten, with worms coming out of their eyes, and water we had been drinking was washing over them. (*Memorias,* 260–61)

Cela's awareness of the historiographic implications of such imprecision becomes evident when the narrator's anonymous interlocutor inquires, "Do you agree with Carlyle that history is the distillation of rumor?" (*Memorias,* 262). The novelist indicates that errors were rife: "One day, it must have been before what I'm telling now, the planes on both sides attacked, first those on our side bombed us by mistake—that used to happen almost daily—and then the enemy shelled us, I guess to pass the time" (270). These recollections help readers to penetrate Cela's apparent impassibility in his novelistic re-creations of the war.

"Torremejía" (*Memorias,* 272–84) recalls the village used as the setting for *Pascual Duarte,* noting that Pascual was born there, "although I didn't meet him personally" (272); he was "one of innumerable scapegoats in Spain's attempt at purging itself" (273). Cela affirms that his knowledge of Pascual's house comes from papers "found by accident"; "I don't remember his house, which isn't surprising, given its insignificance" (277). His troop was lodged in cereal barns belonging to the "Condes del Alamo" (278), and Cela describes the palace, origins of the title, and his own quarters, plus the town's two taverns, citing details reflected in *Pascual Duarte* (279–80). After recuperating in Torremejía, and following the fall of Catalonia, Cela's group was ordered to Levante, where he experienced a near-fatal swimming accident. "Because of a cramp, I began to sink, swallowed water, and they pulled me out unconscious and half dead" (200), initiating another hospitalization in Castellón, during the final, chaotic days of the war (which Charlebois's chronology [con]fuses with the hospitalization in Logroño). This section likewise underscores disorganization and lack of military expertise among the military groups with which Cela associated (echoing major themes of Unamuno's *Paz en la guerra* [Peace in Wartime]). Cela's retrospective commentary on initial postwar mythologization of Franco and recollections of politics in 1939 includes imprisonment of intellectuals such as Julián Marías (308), postwar rationing, and institutionalized sexism: "Women would receive 80 percent of the daily ration for men" (*Memorias,* 329)—initiating scarcities and speculation with foodstuffs portrayed in *The Hive.* When Cela's family went to Galicia to recuperate from wartime privations, a newspaper in Túy published "news" of Cela's and his father's having been killed "in the Red zone." He describes attending his own funeral (another echo of Tom Sawyer): "Both my father and I were very happy because it's comforting to be remembered" (324). Such experiences surely enhanced the ironic sense of life expressed throughout Cela's fiction.

The memoirs end before the flowering of Cela's novelistic career (summarized in this study's biographical chapter), but titles and dates for the next decades appear in most histories of twentieth-century Spanish literature. Lesser known, however, is another aspect of Cela's postwar aesthetic development. After his first poetry collection (whose genesis is discussed in *Memorias*) was published in 1945, Cela was the object of an *homenaje* (public homage) by Postista poets—described by García de la Concha as "nothing more than a mixture of Surrealists and Expressionists."[7] The ceremony in Cela's honor followed publication of some of his poems in the Postista magazine, *Fantasía,* and "Carlos Edmundo de Ory, Chicharro, and Francisco Nieva saluted Cela as one of their own" (García de la Concha, 216; translation mine). This detail significantly attests to Cela's ongoing contact with surrealism—more continuous than generally recognized.

An Insider Biography

Cela Conde's narrative, abounding in anecdotes concerning jokes perpetrated by the novelist, lacks literary polish but overflows with immediate, palpable humanity, exuding admiration and loyalty for his father. His insider view of the circumstances of composition of *The Hive* and other works depicts the novelist writing

> always by hand, dipping his pen in the inkwell rather than filling it, and soiling his fingers in the process. He traces the words slowly, as if sketching them, correcting often, going over and over the drafts. When correcting, he is implacable, crossing out with infinite care the useless part, conscientiously erasing so it can never be read again, even with real effort, then intercalates the new additions, placing diminutive letters wherever there is space . . . margins, between lines, corners, with arrows indicating proper placement crossing the entire page until the whole resembles an indecipherable spider-web. (Cela Conde, 51)

Amplification appears in Darío Villanueva's article on Cela's numerous drafts, his major and minor edits and corrections of successive versions, the laborious process of weighing each word, polishing each phrase. Villanueva affirms that he knows "no other case, among living Spanish authors, of such exhaustive conservation of every single thing related to the creative trajectory, as that of Camilo José Cela" (65).[8] Also illuminating is Villanueva's enumeration of manuscripts collected at the Camilo José Cela Foundation, with the final versions, handwritten in ink, each accompanied by volumes of prior versions, notebooks, working diaries, unpublished drafts, outlines, clippings, commentaries, notations of ideas, and variant versions annotated by the author (68–69). Although Villanueva emphasizes *Pascual Duarte,* he complements Cela Conde's firsthand observations of similar perfectionism in his father's work on later novels.

Cela Conde specifically acknowledges his mother's contributions: "She alone, with infinite care and devotion—often with a magnifying glass—could translate the cryptograph into typewritten pages susceptible of being sent to the publisher" (57). He adds a final "Almost Embarrassing Epilogue" (233–35), which notes that many readers will wonder why he has scarcely suggested Cela's "sentimental adventures." While conceding that the writer "has always been prone to fall in love and never lacked adventures" (233), these are dismissed as transitory infatuations. Silence about his parents' divorce may reflect filial piety, or the separation's not yet being definitive when Cela Conde wrote. He acknowledges omitting many of his father's most fervent likes and dislikes, his "theories about the family," and reaction to the birth of his only grandchild—especially upon learning that the new family member was a girl. Cela Conde stresses his father's love for Galicia and Majorca, and the latter's absorbing passion of the moment, the Camilo José Cela Foundation.

The biographer depicts the novelist's evident delight in the perquisites of Academy membership, including "besides the glory, the right to be addressed as 'Most Excellent Sir' [and] to use stationery with the letterhead of the Royal Spanish Academy" (163), plus a long-outdated meal allowance for the days of Academy work sessions, which Cela never collected, although "he demands and proudly shows the other 'perks,' lovingly saving the business cards with raised lettering destined for the Civil Guards" (166)—a fondness for formality and protocol that may surprise those whose image of Cela is that of the *tremendista* writer or enfant terrible, not the academician. Having attained this exalted status, however, Cela began to enjoy the comforts of his position, and within the same five years that he joined the Academy, he "bought his first automobile and shaved off his beard" (Cela Conde, 166). The biographer emphasizes the dimension of collector—of wines, furniture, artworks—and the novelist's gastronomy and collection of gourmet foods. Referring to his father's "proverbial gluttony," Cela Conde remarks: "Let it suffice to clarify a few details: First, quantity and quality are aspects which CJC appreciates equally, without distinction. Nothing farther from his mind than those 'long and narrow' menus imposed by that silly *nouvelle cuisine* now in fashion" (180). Perhaps reflecting the novelist's lifelong delight in shocking, he states that "CJC has also eaten fried grasshoppers in Africa, monkey in the Caribbean, and something which, according to my father, greatly resembled human flesh in the Orinoco region. . . . And as for the rat that CJC ate in the Majorca village of Sa Pobla, there's an official document completed by Damián Vidal Burull, lawyer and notary of that place" (181). The only thing Cela refuses to eat, says his son, is junk food. The image so sketched harmonizes with the erstwhile surrealist, the enfant terrible of Cela's early literary career, the jokester who so often appeared before his canonization as an academician. By contrast, however, frequently repeated early "blurbs" affirming that Cela had learned English as a child while living with an aunt in England are contradicted by his son, who affirms that "CJC, despite having a British mother, does not speak a word of English. I swear it" (196). Recalling the novelist's lecture tour of U.S. universities, Cela Conde notes that during a formal banquet at Syracuse University, where Cela sat between the president and provost, the writer smiled broadly whenever addressed, invariably responding, "Collonut, Paraguay" (196). If asked whether he knows any language other than Castilian or Galician, "my father replies with the words of Lola Flores: 'God forbid' " (196).

Cela Conde describes his father's working on *San Camilo,* closed inside his largest study, surrounded by newspapers, magazines, catalogs, advertisements, and propaganda of the period, striving to return both historically and emotionally to those troubled times. Writing novels costs Cela an arduous effort: "A writer like my father, who seeks again and again the exact word for each phrase and squeezes out the book drop by drop as if it were a poem, can spend the entire day retouching a single page" (209). Cela's customary production of multiple, variant versions lengthened writing time for *San Camilo,* but what made this novel most difficult, says Cela Conde, was the writer's decision to abandon the facile formula of *costumbrismo* (the biographer refers to certain short stories and *Tobogán de hambrientos*), the litany of names, caricatures, and absurd situations. Although Cela himself rejects attributions of *costumbrismo,* critics mention it somewhat routinely. Cela Conde believes that compatriots were unprepared to understand the "ideological charge" of a novel grounded in the civil war yet distant from the political stance of either of the contending sides. "Spain in 1969 couldn't understand that . . . CJC was ahead of his time, emptying the conflict of ideological passions, choosing as protagonist the individual in his most extreme form, an individual never named, who remains apart from political passions" (210). One key to understanding the novelist's political posture is his "spirit of contradiction, developed to the limits of Nirvana" (211), situating Cela in the tradition of members of the Generation of 1898 such as Miguel de Unamuno and Pío Baroja, who criticized and rejected almost everything traditional, legal, or institutionalized in Spain.[9] Cela Conde's anecdote illustrating his father's "spirit of contradiction" involves an "erudite collector of articles by CJC who complained of finding contradictory viewpoints. 'Surely you don't expect me to agree with my own opinions,' protested CJC, with irrefutable logic" (211). This attitude by no means contradicts remaining traces of surrealist aesthetics and the enfant terrible image that Cela has continued to cultivate, as illustrated by his appearances on the television programs of Mercedes Milá and Gurruchaga:

> CJC quite seriously assured them of his ability to absorb several liters of water through the anus (an ability of Le Pétomane, the French pedomane who astonished the world with his sphincter control). CJC [who had published a translation of Le Pétomane's book] couldn't resist the temptation to attribute the same accomplishments to himself. Both Milá and Gurruchaga kept their cool and challenged him to prove his ability, but when CJC impassively demanded a basin of warm water, that was the end of it. Spanish television wasn't mature enough to continue. (Cela Conde, 226)

During his time as a senator, given the tremendous boredom of proceedings, Cela often nodded off, only to be "curiously persecuted by Fontán, president of the Senate. Once the president spoke to him, without my father—in deepest sleep—deigning to answer. . . . And when he sleeps, CJC really gives a spectacle. Instead of just snoring like anybody else, he sighs, sings, roars, whimpers, recites, laments, coughs, hiccoughs, and murmurs—all at the same time" (229). The president persisted until he interrupted Cela's siesta, then protested, "You were asleep," to which Cela replied, "No, Mr. President, I was not asleep; I was sleeping." Upon Fontán's objection that these were the same thing, the academician responded, "No, Sir! It isn't the same thing to be fucked as to be fucking" (231). Another illustrative incident involves the Madrid production of Cela's operatic oratorio *María Sabina,* well received in New York but repeatedly interrupted by irate audiences in Spain. Cela, "standing up in the box nearest the stage, politely and imperturbably responded with deep bows" (213).

Other Clues to Cela's Character

Deliberately "scandalous" incidents, plus the absence of preaching and overt moralizing in Cela's novels, always impassively narrated, have contributed to an apocryphal vision of Cela as a man who believes in little, if anything, and respects nothing. Yet careful reading of Cela's writings, including his important essay collections and autobiographical works, illuminates his stance on many essential questions. For example, several later novels and nonfiction works mention Cela's opposition to capital punishment. And during the transition to democracy and his active service as a senator, Cela publicly proclaimed his belief in democracy and the principle of equality (although in several places he recognized the existence of de facto inequality). Such sentiments are enunciated more clearly following the demise of the censorship (at the end of 1978) than before, and essay collections such as *Vuelta de hoja* (1981) reprint works written earlier, helping to clarify the evolution of his ideas. Cela's literary apprenticeship under the aegis of Vanguardism and the surrealists initiated him in a hermetic mode of writing: Readers of García Lorca may recall the poet's correspondence affirming his own avoidance of "confessional" writing and his "sense of shame at undressing in public." Although Cela occasionally ventures into the confessional realm in *Memorias,* his novels preserve reticence, resembling Lorca's, concerning his personal beliefs and feelings. Many artists refuse to "explain" their works, believing this to be the proper task of the critic. They do so with still more reason when published clues exist in their essays and other writings (as is Cela's case), and when personal reticence is buttressed both by aesthetic tenets (surrealism) and by the prudent caution imposed by powerful mechanisms of censorship. Much negative reaction to Cela's works (not only in Spain but among supposedly enlightened readers abroad) results from the novelist's failure or refusal to explain what his narratives "mean," or where he stands ideologically. Postmodern thought questions the very existence of "meaning," but many readers (including critics) feel more comfortable when told, "What this means is . . ." They want, as Unamuno charged, to categorize or "pigeonhole" troublesome writers, the more comfortably to forget them. Unamuno actively resisted pigeonholing, preferring to irritate rather than to be forgotten. Cela irritates as well, because he has not made it easy for passive readers to say "Cela's work means this." Difficulties multiply given the frequent subtlety of his irony, the ease with which some readers miss or misinterpret Cela's masterful understatement, and the need to recognize and identify parody, irony, and satire. Despite the seeming objectivity or impassivity of much of Cela's work, it should be taken neither at face value nor out of context, and the larger the context (of Cela's writing) on which readers can draw, the better the safeguard against misinterpreting deceptively "indifferent" poses as complacency. Cela does not moralize or preach about atrocities, but silence can mean many things in addition to indifference.[10]

Cela's acceptance speech before the Swedish Academy at the time of his receipt of the 1989 Nobel Prize cited the essential ethical component of literature, considering the question of "art for art's sake" and whether aesthetic qualities and emotion suffice to justify the creative exercise. His decision in favor of ethics rather than aesthetics as the more important included the significant condition that no ethical compromise is admissible, only the author's own personal beliefs and "intuitions of liberty."[11] Literature can only be fully and honorably "true" literature without coercion, hidden agendas, or *engagement* of the writer, other than with what Cela terms "the human condition" ("Elogio," 146). Literature now and for the foreseeable future requires an author, an individual fount of "ethical and aesthetic intuitions" (148), who functions as a "filter of the current that proceeds from the entire society . . . this connection between man and society best expresses the paradox of being human, subject to individual pride and yet inescapably chained to a collective covering which cannot be removed without risk of madness" (148–49). Cela's essays, his own formulations of his moral, aesthetic, and political principles, significantly illuminate his essential portrait.

Chapter Three
Antecedents and Echoes

Cela, long interested in experimentation and theory of the novelistic genre, has continually varied his novelistic forms. Like Unamuno, Cela holds little respect for a priori definitions of genre, and his own cited earlier ("Novel is whatever says beneath the title, novel") may be the only one permitting consideration of various Cela texts as novels. He has often stressed that his novels differ among themselves, that each constitutes a new experiment. His forms vary more than his themes and style, and although "new" in his repertoire, most forms used in the first half-dozen novels are not unprecedented.

Pascual Duarte

La familia de Pascual Duarte relates the autobiographical confession of a condemned murderer awaiting execution, a violent, uneducated, impoverished villager who composes his life story as a confessional penance in obedience to instructions from the prison chaplain. The first-person monologue, filled with picaresque elements and intertextual echoes of *Lazarillo de Tormes,* alternates episodes of homicidal violence with chapters of quiet, almost lyric reflection. Cela's primary model clearly derives from the classic Spanish picaresque, a ploy rendering the frequently scabrous content more acceptable to the regime's puritanical but strongly traditional and nationalistic censors. Traits of Pascual's mother repeat, parody, or exaggerate similar traits in the mother of the prototypical picaro, Lazarillo, as does the frequent appearance of taverns, roads, and inns. Cela's characteristically squalid settings and marginal characters echo picaresque predilections, and his ironic, pseudoinnocent first-person narratives of progressive disillusionment, delinquency, and imprisonment echo classical models.

Given the death and exile of many writers, Spanish literature languished during and after the civil war. The first significant sign of postwar novelistic rebirth, *Pascual Duarte,* sparked numerous imitations, a "movement" termed *tremendismo* because of its tremendous revulsive impact. Cela steadfastly denied the "movement's" existence, noting antecedents in sixteenth- and seventeenth-century picaresque classics, especially Quevedo's *Vida del Buscón* and Valle-Inclán's grotesque *esperpentos*—expressionistic deformations of heroes and values. *Pascual Duarte* provides the first extensive sampling of Cela's inimitable use of language, a personal style recognizable after minimal acquaintance, with his characteristic *estribillos* (tag lines), folk proverbs and popular sayings, combinations of grotesque caricature with moments of tenderness, and underlying lyricism with ever-present irony. Cela incorporates popular sayings, proverbs, vulgarities, and obscenities within academically correct and "socially proper" passages. His novels evoke vast canvases teeming with grotesqueries, paintings by Goya and Solana among moderns, or Hieronymus Bosch among earlier masters. This latter association is no accident, as evinced by Cela's homage to Bosch in the dedication of *El carro de heno* and his announced intention to dedicate to the same painter another piece (to be subtitled "The inventor of the garrotte" [the Spanish version of the guillotine]). The carnivalesque world of *El carro de heno* (and of several later novels) may succinctly be described as Boschian. Cela's art is painterly because, excepting *Pascual Duarte,* his novels feature little action, with description and dialogue predominating. A painter with words, one of whose favorite subjects is language itself (see his lexicographical works), Cela untiringly records linguistic trivia and absurdities and is always fascinated with nuances. Scrutinizing these, and playing with words, he produces ironic little gems, conversations, incidents, or scenes capable of standing alone—as they often do. This characteristic, for many one of his virtues as a writer, becomes for other critics a vice; they contend that he repeats himself, producing novels with little if any character development, frequently lacking sustained action and traditional plots. *Pascual Duarte* offers the major exception to absence of plot, action, and character development.

Pascual's "family" includes a brutal smuggler father, an alcoholic, beastly mother, and a runaway sister who works as a teenage prostitute. His mother's promiscuity produces his half brother Mario, an idiot born while Pascual's father, locked in a wardrobe after being bitten by a mad dog, was dying of rabies. Mario's abusive putative father kicked the unfortunate child in the head, causing a festering sore; subsequently Mario's ear was gnawed away by a pig as the boy lay sprawled in the street (this particularly grotesque incident has several literary antecedents, traced by McPheeters). Mario's brief, unhappy existence ends when he falls into a large stone jar of oil, where he drowns. Pascual's grotesquely lyric recollection of the child's "beauty" in death, with the golden oil clinging to his hair and softening his deformed features and expression, typifies Cela's art. Mario's burial, attended only by Pascual and the village girl attracted by him, climaxes with Pascual's rape of Lola atop the newly dug grave. Cela characteristically combines Eros and Thanatos, sexuality and death (as had predecessor Ramón del Valle-Inclán),[1] painting humans as sensual animals, whose reproductive instincts are aroused by the presence of death.

Pascual's name alludes to the Paschal Lamb or Easter sacrifice, and the protagonist is in some oblique sense a scapegoat (or Christ figure, a device recurring in *El asesinato del perdedor*). The author's foreword to an American edition of *Pascual Duarte* alludes to society's "pro-rata of guilt" or responsibility for crimes committed by persons produced by that society, suggesting that individuals formed by an unjust social structure are only partially culpable for their acts. Pascual's crimes are usually crimes of passion and, except for killing his mother, were not premeditated. Significantly, Cela carefully creates contexts wherein Pascual proves somehow morally superior to his "victims," a primitive judge and executioner who takes justice into his own hands. Human victims include his first wife, strangled in a knee-jerk reaction upon learning that while he was imprisoned for knifing a man in a tavern brawl, she had survived by selling herself to "el Estirao" ("Stretch"), the pimp exploiting Pascual's sister. Later Pascual asphyxiates el Estirao by crushing his chest. Pascual's ax murder of his mother (who subverted the scruples of his first wife and actively poisoned his second marriage) figures among the bloodiest passages in Spanish fiction, yet readers cannot deem his hatred unjustified. Repeated critical comparisons of *Pascual Duarte* with Camus's *The Stranger* are somewhat inappropriate: the philosophical dimension in Camus's novel scarcely appears in *Pascual Duarte,* although existentialism is not exactly alien to Cela's thought.

A Quiet Interlude

Contrasting with the traditional form and overt violence of its predecessor, *Pabellón de reposo* employs multiple narrative perspectives, ostensibly the diaries of several terminally ill tuberculosis patients. Cela's hospitalizations in 1934 and 1941 provide autobiographical substrata. Identifying characters only by room numbers, producing the "dehumanization" typically associated with Cela's fiction, *Rest Home* emphasizes the indifference of the strong and healthy—doctors and nurses included—who callously laugh at expressions on the faces of the dying and consign the dead to oblivion. Obliquely, lyrically, via an italicized recurring poetic refrain alluding to the tumbling objects transported in the gardener's wheelbarrow, Cela half-conceals, half-reveals the patients' ultimate fate. Presumably to avoid propagating their disease in the city, they are buried in the sanatorium garden—a final depersonalization denying them religious ceremonies or burial in hallowed ground, treating the bodies as fertilizer, negating their humanity. This novel's haunting gothic undertones enhance the desperate loneliness of the diary writers, their almost frantic, morbid eroticism, intimating other dimensions in Cela—an undeveloped potential. As its only violence is psychological, *Rest Home* disconcerted readers of *Pascual Duarte* with its *tempo lento*.

Picaresque Elements

Cela's first novel, with its neo-naturalistic emphasis on the repulsive, ugly, diseased, and criminal, lacks naturalism's scientific pretensions, employing—instead of objectivity—gallows humor, caricature, exaggeration, and other deliberate distortions. Disproportional critical preference for *Pascual Duarte* is as curious as the novel is atypical. Cela resuscitated picaresque form (first-person autobiographical narrative), technique (irony, caricature, pseudoinnocence), ambience (lower-class taverns, inns, hovels, back roads), and borderline criminal characters in this first and best-known work. At the same time, he updated the picaresque novel's social concerns, introducing sufficient contemporaneity to make the work powerfully "relevant," and refined the narrative consciousness. Critics suggested that *Pascual Duarte* drew on another Spanish literary tradition, *costumbrismo* (portrayal of regional customs), although elsewhere Cela disputes such attributions. In any case, he modifies this characteristically idealizing and nostalgic traditional form, unblinkingly presenting unpleasant realities ignored by earlier cultivators of *costumbrismo*. Although antecedents of *costumbrismo* appear in medieval Spanish classics such as the Archpriest of Hita's *Libro de buen amor* (The Book of Good Love), the sixteenth-century *Lazarillo de Tormes* (prototype of the picaresque), seventeenth-century greats such as Cervantes, and the eighteenth-century *sainetes* (one-act popular farces), the term has become essentially synonymous with nineteenth-century variants in vogue during *costumbrismo*'s brief hegemony (between romanticism and realism). With the notable exception of Mariano José de Larra, typical writers of *costumbrismo* were conservatives who idealized backward, rural, patriarchal society, romanticizing the quasi-feudal existence of impoverished peasants and ignoring economic exploitation, injustice, and other ills of the system. A different vision appears in Cela's *"costumbrismo":* remote areas, picturesque villages, ancient towns, or irrepressible lower-class *madrileños,* depicted from grim perspectives, confronting ugly realities, clearly sketching backwardness, ignorance, and primitivism, without disguising lack of schooling as "innocence" or ignorance as naturalness and spontaneity. This mode (which I term Cela's neo-*costumbrismo*) predominates in his short fiction and many volumes of sketches and miscellany, as well as *The Hive*—considered by many critics his masterpiece. *Costumbrismo* variants in Cela's works are ironically or grotesquely deformed, as evinced in *Tobogán,* or such later novels as *Mazurca, El asesinato del perdedor,* and *La cruz de San Andrés.*

Pascual Duarte is atypical; as Cela's best-developed character, he contrasts markedly with the prevalent fragmentary, stylized caricatures or abbreviated, grotesque sketches of most of Cela's fiction. Nevertheless, Gonzalo Sobejano, a distinguished interpreter of the contemporary Spanish novel, identifies as characteristic of most of Cela's novels "the presence of a character, generally of the 'culpable-innocent' type seen in *Pascual Duarte."*[2] The setting likewise proves atypical: no subsequent Cela work is set in Badajoz (Madrid and Galicia—his "typical" geography—are abandoned infrequently, for Venezuela in *La Catira,* a movie set version of the American Old West in *Cristo versus Arizona,* and an unnamed town in *El asesinato del perdedor*).

Nuevas andanzas y desventuras de Lazarillo de Tormes, the least read and least studied of Cela's early works, resuscitates a golden age classic, exploiting the regime's idealization of sixteenth- and seventeenth-century models (the postwar Garcilaso poets group similarly revived pastoral themes cultivated by the Renaissance soldier-poet who introduced the sonnet to Spain). Cela revives the archetypal Renaissance rogue and picaresque prototype to wander Spain's roads and byways once more. Ironic commentaries indirectly suggest the lack of visible progress in the intervening centuries. The novel—a variant of the "stranger in a strange land" motif popular with eighteenth-century writers (e.g., Montesquieu's *Lettres persanes* or Cadalso's *Cartas marruecas* [Moroccan Letters] in Spain)—reiterates picaresque elements in *Pascual Duarte* (echoed in later novels), anticipating aspects of Cela's travel books such as the walking tours of backward areas. Cela's neopicaresque vein has been noted by such well-known Hispanists as Gonzalo Sobejano, Ignacio Soldevila, Ramón Buckley, David William Foster, and Sherman Eoff; and a recent essay studies Cela's use of the "apoc-

ryphal" picaresque,"[3] noting that *Pascual Duarte* and the "New *Lazarillo*"
appear in Ulrich Wicks's *Picaresque Narrative, Picaresque Fictions: A Theory and Research Guide* (Greenwood Press, 1989). These are the only two
Peninsular Spanish works since the seventeenth century to be included
by Wicks among some 60 titles representing all Western literature
(Cabo Aseguinolaza, 152). Cela's bittersweet neo-*costumbrista* vignettes
contain elements reworked in *Mazurca para dos muertos* and *El asesinato
del perdedor.*

One year after publishing *The Hive,* Cela penned an article commenting on his attitude toward the picaresque: "The novelist's duty, today, is
to forget about Madame Bovary, and pay attention—plenty of attention—to Lazarillo. Empty-headed wives, dreamy sentimentalists, have
ceased to be problems for the novel to explore, but hunger is very much
alive, together with bad faith and the despair of the servant of a hundred
masters."[4] Following his receipt of the Nobel Prize, Cela reiterated for
the Madrid daily *El País* his admiration for a classic master of the
picaresque: "Every year I read more of Quevedo" (interview 1989, 21).
Quevedo's impact transcends the caricatures and distortion of *El Buscón
(The Scavenger),* his picaresque classic, cited by Cela among significant
antecedents of *tremendismo;* and numerous critical observers have noted
echoes of Quevedo's style and protoexpressionistic vision throughout
Cela's fiction. Quevedo's later works, especially *Los Sueños (Visions),*
impact Cela's later novels, beginning with *San Camilo, 1936,* and
Quevedo is cited by Cela among his lifelong readings. Quevedo and
Valle-Inclán have been deemed important sources for Cela's peculiar
brand of irony and humor—especially significant in the later novels.

The Critics' Choice

The Hive, Cela's most extensive novel, an experimental work compared
with John Dos Passos's *Manhattan Transfer,* features collage techniques,
incorporating journalistic passages, advertising slogans, and radio propaganda. With a large cast ranging from 200 to more than 360 (by
varying critical counts), *La colmena* has the most characters of Cela's
early novelistic period (and is second only to *Cristo versus Arizona,* whose
cast one critic places at more than 500). *The Hive* presents some three
days in Madrid during the harsh winter of 1942 to 1943, painting
hunger and desperation for many and black market prosperity for others
during the most oppressive years of the Franco police state. Skeletal
characterization, multiple nicknames, variant first and last names, and

tag lines used for identifying purposes make it almost impossible to distinguish new identities from reappearances by other shadowy and variously named character sketches. Experimental aspects include the absence of a protagonist—or use of a collective protagonist—lack of plot, and attempts at simultaneity (resulting in minimization of continuity). Chronology moves forward and backward between the five parts, usually without indicating temporal discontinuity, disorientating readers. Five-part division and unexplained temporal shifts anticipate *La cruz de San Andrés*. *La colmena* (Cela's masterpiece, in the opinion of many critics) and *Pascual Duarte* were the only two of Cela's works mentioned by name in the Nobel citation.

Important aspects of *The Hive* visibly anticipate other later works: similar structure characterizes *La colmena* and such fragmentary, disconnected, presentational novels as *Mazurca* and *Cristo versus Arizona* (and before them, *Mrs. Caldwell*). Likewise, *The Hive* resembles *Los viejos amigos* and *Nuevas escenas matritenses* in characters and setting more than the novels preceding it. These coincide in lacking traditional plots, and (possibly excepting *Mrs. Caldwell*) none has a figure of sufficient stature to qualify as protagonist. Novels of collective focus and collective protagonist, they involve more description than action. Curiously, Cela's treatment of the historical novel has been little examined. Nevertheless, *La colmena* has precise historical parameters and mentions several historical characters, whereas such titles as *San Camilo, 1936* and *Mazurca* recreate Cela's personal vision of the beginning and end of one of the twentieth century's major historical cataclysms, the Spanish civil war. Notwithstanding his repeated expressions of contempt for literary taxonomy and for any classification of novels other than "good," these three novels—all among his best achievements—cannot properly be understood outside the historical circumstances of the Spanish civil war and immediate postwar years (aspects wherein Cela's memoirs are especially illuminating).

Although violence in *The Hive* is limited to the crime implied by the discovery of the strangled corpse of Doña Margot, the novel's impact for many proved as shocking as that of *Pascual Duarte*. Readers were depressed by the near-total absence of "healthy" characters and alienated by the novel's paucity of altruism or common decency, its portrayal of pervasive hunger leading many of the characters to prostitute themselves for a meal, and the prevalent willingness to exploit, humiliate, and abuse others. Prostitution's visibility throughout Cela's work, beginning with *Pascual Duarte*, becomes progressively more visible in

The Hive, San Camilo, Mazurca, and *Cristo versus Arizona.* Umbral, who traces prostitution in these novels and such nonfiction works as *Izas, rabizas y colipoterras,* considers Cela the first novelist to have discovered the appropriate balance for treating a painful reality, distinct from romanticism's idealization or Baudelaire's exaltation, but likewise distant from moralistic condemnation (Umbral, 51–62). *The Hive* inspired catchphrases characterizing Cela's work with respect to the division of humanity into victims and executioners; the prevalence of sexual deviance and furtive eroticism; the preference for ugly, malformed, mutilated, and psychologically repulsive characters; and the portrayal of amorality, indifference, and mankind's cruelty to man (especially women and children). Cela contributed to this perception with various prologues, including such pronouncements as "Life is not good; mankind isn't either." Despite his evident negative aesthetics, Cela insisted (in another prologue), "All I did was go downtown with my camera, and if the models were ugly, tough luck." Cela's affirmation that he invented nothing supports those who consider *The Hive* the first neorealist novel of the postwar era (neorealism, under various names, was the prevailing mode for novels, poetry, and theater during the 1950s and 1960s). From today's vantage point, however, Cela's characteristic expressionistic caricature, abundant in *The Hive,* precludes unqualified classification as neorealistic. *The Hive* anticipates several later novels with its large numbers of ill-defined, sketchy, or caricaturesque characters, discontinuous action, absence of plot, lack of a clearly defined protagonist, and experimental chronology. Deviant eroticism, the grotesque, pervasive evidence of people's inhumanity, and open-ended or inconclusive narrative that avoids closure also appear in many novels of Cela's second period, echoing the prominent characteristics of *The Hive.*

Cela's Personal Favorite

Still more radically experimental, *Mrs. Caldwell habla con su hijo* comprises some 200 brief, untitled "chapters," including ostensible letters, poems, lyric prose, and surrealistic fragments. This novel, long the author's personal favorite, set in another sanatorium and employing a pseudoautobiographical perspective, features one-way dialogue in the second person familiar, as the protagonist addresses her ramblings and recollections to her son, Eliacim (for whom the lady's affection was hardly maternal). J. S. Bernstein's introduction to the English translation observes that "assuming her incestuous love, the problem is how to transform it, disguise it as it were, to reduce its blatant sexuality, the shocking possessiveness Mrs. Caldwell feels towards Eliacim. Herein lies . . . one reason for the tremendous emphasis Mrs. Caldwell gives to the . . . process of transformation in general."[5] Readers slowly realize that Eliacim is long dead, Mrs. Caldwell totally unbalanced, and the sanatorium possibly a lunatic asylum. The final conflagration may be real (Mrs. Caldwell has previously displayed incendiary tendencies) or a psychotic hallucination; alternatively, it could symbolize being "consumed" by her "burning passion." Sobejano suggests that Pascual Duarte's matricidal hate (and his mother's reciprocity) constitutes the counterpart for Mrs. Caldwell's overly possessive maternal love, "as fanatic as Pascual's hatred for the woman who . . . brought him into the world" (1997, 146–47). Formally, *Mrs. Caldwell* is among the most radical experiments of Cela's "early period." Its surrealistic form and content may best be compared with his poetry, *Pisando la dudosa luz del día* (1945), and hallucinatory monologue, *El solitario* (1963); structurally, *Mrs. Caldwell* anticipates *Tobogán de hambrientos* and *Oficio de tinieblas,* where fragmentation is still more extreme. McPheeters termed *Mrs. Caldwell* "as much an anti-novel as has yet been written" in Spain, but he declined to classify *Tobogán.* Although less so than *Tobogán, Mrs. Caldwell* lacks connectedness—as do many of Cela's novels to follow, excepting *La Catira*—and the lyric vein emerges as a structuring principle in several later novels. Mrs. Caldwell, hardly a sympathetic character, figures among Cela's most extensively developed fictional women, one for whom he apparently felt some empathy (he "revives" her in *La cruz de San Andrés*). Her presence as inescapable narrator-protagonist unifies the novel in the absence of plot, continuity, sustained action, and cause-and-effect sequencing. Cela does not explicitly present Mrs. Caldwell as society's victim but suggests that part of her mental imbalance results from restrictions and repression imposed by a traditional, puritanical, and hypocritical culture.

Geographic Exoticism

Contrasting with the experimentalism of *La colmena* and *Mrs. Caldwell, La Catira* seems relatively conventional and, according to some critics, imitates Rómulo Gallegos's classic *Doña Bárbara.* The presence of strong-willed, larger-than-life "heroines" of the Venezuelan plains in both novels probably explains this attribution, but enormous differences exist in plot, tone, values, and details. The female protagonist—atypical for Cela in possessing unparalleled empowerment—seems diminished by comparison with the model's barbaric force. Indeed, little remains of the presumed model as *La Catira* accumulates varied, curious acts of sexual deviation and violence, accompanied by gruesome deaths (e.g., characters fried in the sidewalk doughnut vendor's vat of oil, eaten alive by piranhas, murdered and afterward sodomized by a homosexual necrophiliac). Despite the shock value of *La Catira, Cristo versus Arizona* emphatically surpasses it in portraiture of deviant sexual acts and bizarre, cruel, inhuman ways of dying.[6] Unlike other early novels, *La Catira* seems insignificant as an antecedent for Cela's later period, as its sole distinctive, reappearing characteristic—extremes of deviant sexuality and violent, shocking deaths—does not originate with this one "Venezuelan" novel, although exaggerated to a degree unparalleled before *Cristo versus Arizona*.

In 1962, when Cela published *Tobogán de hambrientos,* his first piece of long fiction since 1955, he had completed three travel books, five volumes of brief fiction, an anthology, a half-dozen volumes of essays and criticism, and the first installment of his memoirs during the intervening seven years. Many of these works, as well as those shortly after *Tobogán,* emphasize the visual image at the expense of the verbal or privilege the pictorial. Several offer brief texts written primarily if not exclusively to accompany illustrations, be these the eerie, hallucinatory pen-and-ink drawings of *El solitario,* the candid crayon sketches of *Once cuentos de fútbol* (1963), the stark, grainy photos of *Izas, rabizas y colipoterras* (1964), or the naturalistic photography illustrating the seven series of *Nuevas escenas matritenses* (1965–1966). Together with other limited-edition "coffee-table books" produced for the collectors' market, such works exemplify certain predominantly descriptive techniques of *Tobogán,* which is presentational and "invertebrate," with minimal and nonsequential narrative content often more implicit than explicit— "action" is scarcely suggested by juxtaposition, silence, or changes in the interim since the first appearances of the characters. *La colmena* had moved in the direction of the antinovel, eliminating plot and protagonist, tentatively experimenting with simultaneity (action occurring in multiple places at the same time), and breaking with linear chronology. *Mrs. Caldwell* went further, with its obsessive interior monologue structured in some 200 disconnected fragments, united only by the personality of the narrative consciousness, while lacking plot, sequencing, connected action, and chronology. *Tobogán,* a more radical antinovel, lacks all of these and more.

The Antinovel

A "novel" with an excess of insignificant characters and truncated tales, but little else other than an easily identifiable, symmetrical architecture, *Tobogán* employs the structure of an equilateral triangle with the bottom missing, somewhat resembling a mountain that the figurative toboggan ascends only to hurtle downward. A novel by Cela's own definition (the word "novel" appears beneath the title), *Tobogán* comprises two series of 100 vignettes (one ascending, one descending), linked by invisible degrees of contact: Series 1, 10 vignettes constituting a sort of chapter, presents character A with his or her family, neighbors, associates, and so on, among whom is B, who has a fairly peripheral relationship to A's group (e.g., B lives in the same building as A's lover, is the garbage collector for that building, etc.). Series 2 presents B with his or her family, neighbors, and associates, among whom is C, whose degree of contact with these is also peripheral (perhaps one is a coworker of C's brother, or his building janitor, etc.). Series 3 will focus on C and his or her family and associates, including another peripheral contact, D, known only to one of C's group, whose circle becomes the focus of series 4, and so on. No one in A's group knows anyone in C's group (the only intermediary is B). After presenting 10 series—100 vignettes, involving all the characters—the toboggan ascending the mountain, the narrative focus reverses, retracing its steps exactly (descending the mountain), finally arriving back at the point of departure, character A, having revisited the other 99 in rigorous reverse order. Possibly this structure illustrates the notion of "six degrees of separation." Alternatively, it might demonstrate existential otherness and radical isolation, notwithstanding the invisible connections linking each of us to others we have never seen or even imagined. McPheeters points out that the cycle is broken when upon reaching the 200th vignette, the character of the first sketch kills himself after his mother dies (McPheeters, 141). Readers familiar with symmetrically structured collections based on tens may recall the *Decameron* or María de Zayas's two collections of 10 novellas about the "enchantments" and "disenchantments" of love. When such possible antecedents are juxtaposed to *Tobogán,* however, there appears to be no connection beyond the purely structural.

The primary mode of discourse is descriptive rather than narrative, and character presentation seldom goes beyond superficial portraiture of physical appearance—bodies almost without personalities, scarcely a hint of psychology or "life story." So little "action" happens that even transitions from A to B occur in narrative silence, in the blank space between vignettes, making it inaccurate to speak of cinematographic technique. Readers must deduce intervening "action" based on changes between "ascending" and "descending" appearances of the characters. The portraits come closer to stills than movies (and sound—conversation—is minimal, trivial, superficial, as well). The common denominator—hunger and economic want—suggests a "social" motive inasmuch as *Tobogán* appeared during the heyday of Spain's "social novel," which indirectly denounced social inequities and injustices (implicitly blamed on the regime). Actually, other forms of human "hunger" are insinuated as well (especially emotional and existential). Although similar figures and techniques appear in Cela's brief fiction of the period, the difference is that other neo-*costumbrista* snapshots are neither termed a novel nor arranged in an identifiable pattern (the novelist might disagree, but his son terms *Tobogán* "*costumbrismo*"). Some ingredients are used in *Oficio de tinieblas* (an even more extreme experiment, which eliminates recognizable characters and environments—nearly all that remains of the traditional novel in *Tobogán*). McPheeters cites Cela's analogy between the skeleton of *Tobogán* and that of a snake, "because in this life everything is a concatenation, with no unattached pieces" (141). As in the travel books, Cela simply interrupts the presentation with extraneous conversation, speaking directly to the reader, to himself, or with a third party. McPheeters notes that antecedents for this interpolated, usually irrelevant dialogue appear in the travel books (and similar absurd, non sequitur conversations are frequent in later novels).

Antecedents for several aspects of Cela's later fiction appear in his nonfiction, especially his travel books, as Zamora Vicente observes in his overview of five decades of the novelist's development (see Zamora Vicente 1997). This critic stresses the travel books as sources for characters, settings, and types in *Apuntes carpetovetónicos* and many short-story collections (particularly those set in rural areas and villages), as well as in *Mazurca*. Another nonfiction text, the oratorio *María Sabina* (1967), pioneers the litany-like techniques in *Oficio, Mazurca, Cristo versus Arizona,* and *La cruz de San Andrés* (as well as the latter's division in five "melopeyas").[7] Cela's highly personal literary style employs alliterative, rhythmic prose, parallel constructions, grotesque caricatures sometimes juxtaposed to lyric tenderness, ever-present ironies, abundant tag lines, popular sayings, vulgarity, and obscenities, often alongside euphemisms in academically correct passages. Playfully examining words and language, trivializing or reducing to absurdity, he produces scenes, conversations, and incidents of exceptional artistry while avoiding narrative closure, traditional plots, connected action, and sequentiality. Critics have repeatedly questioned Cela's ability to create characters, since his only well-developed personality—Pascual Duarte, neither hero nor protagonist in the strict sense—does not act so much as react, almost always destructively. Innumerable sketches of beggars, the blind, prostitutes, the poor and indigent, and exploitative black marketers and merchants remain largely undeveloped; the characters are seen only externally, usually dehumanized, often reduced to animalistic levels. Besides assorted mental and sexual aberrations, Cela depicts violent, sadistic, or irrational crimes (which multiply in his later works). His minimal character development, frequently open-ended narratives, omission of traditional "required ingredients" (plot, protagonist, continuity, etc.), and works without identifiable temporal parameters have prompted many critics to question whether Cela is "really a novelist." The query may conceal deprecatory intent, but such queries reflect an underlying problem of genre, elegantly articulated nearly four decades ago by Guillermo de Torre:

> The question remains: is Cela fundamentally a novelist? . . . It is not only the numerical superiority of his books of short fiction, miscellany and travel, his volume of poetry and another of memoirs . . . but another, more significant contrast: the predominance of certain elements— descriptive, picturesque, landscape- or environment-related, even in what concerns characterization—constituting what is developed most fully.[8]

Torre concludes (as have many others) that Cela is essentially a stylist, an artist "of everyday language, of vulgar, aggressive expression, who raises popular sayings and fixed phrases to the level of art" (164). Cela's abundant clichés, idioms, proverbs, slang, popular sayings, silliness, verbal crutches, and tics of living speech thus accord with a conscious aesthetic purpose, simultaneously crude and cultured. Combining the colloquial with the academic or esoteric is indeed a hallmark of Cela's style. More recent studies have better articulated relationships between Cela's nonfiction and his fiction. Zamora Vicente elucidates further the travel books' significance as sources for portraits of rural people—peasants, farmers, shepherds, tradesmen—contrasting Cela's authentic paintings with Azorín's idealized reproductions of sixteenth-century rustics who speak with "all the elegance of Fray Luis de León" (1997, 19).

On the threshold of the third millennium, when concepts of genre and rules of established models have yielded to the aesthetics of postmodernism, questions of whether Cela is "really a novelist" can scarcely inspire polemics. Even ardent admirers of Cela find models for his later novels in other forms. Sobejano (1997) affirms that the paradigm operative in the first three novels and *Mrs. Caldwell* is that of the individual confession; that of *La colmena, La Catira,* and *Tobogán,* the chronicle; and that of *San Camilo, Oficio, Mazurca,* and *Cristo versus Arizona,* the litany. Given the antinovel and innumerable twentieth-century revisions of the novel as genre, no single, dominant definition of "novel" remains— although this may still be a logical prerequisite for defining "novelist." Nineteenth-century novelistic theory and practice would probably recognize only *Pascual Duarte* and perhaps the "New Lazarillo" as novels, yet few contemporary critics would define novel and novelist by criteria of centuries past. Spanish philosopher Miguel de Unamuno maintained that something can be defined or definitively described only when it is dead. Like Unamuno, Cela has long resisted conventional boundaries of genres, and like Unamuno (as well as Baroja), he believes that "life has no plot." Critics may debate the "death of the novel," but doing so will not affect the continuing production of "novels." Cela as novelist has moved from neo-naturalism or neorealism through several experiments to arrive at his present postmodern practice.

Cela's two novelistic periods presently exhibit approximate numerical equilibrium. Critics may not agree on descriptions of periods and their characteristics and duration in Cela's work, but most generally recognize that certain aspects (lexicon, form) have evolved considerably while others have remained relatively constant (theme, techniques). In general, the sober, controlled style of his initial works becomes progressively more baroque, the vocabulary more extravagant, syntax more complex, linguistic experimentation more extreme. Grotesque and expressionistic distortions intensify; characters become more exaggerated and bitter, with situations increasingly absurd. Arguably, however, these elements have been present to varying degrees since the beginning, and later works do not introduce new ingredients but intensify old ones, varying emphases and recombining elements already present.

Chapter Four

One Week in July:
San Camilo, 1936

By ironic coincidence, 18 July (when the Spanish civil war began) was St. Camillus Day. Cela's preface to *San Camilo, 1936* indicates that Camillus of Lelis is the patron saint of hospitals, the patron of curing, not killing. That week witnessed the invasion of the peninsula by rebellious officers of the Spanish army in Africa commanded by General Francisco Franco, plus uprisings by pro-Franco Falangist cells. Tragic events included the assassination of Federico García Lorca in Granada, together with hundreds of others with liberal associations or socialist leanings. In *Vísperas, festividad y octava de San Camilo del año 1936 en Madrid* (1969; *San Camilo, 1936; the Eve, Feast and Octave of St. Camillus of the Year 1936 in Madrid*, 1991)—known by the shortened title, *San Camilo, 1936*—Cela portrays official confusion, indifference, and misinformation, plus public reactions ranging from anguish and panic to right-wing elation.[1]

Although sharing aspects of the historical novel (specific time and place, numerous historical characters and documented events combined with fictitious ones), *San Camilo* departs radically from traditional historiography. Cela makes no pretense of objective presentation or "scientific" perspective, nor does he record acts of heroism and courage. This postmodern novel, with its demythologizing and revisionist thrust, subverts "history" as purveyed by the Franco regime and could be termed an "antihistorical" narrative. Indeed, this term is used by John H. R. Polt, translator of the excellent English edition. History—actual happenings during the time in question—becomes an obligatory intertext: readers must understand the novel against the background of historical events, historiographic assumptions concerning genre, and Francoist historiography. Separating those momentous days and historical events from bitter memories involved powerful emotions producing strong negative reactions among readers.

San Camilo signaled Cela's return to the novel and was reviewed by many prestigious critics within weeks of its release in December 1969.[2]

Charlebois sums up the controversy: "Critics have labeled it everything from historical and testimonial to mythical and structural" (53).[3] Frequently cited is Paul Ilie's denunciation, accusing Cela of "political pornography" and irresponsibility in omitting or obfuscating political issues underlying the civil war.[4] Perhaps equally intolerable for Ilie was Cela's juxtaposing events in both political camps, portraying both sides as equally inept and perverse, equally corrupt and violent, equally culpable. Because for many observers, the contenders were far from comparable, Cela's blurring of political divisions and presentation of opposing sides as equally wanton and indiscriminately promiscuous seemed outrageous. Ilie denounced Cela's emphasis on sexuality, both "normal" and deviant (leading one Spanish reviewer to dub the novel "Brothel Toboggan"). Jo Labanyi observes that censors, surprisingly, approved it without Cela's even hinting that the Falangist uprising would bring anything other than bloodletting.[5] Labanyi suggests that the novel represents "refuge in Eros as a release from history" (179), and that Cela demythologizes official versions of history not because these are mythical but "because they attempt to pass themselves off as history: that is, because they take history seriously" (179).

Maryse Bertrand de Muñoz examines *San Camilo* specifically as a war novel, representing a "fourth moment" of civil war novels, belonging to Franco's final decade and benefiting from Spain's Press Law of 1966, which allowed writers a certain margin of freedom from censorship.[6] Bertrand stresses predominant corporal and sexual violence, accompanied by verbal and psychological violence throughout (78), reinforced by crude, vulgar, obscene language and obsessive motifs of foul smells, nauseating odors, blood, death, cruelty, and animalistic behavior (80). Bertrand notes the polemic that *San Camilo* produced, but she suggests that the "real obscenity" for Ilie resided in what he perceived as Cela's "anti-Republican and antidemocratic posture, not in the erotic obsession" (Bertrand, 77–78). She observes that José Domingo judged the novel to be "politically neutral" (78), perhaps more intolerable for some than partisan advocacy of one side or the other. The near deification of Franco and the Falangists by regime historiographers made it sometimes difficult to "take history seriously." *San Camilo* replaces official myths with countermythification, "because Spanish history is written off as beyond redemption" (Labanyi, 178–79). Cela rejects no particular history in *San Camilo;* he expresses skepticism concerning the writing of history per se, citing Carlyle's observation "that history is the distillation of rumor" (*Memorias,* 262).

Literary Contexts of *San Camilo*

San Camilo has attracted more critical attention than any work of Cela's second period. Cela for the first time deals directly with the Spanish civil war (revisited in *Mazurca para dos muertos,* 1983). *San Camilo*'s action chronologically antedates *La colmena;* both novels portray panoramic cross sections of Madrid at specified dates (1936, 1942), covering brief periods, featuring huge casts, and emphasizing what Unamuno called *intrahistoria*—routine, quotidian happenings omitted by historiography, representing everyday reality rather than isolated larger events, and focusing on the masses of anonymous, pedestrian individuals rather than solitary heroes. Both novels, essentially plotless, rely on their tight chronology and historical context for structure, and both feature collective protagonists—less apparent in *San Camilo* because its narrative perspective involves a "focalizer" consciousness easily confused with a narrator-protagonist. Nevertheless, this figure is primarily a spectator (Unamuno would call him an "agonist"; he acts too infrequently and indecisively to qualify as protagonist). As does *The Hive, San Camilo* employs numerous "cuts," abrupt changes of scene, shifts of focus, and subsequent returns, weaving complex patterns whose most essential features are repetition and parallels. Significant differences exist as well. *San Camilo,* set in Republican Spain, imparts impressions of freedom, even license, absent in *La colmena* (not lacking licentious behavior). "History" looms larger in *San Camilo*—the days in question are momentous, whereas those in *La colmena* are not, and many more historical personages appear in *San Camilo,* whose characters are understandably more preoccupied with current events. In both, however, characters spend more time and effort satisfying their physical appetites than in any other activity.

The external, pseudo-objective narrative viewpoint employed in *La colmena* contrasts with the subjective, internalized perspective in *San Camilo.* Plotlessness notwithstanding, some unity results from retracing the historical events of July 1936, whose linear cause-and-effect relationship strands replace plot, providing apparent narrative continuity and acquiring further coherence thanks to repetitive presentations from varying viewpoints—another difference with respect to *La colmena.* In *San Camilo,* repetitions serve as structuring devices, anticipating more visible lyric structures in later novels. The structuring power of temporal constraints, continuity, and cause-and-effect sequences gives coherence to *San Camilo.*

Thematic repetition also exercises significant structuring functions in *San Camilo,* together with what may be called a *sí/no* dialectic of construction, using constant shifts of focus by the narrative consciousness, accompanied by a sameness of tone of the auto-dialogues and varied, obsessively repeated motifs. Repetitive themes include sexuality, death, suicide, fear, disguise or concealment, name changes, ignorance (*no saber*—not knowing), defining mankind, hypocrisy, and venality. The most oft cited recurring motif is the mirror and mirror mutations. Other repetitive motifs include the death mask, odors, blood, flies, crimes, sicknesses, and deformities. Similar themes and motifs appear in *Oficio de tinieblas,* which includes numerous constants of Cela's writing. Metaliterary allusions occur repeatedly as Cela directly or indirectly quotes Unamuno, Joaquín Costa, Angel Ganivet, Antonio Machado, José Ortega y Gasset, and others. Yet another repetitive device involves interpolation of short stories and childhood memories. As repetition constitutes a significant lyric device, recurring motifs contribute to lyric structures in *San Camilo,* and in increasing proportions in later novels.

Significantly, although Cela avoids a ludic treatment, he handles historical raw materials most unconventionally. Blended indiscriminately with the quotidian, the trivial, and the absurd, the larger "historical" events are interspersed with daily routines and chance happenings in the lives of the populace. Unamuno's concept of *intrahistoria* offers an alternative to historiography that Cela may have considered more revelatory of reality than what historians usually record. Arguing that major battles, decisive ruptures or catastrophes, and larger-than-life acts of heroism constitute exceptions rather than the norm, Unamuno concluded that to base "history" on these would be an aberration: what history should record is daily lives, unsung heroes, underlying continuity. He compared "history" to the storm-tossed waves of ocean tempests, and "intrahistory" to mighty, invisible marine currents, perpetually flowing in the ocean depths, calm or storm notwithstanding. Several observers have detected similarities between *San Camilo* and *intrahistoria* (although Unamuno would have recoiled at Cela's emphasis on the erotic and obscene). Cela probably read Unamuno's "intrahistorical" treatment of the last Carlist war (a nineteenth-century civil conflict) in his first novel, *Paz en la guerra* (1897; Peace in War).

San Camilo's anonymous personal narrator enhances the novel's impression of unity, as this spectator's obsessive monologues involve regular repetition, a stylistic feature of Cela's novels at least since *La Catira*.[7] Spain's civil conflict inspired some 8,000 novels worldwide, including some 1,300 written in Spain, according to studies by Bertrand. Many were fiercely partisan; nearly all portrayed heroism or virtue on one side or the other rather than abjection on both. During the Franco era, the conflict was officially deemed "Our Glorious National Crusade," a mythification and sanctification that Cela violently subverts. Antolín Rato recalls reactions among Spanish university students when *San Camilo* appeared:

> [Cela's] new novel was not aimed at adding anything to the anti-Franco struggle which for the most part consumed our attention and energies. The novel was ambiguous. The Reds were not good and the Franco forces were not bad, as we wanted them to be represented. The structure was considerably more complicated than that. There were no heroes with whom we could identify.[8]

Narratologically, *San Camilo* resembles James Joyce's *Ulysses:* an interminable internal monologue by a perambulating "narrator" who wanders about the city, not for 24 hours but for approximately two weeks,[9] accomplishing nothing, haphazardly observing demonstrations, street skirmishes, and funerals, listening to political harangues, randomly overhearing conversations and radio communiqués of doubtful validity, all the while obsessively preoccupied with libidinous memories and fantasies. Other scholars mention John Dos Passos's *Manhattan Transfer,* citing Cela's adoption of similar collage techniques: intercalation of newspaper clippings, obituaries, popular attractions, cultural references, want ads, and other advertising (including signs on commercial establishments passed in the narrator's wanderings). Spanish critics also repeatedly cited the final soliloquy of Joyce's *Ulysses,* "delirious" monologues in several Faulkner novels, Michel Butor's *La modification,* and Carlos Fuentes's *La muerte de Artemio Cruz.* Cela combines authentic and parodic or apocryphal documentation, further blurring the boundaries between fact and fiction, undermining media credibility as journalists are caricatured or depicted in grotesque sexual activities. Intertextual references juxtapose writers from the time of Heraclitus to the novelistic present (i.e., 1936), reinforcing impressions of supratemporal discourse or, conversely, of timelessness.

Sanz Villanueva mentions formal experiments and stylistic virtuosity but contends that Cela's greatest achievement in *San Camilo* is second-person narrative perspective and success in conveying the difficulty of communicating certain states of consciousness, especially the character's anguished quest for self-encounter.[10] Several critics have termed the narrative consciousness a narrator-protagonist, but he does not so much as act as react—psychically—and observe. According to Genaro Pérez, any protagonism of this youthful observer stems from "his function as Orteguian spectator [and] . . . screen upon which are projected other consciousnesses, episodes both historical and intrahistorical, commercial announcements and political propaganda."[11] Insofar as "protagonist" implies action, the term is inappropriate; the narrative consciousness is largely passive and lacks goals, except for his erotic activity. The novelist himself, in an interview with Stephen Miller, states clearly that the nameless narrative consciousness is simply that: "He's not a protagonist. In *San Camilo,* as in *La colmena,* the protagonist is an entire city."[12] For Cela, the figures of Martín Marco in *The Hive* and the anonymous narrative consciousness of *San Camilo,* "rather than protagonist, are the link between all the novel's situations, or nearly all . . . not a hero, but an anti-hero" (interview 1992, 12–13).

Typographically, *San Camilo* recalls Vanguardist works with its unconventional punctuation—largely consisting of commas, initially indicating transitions; then punctuation progressively diminishes. Likewise omitted are normal paragraph breaks; sentences often run for pages. The narrative consciousness sometimes uses the first person, but the predominant person of discourse in this schizophrenic monologue or "monodialogue" with the narrator's "other self" is the second person familiar (*tú,* which unlike its English equivalent "thou," is not obsolete in Spanish). Cela had already experimented with writing largely in the *tú* form in *Mrs. Caldwell habla con su hijo* and subsequently uses it extensively in *Oficio de tinieblas.* Few indications of changes of speaker or interlocutor appear, but the narrative consciousness shifts and metamorphoses. The primary consciousness represents an emaciated young man resembling Cela in age (then 20 years old), social class, philosophical bent, erotic penchants, and ill health (both have tuberculosis). Occasional skeptical comments obviously represent the viewpoint of the mature novelist, not the young man emerging from adolescence.

As in *Mazurca para dos muertos,* this alter ego/interlocutor is acquainted with Camilo José Cela, aspiring writer, and exchanges occasional words with him—in other words, Cela makes "Camilo José Cela" a minor character in *San Camilo* and other subsequent novels. His use of writers as characters or narrators, and the presence of their text(s) within the novelistic discourse begins with Pascual Duarte, who writes his life as confession. The several significant characters of *Pabellón de reposo* all keep diaries, and *Mrs. Caldwell* includes poems and letters that the title character has written to her son. Martín Marco in *The Hive* is another aspiring writer. Metafictional dimensions, enhanced by the heightened visibility of writers among the characters and their self-referential commentaries, expand in Cela's later novels. Two (or more) aspiring writers appear in *Mazurca,* and the variously named narrator-writer of *Cristo versus Arizona* peppers his text with comments, questions, opinions, doubts, and meditations inspired by the writing act. Increasingly distant from omniscience, the narrator-writers of Cela's later novels continually restate, retract, and self-critique, plagued by their own limitations, ignorance, and insecurity, "cringing," as Bakhtin would say.[13] Observers disagree about the significance of the role of the narrative consciousness in *San Camilo;* José Domingo asserts that there is no "major character,"[14] but opposing interpretations stress the novel's subjectivity, affirming that the "narrator-protagonist" dominates the text entirely. More accurately, the narrative consciousness constitutes an inescapable presence, through which events, as they are focalized, are fused with his obsessive monologue. This device subverts traditional hierarchies of importance: incidents of international significance occupy the same undifferentiated level as trivia, and historical events (objective, major happenings) merge into fantasies in the narrator's mind. Distinctions between minutiae and national concerns are similarly blurred. Whether calculatedly or not, *San Camilo* proved surrealist in its seeming disrespect for all the war signified (including a million dead), emphasizing the unheroic and antiheroic, venality, stupidity, blood lust, vulgarity, absurdity, triviality. Surrealism insinuates its presence elsewhere in bizarre behavior, underlying Freudian concepts, the unreality of events for many, and numerous metaphors, images, and perceptions. Stream-of-consciousness technique and hallucinatory episodes simultaneously evoke Joyce and enhance surrealist effects, alienating the reader just as the narrative consciousness appears radically alienated from all that surrounds him.[15]

As already noted, Cela's novels before *San Camilo* were written under the aegis of neorealism, whereas aestheticism and subjectivity return to prominence in the Spanish novel of the late 1960s, with neo-baroque style often combined with modified surrealism (as in works of Juan Benet).[16] Although language again becomes an end in itself, numerous works also subvert Falangist myths, Franco's mythified traditions, and conservative values. Several cultivators of the so-called New Narrative make extensive use of obsessive monologues, second-person narration, and shifting viewpoints found in *San Camilo,* which critics identified as neo-Vanguardist New Narrative, forgetting that Cela had employed these techniques some 15 years earlier in *Mrs. Caldwell*. Insofar as experimentation with the form and limits of the genre is integral to the New Narrative, several previous Cela novels contain precedents. Language per se and linguistic experimentation as ends in themselves for the "new novel" also have antecedents in Cela's work, and the New Narrative's experiments with time and perspective, shifting or fragmented chronology, duplicate or parallel sequences, and multiple story lines—all present in *San Camilo*—appeared in varying degrees in *Mrs. Caldwell, La colmena, Tobogán de hambrientos,* and *El solitario,* with tentative examples in *Pabellón de reposo.* Yet given his repetition of certain themes and formulas, Cela acknowledged that certain veins of inspiration were becoming exhausted: "I realized that that road was a blind alley . . . and rejected many of my most characteristic forms of expression, because if I had continued them, they would have put me in danger of becoming a kind of plagiary of myself."[17] Cela renovated form more than content, however, and techniques and structures more than style, so that many themes remained constant. Modified surrealism, present in many New Narratives and Cela's later novels, has antecedents in his own work dating back to *Pisando la dudosa luz del día,* composed in 1936—and thus contemporaneous with the action of *San Camilo.* The two books share similar dedicatory epigraphs, and as attested in *Memorias,* traumatic experiences suffered by the 20-year-old Cela during the bombardments of Madrid in 1936 inspired portions of both works.[18] Thus *San Camilo* coincides with numerous aspects of Spain's renewed aestheticism, but many are new for Cela; his own sense of needing renovation notwithstanding, plus many observers' perceptions of *San Camilo* as part of a larger novelistic renewal, "newness" is relative, consisting in varying proportions of ingredients already present to some degree in earlier writings.

Historical and Cultural Context

The novel's full title *(Vísperas, festividad y octava de San Camilo del año 1936 en Madrid),* alluding to a specific historical time and place, simultaneously comprises the subtitles of the three main parts. *Vísperas* not only means eve (of the saint's day) but loosely encompasses its antecedents, five or six days preceding; it also means vespers (another allusion to a religious service appears in the title of Cela's next novel). *Festividad* and *octava* (colloquially, a week is "eight days" in Spain) together comprise a novena (nine-day divine service). The following novel's title reference to the service of darkness *(Oficio de tinieblas)* similarly mentions forms of the mass in a context that no doubt struck many Spanish observers as sacrilegious when combined with these novels' pervasive eroticism, violence, and amorality. Another instance occurs in *Cristo versus Arizona*.[19] Subtitling *San Camilo*'s three main parts with the names of religious services heightens ironic contrasts with the content.

Labanyi suggests that the cyclical structure of *San Camilo* undermines the superficial chronology of events because the novelist rejects the linear progression that historians impose on past events. The absence of causal analysis, combined with persistent repetition, creates a sense of uncontrollable escalation (Labanyi, 181–82). The three parts of the novel form a symmetrical structure, with the pivotal central section— 18 July—being situated between two parts of exactly 168 pages each. Labanyi detects "contrapuntal interweaving of the vast cast of characters, with the end of Part 3 recapitulating the motifs and characters introduced in Part 1" (182). The first date encompassed in the "Vísperas" (Vespers) section is Sunday, 12 July, which historically saw the political assassination of Lt. Castillo of the Republican Guardias de Asalto (paramilitary riot police, then mostly Socialist). Three months earlier, Castillo had participated in a skirmish between conservatives from the Guardia Civil and his own police corps during the funeral of a pro-Falangist Guardia Civil who had been killed by an Asalto. Castillo killed Andrés Sáenz de Heredia, cousin of José Antonio Primo de Rivera (founder of the Falange), and retaliating Falangists ambushed Castillo in retribution—the second Asalto assassinated that summer. Vengeance for Castillo's murder was the gangster-style execution of parliamentary conservative opposition leader Calvo Sotelo (a Monarchist) on 13 July. Around 3:00 A.M., Calvo Sotelo was "arrested" at his home by Asaltos and Socialists posing as police, who executed the politician as the car sped away at 70 miles per hour. The body was handed over to a cemetery attendant and not identified until many hours later.[20]

Murder of Parliament's opposition leader, supposedly by regular police, horrified the middle class. Given public reaction, the date planned for the revolt (and Franco invasion) was advanced. On 16 July, the Spanish army in Morocco (under Franco) seized control of Spain's erstwhile North African provinces of Ceuta and Melilla, and two days later, the government responded to the insurrection by distributing arms to the populace at midnight on Saturday. Meanwhile the funerals of both victims (Castillo and Calvo Sotelo) were held the same day, 14 July. Cela presents these events from multiple perspectives in *San*

Camilo, insofar as they are witnessed by multiple characters from several vantage points, but underlying reasons are not elucidated, nor are historical antecedents mentioned (as in conventional historical novels). Additional specifics concerning the deaths of Castillo, Calvo Sotelo, and other victims of political assassination can be found in Ian Gibson's *La noche en que mataron a Calvo Sotelo* (Barcelona: Argos Vergara, 1982).

These events, the most historically significant of many in "Vísperas," provoke growing unrest in intervening days, with government crises, prevailing apprehension and uncertainty, and demands that the populace be given arms counterpointed by speeches from peace advocates. Sensations of growing tension and pent-up violence are conveyed and subliminally reinforced by presenting a series of minor crimes with accidental deaths, actual and attempted political reprisals by both extremes, repetitive motifs of blood and suffering, and an irrational, accelerating desire by the narrative consciousness to kill—his hypothetical victim being the foul-smelling prostitute Magdalena, with whom he has frequently spent the night. One message of *San Camilo* (recalling the notion of society's pro rata share of guilt mentioned in the prologue to the American edition of *Pascual Duarte*) is that everyone has the potential for violence; the novel's series of crimes, pervasiveness of blood and death, and irrational desires suggest the undermining of socialization and "normal" behavior in an atmosphere of confusion, terrorism, and opportunism, exacerbated by the summer heat, near anarchy, and misinformation.

Labanyi observes that "the impression that time is revolving on the spot is reinforced by the parallel description of events taking place simultaneously in different parts of Madrid. Indeed, time literally stops with the narrator's watch at the start of the novel. A Republican militiaman—echoing the 1848 July Revolution in Paris—shoots at the clock on the Ministry of the Interior, as if trying to put a stop to politics and with it history" (182). Pascual Duarte remembers the clock on the town hall of his village with its hands fixed forever on the same hour. Another conventional symbol of passing time—flowing water—is similarly immobilized in Cela's first novel as Pascual reminisces about the lavishly decorated town fountain where he has never seen a drop of water. Such failures of the municipality, which in *Pascual Duarte* symbolize stagnation, dysfunctional government, and a lack of progress, have become a philosophical statement with obvious historiographic implications: history repeats itself, time does not pass, the circle is a labyrinthine nightmare, and for Cela in *San Camilo,* all political activity seems actually or potentially criminal. The narrator's Uncle Jerónimo (a kind of lay prophet) denounces the religious incendiary he detects in every Spaniard's soul, viewing history as a curse: "Everyone comes into the world with his destiny marked; nobody can escape from what is written" (*San Camilo,* 311). There is no salvation, no redemption, and conversely no apocalypse (cf. 422), no new millennium.

The short second central part, covering only 18 July, St. Camillus Day, is the only part not subdivided into four chapters (which in the first and third parts unobtrusively correspond to respective days—another novena). Shifting narrative focus concentrates alternately on people attempting to flee the impending conflict, others who conceal themselves in the city, and others preparing for active participation. The primary narrative consciousness, with friends and acquaintances from both contending groups, does not appear more inclined to one side than the other, sustaining the impression of neutrality, indifference, or noncommitment to novel's end. Historical elements loom larger in *San Camilo* than in *La colmena* (or subsequently in *Mazurca*). No major historical events occurred in Madrid during the winter of 1942 to 1943 (portrayed in *La colmena*). The historical characters and events in *San Camilo* are underscored by real politicians, cultural figures, generals and military leaders, diplomats and intellectuals (including Alonso Zamora Vicente, Manuel García Morente, Pi y Margall, Gregorio Montes, Julián Marías, and Cela himself—not as author or narrator but simply as a disoriented adolescent suffering through events from a spectator's position). Cela inserts references to numerous Spanish writers, literary works, and characters, past and present. *Mazurca,* by contrast, is suprahistorical, given its mythic and lyric dimensions, and some characters are taken from real life or based thereon (again including Cela himself), but none have historical prominence.

Obsessive sexuality, without idealism, love, illusions, or joy, occasionally even without enthusiasm, becomes—like death—another equalizer. The one activity seemingly shared by all—sexuality without scruples—appears almost mechanical, routine, and compulsive. Leo Hickey points out the high degree of machismo, as women are considered exclusively as sex objects.[21] Uncle Jerónimo, the spokesman for "nature," advocates the crudest sexuality, affirming in the epilogue that the Spanish national disease is sexual repression: "If Spaniards were to fuck more and better, they'd be less brutal, stupid and messianic, there'd be fewer heroes and martyrs, that's true, but also fewer murderers, and things might even get better" (*San Camilo,* 319). But sexual liberation in *San Camilo* bears little resemblance to women's liberation, as Jerónimo's utopia involves providing prostitutes free of charge for all males. In what Labanyi deems "an extraordinary semantic distortion" (189), Cela terms this institutionalized male gratification "women's liberation." Sexuality becomes another image of endless repetition, a mirror of history, equated to a spinning top and water wheel in its endless monotony. Its emblem is the image of Narcissus (which partially explains the pervasive mirrors).

The nameless narrative consciousness of *San Camilo (tú)* remains a shadow, scarcely developed as an individual personality, functioning primarily as focalizer for the real (collective) protagonist, the masses of Madrid. This persona, who is studying for *oposiciones* (public examinations) for the Customs Service—as did Cela—has a steady girlfriend named Tránsito and is 20 years old (like Cela, who was born in 1916). His father is a customs officer, as was Cela's; he enjoys normal health, writes poetry, and—like Pío Baroja's autobiographical protagonist in *El árbol de la ciencia*—has an uncle with whom he converses about life's meaning. Hickey deems this character an "alter ego" of the author (227); he is *not* Camilo José Cela (as character), although they have a common circle of friends. A characterizing device for the narrator is the mirror, wherein he repeatedly (often initially, sometimes later in each of the 10 chapters or divisions) confronts his image. The mirror provides another (implied) interlocutor for the narrator's mono-dialogues, and the final pages list continually metamorphosing mirrors: "flat mirror pock-marked by humidity, parallelipedic mirror of multiplying intentions, a football-shaped mirror, monotonously fetal, an almost spherical, vicious and anaesthetizing mirror, a mirror in the shape of a bloody Medusa with a sickness hanging from every strand" (*San Camilo,* 427). Genaro Pérez suggests that the mirror's shattered identity reflects war's shattering of peace, security, and prewar reality (45). Sanz Villanueva notes the character's "identity problem" (68–69), elsewhere underscoring the theme of guilt: Cela "appears convinced that the bothersome problem of guilt can't be transcended if it is not projected in a moral sense . . . as a problem that affects the individual consciences of each and every Spaniard . . . all Spaniards must begin by recognizing their guilt" (207). The mirror also evokes memory, and because memory (equated with history) does not fade, Labanyi suggests that *San Camilo* "rejects the traditional concept of history as the record of the past in favor of a concept of history as fiction, as oblivion" (191). Thus the narrator's mirror, which initially appears to reflect history, eventually acquires the explicit function of blurring or erasing. Rather than reflecting a systematically distorted image, it distorts itself, constantly changing shapes. The confused, immature, self-contradictory narrator (anticipating the "unreliable narrator" of later works) is revealed ultimately as a liar; he has lied about many things, including whether he even has a mirror. So numerous are the contradictions and so blurred and fluctuating are the perspectives that readers cannot be sure who is speaking at times. The ambiguous, frequently used *tú* form could signify another character addressing the narrator, or the narrator addressing himself in the mirror. Charlebois observes that "as the primary structuring motif for the novel, the mirror is the symbolic thematic counterpart of thirty years of reflection, something the narrator calls a 'recapitulation.' . . . Being one of the significant common threads of the novel, the looking glass is strategically positioned at the beginning of five of the novel's ten chapters" (54).

The nameless narrator repeats time and again that he is not Napoleon, not King Cyril of England (apparently an apocryphal monarch, for whom no dates or other details are given, aside from reiterated allusions to his gruesome death by anal impalement). The point seems to be the impossibility of being a singular historical figure, ruler, or emperor, real or imagined, with obvious implications for novelistic theory: the only "hero" possible for contemporary narrative is a collective one. The collective aspect is subliminally underscored by the multiple intertexts from the mass media (radio and periodical news reports, advertising, public announcements, etc.). Personal identity crises notwithstanding, the narrator, with occasional implausible omniscience, speaks of other characters' most intimate thoughts and feelings, comments on their attitudes, and intervenes as narrator to contradict other characters and comment on political events. Such commentary, initially minimal, increases to occupy center stage and then gives way to anecdotes concerning other characters.

The third major division, "Octava," begins on the novel's second Sunday, one week after the assassination of Lt. Castillo, covering the succeeding days until Wednesday, 22 July. An undated epilogue comprises an incongruous, one-sided dialogue between the narrative consciousness and Uncle Jerónimo, who repeats with growing fervor, "Make [free] love not war." No significant time elapses between the body of the novel and the epilogue: the city's situation and characters' psychic states remain unchanged, placing the epilogue's probable date sometime during the "octava" (i.e., before the third Sunday, 26 July). Such are the temporal parameters of *San Camilo;* these, with the historical background, lend themselves to summary and exposition far more simply than the secondary story lines and viewpoints (each narrative thread corresponds to a different focus, surveying the actions and concerns of a different character or group). Although Cela includes members of all social classes, the most significant groups comprise politicians of both extremes, Left and Right—all of whom spend disproportionate amounts of time in bawdy houses, brothels, or more elegant establishments of prostitution. Readers unavoidably conclude that Cela implies that both sides made most of their decisions concerning the war in whorehouses. Observing that the novelistic cosmos representing Madrid in 1936 is peopled almost entirely by prostitutes, madams, and their clients, plus a number of homosexuals and persons with sexual obsessions or aberrations, Hickey expresses surprise that some critics have seen this world as not symbolic (228): probably Cela selected it to represent prevailingly low moral values and the overpowering importance accorded to physiological necessities in Madrid, Spain then and now, and the world now and forever. This vision initiates a quasi-allegorical portrayal of Spain found in several novels of Cela's second period, which in *Oficio de tinieblas* and the two most recent novels is carnivalesque. The population's lack of interest in anything transcendental and their obsession with physiological needs and biological processes (fornication, masturbation, drinking, eating, sleeping) reinforce the animalistic vision of humanity pervading Cela's fiction generally. Hickey further cites Cela's declaration that "the Civil War offered Spaniards the freedom to release and activate their pent-up hatred, repressed aggressive instincts and innate cruelty" (166). Antonio Iglesias Laguna suggested that Cela's use of so much vulgarity and sexuality was intended to challenge Spanish society for being falsely puritanical, falsely chaste, and falsely Christian, to combat Spain's repression of life and vitality.[22]

Language and Rhetoric

Leitmotivs, obsessive images, frequent repetitions of litanies of several sorts, and interrupting and retelling incidents already presented all figure among postmodern devices that anticipate narrative techniques in Cela's later novels but also function in *San Camilo* to emphasize the sense of collectivity: collective protagonist, collective voices (via the mass media), and collective narration that incorporates innumerable popular sayings, proverbs, fixed phrases, colloquialisms, slang of the day, names of typical brands and products, and clichés. Enhancing collective, undifferentiated, multivoiced narration are innumerable abbreviations—initials representing the names of political parties and organizations. Intertextual allusions range from Bible verses and liturgy fragments to popular songs, contemporary theater and movies, restaurants, and foreign authors and characters. Such allusions sometimes involve details of Spanish culture in the 1930s (including customs associated with death or dying, and with mealtimes and special celebrations) that would be unfamiliar not only to foreigners but to today's younger generation of Spaniards. The effect is alienating, defamiliarizing, with potential for producing reader discomfort, especially when juxtaposed with the oft-cited vulgarity, obscenity, and pervasive sexuality and served up to readers still influenced by political connotations and realities of the war and its aftermath. Consequently some more recent critics who treat *San Camilo* as a "civil war novel" do so with certain qualifications, treating it as a form of antihistory,[23] and Cela himself repeatedly declared *San Camilo* to be a novel "immersed in the civil war" rather than written about that conflict. In an interview with Edmundo Vandencammen, Cela explains the novel's conception as a "'fresco' of the anguish and insanity of men who understood nothing of what was happening" when the war officially began.[24]

The writer's passion for words is the focus of several analyses, and his idiosyncratic use of language in *San Camilo* is no exception. Diane Wilder Cornwell observes that this novel

> participate[s] fully in the contemporary revolution of expectations surrounding literary language which has elevated language into the role of a protagonist . . . [Language is primarily] expressive of theme—no longer . . . a mere passive conveyor of meaning but rather duplicating in its own form and structure particular narrative moments, interrelationships between characters, the dynamics of an episode, or entire states of consciousness, recreating what traditional language could only name.[25]

The long internal monologue of the narrative consciousness exercises several of the foregoing functions, duplicating them "in its own form and structure." The forms and functions of repetition—and rituals—likewise achieve certain rhetorical and structural effects, sometimes deliberately negative. Cornwell indicates that excessive repetition subverts rather than strengthens (64–65). In the "duplication in form and structure of particular narrative moments," Cela deliberately eliminates distinctions between text and context, literature and history.

New Historicism

Perhaps not coincidentally, the New Historicism is uniquely interested in "thick description, trivia and detail," the "historeme" (abundant and pervasive in *San Camilo*). And unlike the "old historicism," traditional historiography, which recorded only the great events, the New Historicism attempts to incorporate the marginalized or excluded (as in Unamuno's *intrahistoria* cited earlier, an approach adapted in *San Camilo*). Resulting texts challenge accepted historical "truth" to present a broader, more "complete" picture. Theorists of New Historicism often coincide with Cela's practice in *San Camilo* and later novels. One significant concept involves the fictitious condition of History (with a capital *H*), or the historicity of fiction. History is fiction; fiction is history. In his preface to the fourth edition of *La colmena* (Raquel Asún's critical edition), Cela affirmed, "This is a book of history, not a novel."[26] Curiously, Unamuno also titled his polemical historical memoir and political diatribe against Primo de Rivera's dictatorship *Como se escribe una novela* (How to Write a Novel), affording Cela ample precedent in blurring genre distinctions between history and novel. J. H. R. Polt notes that *history* and *life,* in Cela's comments, mean "much the same thing . . . because history is here used in the sense of the history that one makes by living."[27] Polt cites Cela's prefatory note to the third edition of *La colmena,* "History is like the circulation of the blood or digestion of food," and mentions its similarity to "Unamuno's *intrahistoria,* the minute, biological flow of many individual existences" (445). Most New Historicists affirm that meaning does not transcend the context but is produced within it, leading to relativism and an open-ended universe where time's passage brings new realities and meanings. According to Stephen Greenblatt,[28] who apparently invented the term, the so-called New Historicism is an oscillating textual practice, without fixed doctrine or formal discipline, lacking unequivocal poetics (by virtue of these omissions, both Unamuno and Cela might be designated New Historicists). New Historicism blurs boundaries between types of discourse and denies the importance—or even the existence—of genres, another point of coincidence with Cela's practice. Despite undeniable Marxist substrata in emphases on class conflict, New Historicism does not serve the interests of any given political ideology (certainly relevant for *San Camilo*). In this sense, it is postmodern and would accommodate attitudes expressed in several of Cela's later works, especially *Cristo versus Arizona* and subsequent novels. New Historicists affirm the absence of clear or essential differences between literary and historical texts.[29]

This observation applies most clearly to *San Camilo*. Hickey agrees that *San Camilo* is not a historical novel according to criteria of Lukacs, but it is "full of history," reflecting one of the most historically significant weeks in modern Spanish annals, and "the reality of the empirical world plays an essential role," as in the historical novel (Hickey, 227). Gemma Roberts figures among those critics who have praised *San Camilo* for its rejection of history and preference for reflecting individual experience, in other words, for an "intrahistorical" vision.[30] Polt offers an illuminating analogy with his remark that whereas other novelists of the Spanish civil war offer a "bird's-eye view," *San Camilo* gives a "worm's-eye view" (445). The unreliability of memory and of narrators is a recurrent theme in *El asesinato del perdedor* and *La cruz de San Andrés*— together with the tendency of eyewitnesses to contradict one another. Thus Cela offers multiple conflicting versions of the assassination of Lt. Castillo (*San Camilo*, 70, 71, 85), following a similar procedure with the murder of Calvo Sotelo (cf. 85 – 86). The novel thereby reflects the experience of individuals who, immersed in events that are embedded in their context rather than extracted from a matrix of apparently irrelevant information, necessarily lack the abstract vision of the historian. Cela's preface to the third edition of *La colmena* contains a relevant affirmation: "To *make* history, one must have no ideas. . . . Ideas are atavisms . . . never a culture and even less a tradition. Human culture and tradition, like the culture and tradition of hyenas or ants, could be guided by a compass with only three points: eating, reproducing, and destroying." This line of thought appears in the actions of characters in *San Camilo*, reducible to eating, eroticism, and killing. Rendering a historical event requires apprehending, ordering, and classifying countless individual actions and experiences, most of them "inevitably not experienced directly by the orderer and classifier" (Polt, 444). Cela's re-creation of the broad historico-social-cultural context of July 1936 suggests awareness of the New Historians' belief that the full historical context is not only important but essential (exact dates, contemporary milieu, ephemera, etc.). Presumably he would also agree with Roland Barthes that history is merely "meaning," which must change to satisfy the needs of changing civilization—changing governments, ideologies, and attitudes.[31]

San Camilo suggests that ideologies lead to violence, with crimes committed in the name of ideas, history, and religion (concepts that reappear in *Mazurca*), and that abstractions are dangerous—an idea found again in *El asesinato del perdedor,* where Cela's target is "justice" and its self-important minions. Slogans, myths, rituals, and symbols (flags, insignias, party-related gestures and signs) are not only dangerous but interchangeable: extremes of Right and Left are indistinguishable in their behavior and even their pronouncements. The narrator's Uncle Jerónimo, identified by several critics as Cela's spokesman, advises his nephew, "Try to believe in something other than history, that great fallacy, believe in the theological virtues [faith, hope, and charity] and in love, believe in life and in death—as you see I'm not asking for much" (*San Camilo,* 329). Via the pronouncements of Uncle Jerónimo, *San Camilo* emphatically states the primacy of the physiological over ideology and abstractions, offering an orthodox Freudian elucidation of the underlying causes of the civil war: an explosion of fratricidal violence motivated by massive sexual repression and aggravated by messianic demagogues on both sides (*San Camilo* echoes various Spanish intellectuals and essayists who have seen violence as endemic).[32] Such an explanation is consistent with Cela's insistence on the primacy of biological and instinctive forces over moral, intellectual, and ethical behavior, his depiction of humanity as a plaything of blind, uncontrollable forces. Despite frequent suggestions of contempt (and pity) for humanity, *San Camilo* also expresses Cela's bittersweet, tragicomic affection for concrete, suffering individuals caught up and crushed by larger events. At the same time, the novel rejects history, insofar as it is an abstraction, and insofar as history, ideology, and other abstractions inspire violence and the mistaken sacrifice of everything—possessions, love, life itself— on the altar of ideologies.

Chapter Five
Midnight Mass: *Oficio de tinieblas*

Neorealism was waning when Cela published *San Camilo, 1936.* The first and aesthetically weightiest challenge came from *Tiempo de silencio* (1962; *Time of Silence,* 1970), by Luis Martín Santos (1924–1964); the death knell was sounded by the neo-baroque tour de force *Volverás a Región* (1967; You Will Return to Región), by Juan Benet (1927–1993). As literature of engagement, neorealist "social literature" aimed to make a political statement, albeit surreptitiously, skirting the totalitarian regime's censorship. Style and concern for form were deemed unjustifiable unless they contributed directly to a critical (politically subversive) message. In reality, Cela's sardonic, sarcastic style, his tendency to comment at will on characters, their pasts, and motivations, and his lifelong use of deformation and caricature should discourage attributions of neorealism or its variants to his fiction. However, works such as *Tobogán de hambrientos,* with its multitude of poor, indigent, starving, or desperate characters, do exhibit certain characteristics of the movement, as everyday life dominates, with the routine, the quotidian, the typical and usually unremarkable displacing the exceptional, the heroic, the idealized.

Spain's New Narrative and Cela's "Renovation"

Post-neorealist literature in Spain (especially the novel, but also poetry and theater) moves in the direction of neo-baroque language and structures, or neo-Vanguardism, surrealism, and experimentalism. Spain's "new narrative" exhibited certain easily recognizable typographic characteristics: the suppression of orthodox punctuation, capitalization, and syntax and the omission of normal structural divisions such as paragraphs and chapters (observable in *San Camilo* and *Oficio*). Occasionally, pictorial or graphic elements appear within the text of *Oficio de tinieblas, 5.*[1] "New" novelists with their neo-baroque prose rejected neorealism's colloquial, accessible discourse in favor of complex, convoluted sentence structure or Latinate syntax, with sentences frequently running three or four pages (in extreme cases, novels have only one sentence). Vocabulary expands, incorporating neologisms, foreign words, scientific terms, archaisms, and esoteric terminology. Imagination and fantasy acquire new prominence, with everyday reality often relegated to the background or obscured by the mental meanderings of a befuddled narrative consciousness. Writing *San Camilo* obliged Cela to relive experiences long repressed and to read about others in period newspapers and magazines. Reliving horrifying aspects of the war possibly prompted his writing *Oficio de tinieblas* (as suggested by several commonalities): both are governed by Eros and Thanatos, written primarily in the second person singular *(tú)* form, and filled with darkness. Shared symbols include the mirror (related to self-encounter and facing unpleasant truths), and motifs of enclosure or imprisonment abound, together with symbols of the absence or impossibility of communication. Other common motifs include disease (and the view of humanity as a sick animal), deformity, mutilation, and torture. Surrealist sources and devices proliferate, as do iconoclastic attitudes. Common to the two works is the motif of not using or mentioning real names, which reappears in *El asesinato del perdedor.* Additional similarities include the presence of mutations and fusion, dissociation, fragmentation, and increasing absurdity—all of which grow in visibility and significance in the later novels. *San Camilo* is in many ways a pivotal work between Cela's earlier novels and more difficult narratives to follow. Not only does it occupy an important chronological position, ending a period of novelistic silence and introducing a new era of intense experimentation and subjectivity, but it also initiates significant narratological changes, reaffirming aesthetic preoccupations. The magical and mysterious, mythical and symbolic, acquire new visibility in post-neorealist works, as does the author's culture, rhetoric, personal concept of literature, and Weltanschauung. In *San Camilo,* and more so in *Oficio,* subjectivity displaces the pseudo-objectivity of critical realism, and introspection, emotions, memory, and psychological analysis take center stage. "New Novel" experiments with time and with narrative perspective are numerous, involving shifting or fragmented chronology, multiple time planes, duplicate or parallel sequences, multiple story lines, and absent, dead, or abnormal protagonist-narrators. Characters often lack depth and direction, exemplifying the *homo absurdus* (an archetype of the subgenre), employing first person while taking refuge in anonymity, and remaining too diffuse for the reader to capture or understand. Second-person narrative sometimes fulfills similar functions. Cela and Juan Benet increased potential confusion for readers by giving several names to individual characters, or the same name(s) to several different characters; omitting names similarly deprived readers of making definitive identifications, often excluding knowledge of the characters beyond their acts and words. Many such traits, already present or implicit in *San Camilo,* become more visible in *Oficio de tinieblas* (and recur in Cela's later novels).

Increased subjectivity and experimentation in *San Camilo* and *Oficio de tinieblas* are especially striking when compared to neo-picaresque and neo-*costumbrismo* content in works of neorealist focus, for instance, *Tobogán de hambrientos.* While news flashes, advertisements, and so forth counterbalance the narrator's subjectivity in *San Camilo,* in *Oficio,* nothing interferes with subjectivity. Second-person narrative reappears, but the omnipresent *tú* is even less a person than in *San Camilo.* One cannot accurately speak of either narrator or narrative in *Oficio,* which narrates nothing. *The Random House Dictionary of the English Language,* unabridged edition (1971), defines narration as "an account or story . . . a recital of events, especially in chronological order, as the story narrated in a poem or the exposition set forth in a drama." Synonyms include chronicle, tale, and history. *Oficio de tinieblas,* with its nearly 1,200 separate fragmentary entities, or "monads," ranging in length from less than a line to some two pages, is none of these.

The Antinovel and *Oficio*

The term "antinovel" denotes novels lacking traditional plot structure and other traditional novelistic ingredients (hero, relatively straightforward chronology, etc.). *La colmena* could by such criteria constitute an antinovel, and McPheeters (writing before either *San Camilo* or *Oficio*) termed *Mrs. Caldwell* "as much an anti-novel as has yet been conceived in Spain." *Mrs. Caldwell* offers a structural antecedent for *Oficio,* with some 200 unconnected fragments anticipating the nearly 1,200 monads of *Oficio.* But the resourceful reader of *Mrs. Caldwell* can reconstruct a semblance of the protagonist or narrative consciousness (apparently a madwoman) and deduce probable sequential action. Neither is possible for readers of *Oficio,* as fragmentation increases, and the fact that the latter belongs simultaneously to the confessional mode (to which Sobejano assigns *Mrs. Caldwell*) strengthens connections between the two, even though the former is assigned to the seemingly contradictory classifications of vast, collective chronicle and litany (Sobejano 1997, 139, 140). *San Camilo* returns fully to Vanguard-style narrative, reflecting Cela's prewar admiration for Joyce. The element of litany (an enhanced and intensified adaptation of the tag line technique and refrains characterizing Cela's fiction from the inception) acquires increased significance in later novels, incorporating recognizable liturgical forms in *Oficio* and several successors. Aspects of the litany—rhythmic, repetitive sequences— reappear with structuring functions in *Mazurca para dos muertos, Cristo versus Arizona, El asesinato del perdedor,* and *La cruz de San Andrés,* whose form is more lyrical than narrative.

Some critics term *Oficio* an antinovel, but this is a far more radical experiment. The antinovel is still a novel, with describable characters and setting, identifiable events, and relationships between these, albeit lacking clear-cut plot or sequentiality. *Oficio* suppresses plot, describable setting, identifiable characters, definite time and space, sustained action, meaningful sequence (of events, reflections, memories, or meditations), and identifiable chronology. Novelistic chronology has historically provided the framework for sequential action; without action or continuity, chronological data become meaningless, as in *Oficio,* where readers can scarcely affirm that time passes or anything happens. *Oficio* lacks characters in any normal sense, although the shadowy, anonymous narrative perspective occasionally refers to family members—vague, abstract, unnamed figures known only generically by familial role relationships: *tuprimo* (your cousin), *tu padre* (your father), *tu madre* (your mother). These faceless, nameless, nearly mindless constructs function as abstract axles on which to hang a collection of vices. In *Oficio,* Cela intensifies the minimalist characterization typifying many of his early personages, usually caricatures or social stereotypes, often grotesque, occasionally pathetic, rarely developed at length. Characters in *Tobogán de hambrientos* are exclusively two-dimensional, merely names with circumstances (spatial, familial, social): personality and subjectivity remain deliberately undeveloped, suggested on rare occasions by details such as a letter in the pocket of a corpse. *Tobogán* provides the most relevant antecedent for *Oficio*'s vague characters and lack of sequential action.

Yet *Oficio* is not fully antiliterature, due to its art and artifice of language and structure. Notwithstanding the absence of characters, setting, action, and connected narrative, *Oficio* is not simply an essay or tirade, a jigsaw puzzle with key pieces missing. Robert Saladrigas, in an early review of *Oficio,* inquired: "Is it possibly a poem? I wouldn't dare deny it, although . . . here again Cela breaks with every trace of [lyric] convention."[2] Gonzalo Navajas detects a radical questioning of the most fundamental premises of modernity, a minute examination of underlying presuppositions, and what modernity conceals or represses because it is incapable of assimilating or explaining it. "Cela is the Unconscious of Modernity which emerges when civilizing mechanisms are not functional or have become aberrations because of deformation of their constitutive nature."[3] Navajas argues that although various contemporary novelists have made emergence of the unconscious a central theme of discourse, what differentiates Cela is his concentration on the most primordial conduct, those aspects preceding the elaboration of consciousness.

Oficio, rejecting all existing models, fits no recognized definition other than Cela's own tongue-in-cheek suggestion, "any book which includes beneath the title the word 'novel,'" qualifying *Oficio de tinieblas* as novel, as evinced by its lengthy title:

> *Office of darkness* or thesis novel written to be sung by a choir of invalids as ornament for the liturgy celebrating the triumph of the blessed and the circumstances of blessedness, to wit: the torture of Saint Theodora the martyrdom of St. Venancio the exile of St. Macarius the solitude of St. Hugo whose transit took place beneath a rain of abject smiles of gratitude and is commemorated the first day of april. (*Oficio,* title page)

Concepts such as sickness, torture, martyrdom, solitude, and abjection—already enunciated in the title—foreshadow the content. Equally emphatic suggestions of sanctity, spiritual triumph, and blessedness, however, mislead and disappoint readers naively expecting counterbalancing virtues. Having termed the work a thesis novel, however, Cela states on the following page, "Naturally, this is not a novel, but a purging of my heart." Cela seems to have been sincere in proclaiming his novelistic abdication at a press conference at the time of the book's release, as he published no novels for more than a decade. Rafael Conte considers *Oficio* (which he terms Cela's "ninth novel") "the strangest, most obscure, darkest, and most disquieting of all, the apex of his experimentalism, his most-misunderstood book, still insufficiently evaluated."[4] Another overview of Cela's work terms *Oficio* a "thesis novel" that "has no equivalent in the literature of the world, with its bestiary and its panoramas of peoples and animals and monsters, singing an infernal anti-liturgy, where man is initiated into nothingness and death."[5] Cela's ironic classification of *Oficio* as a thesis novel begs commentary: while clearly not a thesis novel, what it is proves less clear, as demonstrated by the diversity of critical reactions.

Classifications of *Oficio*

José María Alfaro, writing in *ABC* (15 November 1973), termed *Oficio de tinieblas* "poetry," and José Domingo's review in *Insula* 327 (February 1974) deemed the book poetic prose or a group of little prose poems. For Rafael Conte, writing in *Informaciones de las Artes y las Letras* 285 (27 December 1973), *Oficio* was "an experiment, a broken mosaic." Cela often affirmed that each of his novels was innovative, an experiment in its own way—an attitude reaffirmed in another interview published a full decade after *Oficio*. "Whenever I've written a novel, I've leaped into thin air," he stated in *El País Semanal* 523 (19 June 1983), reiterating the notion that his duty as a writer consists in exploring different pathways. In a postpublication Madrid colloquium, Cela described *Oficio* as a work of "internal reality." Alluding to Stendhal's concept of the novel as a mirror passing along the road, Cela clarified that *Oficio* follows a route leading not along a road but inward—a risky trajectory through dark, turbulent pathways of the soul, requiring writing and structures coherent with the soul's chaotic nature.[6] The colloquium, reported in *ABC* (3 February 1974), associates *Oficio* with narratives requiring reader participation—as experimental novels typically do. Readers must counter the scarcity of external circumstances and peripeteia, the vagueness of the abstract and problematic characters, frequent and seemingly arbitrary temporal breaks, the absence of elementary typographical conventions, enormous linguistic difficulties, and monotony and lack of pleasure or entertainment afforded.

Torrente Ballester, long-time professional critic and leading exponent of another variant of the "New Novel," wrote of his difficulties with *Oficio* (not identified by name):

> It's a novel that tells something quite unclear about some abstract entities, without any reality but the merely verbal. Man, humanity, is nowhere; I can't remember anything in which dehumanization has been taken to such a radical extreme. . . . Poetry and wit have been excluded. As invention, it is impoverished, repetitive, monotonous. This road will lead us nowhere. . . . It isn't a novel, nor is it a work of art.[7]

Torrente Ballester questioned the contemporary Vanguardist vogue, inquiring, "Can we truly no longer write anything where something happens to somebody?" (233).

At the opposite extreme is the reaction of Mariano Antolín Rato, a novelist of the younger generation (whose disappointment with *San Camilo* was cited in the previous chapter):

Oficio revealed to us, unhesitatingly and definitively, how great a writer Camilo José Cela really was . . . [and] succeeded in making familiar in Spain the kind of novel which until then had come from abroad: a modern narrative (as was my novel, according to the critics)—a novel which, while being Spanish, seemed moved, even shaken, by the problems assailing all men in the 1970s. (35)

Antolín Rato observes that Cela presents a discourse "whose world of reference is not supported by external or visible material . . . [but] discontinuous narration in which meaning resides in the dynamic process of a mind devoted to complicated plays of images whose sparks reach the realm of ideas . . . like hallucinatory arabesques" (35). Creative imagination "flows in uncontrollable currents, its only concretion being the grammatical skeleton" (36). Beneath the experimentalism runs an "undercurrent of terrible beings and situations . . . Cela's is a world ruled by atrocity, torture, and the sadism of a humanity impelled toward horror by a pervasive and barbaric schizophrenia that is his environment, a world akin to that presented, for example, by Robbe-Grillet in *Project for a Revolution in New York* or by William Burroughs in *Naked Lunch*" (36).

Cela himself called *Oficio* "probably the most difficult book ever written. . . . you have to be very much into what we call 'the literary phenomenon' or the 'cultural phenomenon' . . . in order to sink your teeth into it."[8] In masterful understatement, Martínez Cachero notes that for once, Cela, his critics, and readers agree: *Oficio* is not a novel in the strict, generic sense of the word (347). Rafael Conte, from the perspective of intervening critical commentary, still questions:

Is this book a novel? Its author says so, and we should remember that his famous definition of the novel—"any book that says 'novel' beneath the title"—is not a joke, but a cry of liberation, an heir of Baroja's "tailor's box," a correction of the quantitative E. M. Forster, a return to the novel's hybrid and impure origins, perhaps even the conscious project of its own self-destruction. (66)

Ideas in *Oficio*

Cela's proclamation of his "abdication" and his pronouncements concerning *Oficio* must be taken in context, including the novel itself with its convincing cumulative evidence of personal crisis, such as the reiterated notes of self-accusation—new in Cela's work, and present from the opening lines:

it's comfortable to be defeated at twenty-five without a single gray hair in your head without a single cavity in your teeth without a single cloud on your conscience with only two or three lacunae in your memory and to look at the world from the heavens from purgatory from hell from beyond the Pyrenees and the Andes with frigidity with indifference with stupor (11)

don't take advantage in sports don't take any advantage for yourself at the starting gate it's comfortable to be defeated in the prime of youth don't forget it (35)

you shouldn't be obsessed by the idea that it's comfortable to be defeated at twenty-five you should get used to the idea of living with your back turned to all ideas a gentleman doesn't have ideas (110)

Cela reiterates the notion of having given up too easily, having taken the path of least resistance, retiring from the fray in the prime of youth. Another self-accusation affirms that the narrative consciousness "cannot escape the feeling that for years you've been wasting your time fooling everybody around you . . . and it shows . . . that you are far from telling the truth far from thinking the truth" (799). The narrative consciousness appears obsessed with concealing certain things (for example, concern over revealing names and the frequently reiterated injunction "not to pronounce his name" whenever his father is mentioned). Silence regarding family nomenclature enshrouds his mother, grandmother, grandfather, and cousin, as well as the cousin's girlfriend and generic characters such as the executioner. Monad 1017 lists several women whose names have never been mentioned and will not be again: "zenaida the woman dressed as Colombine," "leocricia the woman dressed as a gypsy," "hugolina the woman dressed as a man," "modalda the woman who paints her eyes with tailor's soap," among others. Accompanying the compulsion to concealment is the narrator's preoccupation with silence and control: "don't let your words flow freely and copy the customs of the convent's silent mummies" (462). These writerly virtues or failings, like revelation or concealment, are related to the concept of confession. Monad 332, deemed significant by several commentators, states: "you never doubted the words you heard and you lost now it is too late to turn back and even to make an examination of conscience." The notion of "too late" or not having acted in time is another insistent, recurring motif.

The text comprises 1,194 fragments whose most frequent length approximates a modest paragraph. Sequencing of the "monads" appears arbitrary, although a small percentage of these discrete numbered segments are juxtaposed to others that are related to them thematically, logically, or syntactically. Occasionally, related monads may be arranged sequentially, but fragmentation and isolation prevail. Those who have commented on the monad as concept relate it summarily to Gottfried Leibniz (e.g., Charlebois calls it "an intentional borrowing from Leibniz to refer to the simplest, indivisible units of living things" [64]).[9] A more literary and relevant antecedent, however, is poet Antonio Machado, a pioneer of existentialism in Spain and martyr of the civil war. Writing via his heteronyms Abel Martín and Juan de Mairena, Machado modified the concept, emphasizing that the monad had neither windows nor doors (an emblem of radical solitude and the impossibility of communication) yet yearned for (comm)union with the Other. The existential absurdity of the monad's situation as described by Machado better suits the surrealist mode of *Oficio,* contrasting with the essentially combinable nature of Leibniz's monads (as basic building blocks of all matter). The fragmentary nature of *Oficio* enhances and is enhanced by the monads' inescapable solitude. One of the novel's oft-reiterated motifs, solitude figures among numerous links to *San Camilo.* From *San Camilo* onward, Cela increasingly employs religious allusions, incorporating litanies, parts of the Rosary, and in *Oficio,* the ironic analogy with Catholicism's holiest High Mass. Still more visible is the novelist's gesture toward religious contexts in *Cristo versus Arizona,* and litanies are prominent in *El asesinato del perdedor* and *La cruz de San Andrés.*

Carol Wasserman notes criticism of traditional religion in *San Camilo,* including observations attributed to characters who in her view speak for Cela; for example, "it's necessary to detoxify Spain from its religious superstition" (*Oficio,* 216), and Uncle Jerónimo's observation that "inside every Spaniard dwells a religious incendiary . . . reactionaries burn heretics and books and revolutionaries burn churches and images, the idea is to burn something" (227). Elsewhere the narrative consciousness of *San Camilo* reflects (in terms clearly anticipating *Cristo versus Arizona*) that "God has nothing to do with what mankind does, He contemplates us with infinite scorn with infinite pity also with an infinite burden weighing upon Him" (110). The God portrayed in Cela's work pities humanity's exaggerated religious beliefs and the wars these produce— important for understanding *Oficio.* Wasserman cites an interview with the author: "My opinion of religion and the Church in Spain isn't very good" (135), adding Cela's belief that "religion in human history has fulfilled a function of moral control, so that people don't commit more barbarities than they already do" (135). Concerning numerous obituaries in *San Camilo* and *Oficio,* Wasserman affirms that despite much talk of death in wars and by natural causes, *Oficio* and other writings show Cela to be completely against the death penalty (136). Several monads suggest textual confirmation; for example, "your father don't pronounce his name was against the death penalty" (*Oficio,* 657). Another generic type, the executioner, proclaims opposition to "distributing licenses to kill" (660); furthermore, "only rich merchants who made their fortune with blood defend it [the death penalty] very conservative men still believe that blood washes away blood[.] it's essential to hand over your savings to the committee to combat the death penalty" (757).

Among the novel's characters—including familial archetypes, literary types (e.g., masks of the commedia dell'arte such as Colombine and Pierrot), and numerous historical figures—appear various generic representatives of trades connected with death: the executioner, grave digger, and stonecutter (engraver of tombstones). Cela also criticizes discrimination on the basis of race, ethnicity, and social class (a topic enunciated more emphatically in *Cristo versus Arizona*). He criticizes pollution, unemployment, abuse of authority (excoriated in *El asesinato del perdedor*), the high price of health care, the marginalization and abandonment of senior citizens (cf. *Oficio,* 59), and other perceived injustices, including military conscription. One of Cela's most enduring themes, man's inhumanity to man, figures emphatically in all the later novels. *Oficio* includes interesting statements on gender relations that may surprise many readers, as Cela portrays women quite negatively: swarms of prostitutes, gossipy matriarchs, bored concubines, and faded housewives. Man is repeatedly portrayed in *Oficio* as weak: "man is an awfully weak animal" (403); "man is weaker and more cowardly than woman he tires sooner and gives up the fight sooner dies sooner"; "man and woman love in different ways" (964). Woman appears stronger, implicitly more likely to fight and win, according to the foregoing affirmations (while not biologically accurate, these affirmations are often borne out by Cela's portraits of women). Cela's novel that best portrays the strength and fighting qualities of certain female characters is his next, *Mazurca.*

The narrative consciousness of *Oficio* exhibits symptoms suggesting crisis and depression, with endless references to pain, punishment, death, cowardice, torture, cadavers, fear, mutilation of bodies, hunger, exile, blood, absurdity, falsehood, boredom, cruelty, despair, lies, vanity, pride, defeat, humiliation, revenge, resignation, venality, misery, suicide, poverty, murder, execution, killing, cemeteries, grave diggers, tombs, vermin, sadism, varied forms of suffering, and every imaginable perversion of "love" and sexuality. One significant self-accusation appears in the repeated affirmation that "you were a very inexpert spectator, that is your grave sin, the sin for which there can be no pardon without penance without penitence of blood" (21). Existentially, the persona's self-recriminations concern lack of engagement and of authenticity. The narrator's self-loathing and prolonged identity crisis do not fully camouflage his lack of coherent personality. Although the omnipresent *tú* seemingly speaks at times for the author, no sooner has an illusion of personality been created than it is contradicted or negated.

Critics have tended to overlook the fact that *Oficio* is Cela's only long "fiction" published in the 15 years separating his two novels about the Spanish civil war, *San Camilo* (1969) and *Mazurca* (1984), suggesting meaningful connections between the three works. Conte does not link *San Camilo* and *Oficio* to Cela's next novel about the civil war but does point out that whereas *San Camilo* treats the war's outbreak, there is a specific textual connection between *Oficio* and the civil conflict's end (the title reference to "the first of April" or "Day of Victory," when Franco's military communiqué notified the nation of the unconditional surrender of the remnants of the Loyalist Republican army). Because the temporal parameters of *Mazurca* almost coincide with the civil war's beginning and end, and incidents falling beyond these parameters involve earlier civil strife, a closer relationship may exist between the three novels than critics have yet identified. Indeed, the three novels could be termed Cela's trilogy about the civil war. Such a hypothesis would open new avenues of interpretation of *Oficio*. References to 1 April throughout the novel suggest that date's obsessive importance for the work as a whole, and readers should remember that it saw not only the Republic's surrender but the beginning of Franco's dictatorship and totalitarian police state.

Other postwar novelists (e.g., Ana María Matute) have repeatedly mentioned the "horrors of peace" following the horrors of war. Hundreds of thousands of Republican partisans and sympathizers were systematically rounded up and summarily executed or imprisoned, including one of Cela's youthful drinking companions, Republican soldier-poet Miguel Hernández, who died in a Franco prison because of a lack of medical care. Novelist Angel María de Lera, formerly a minor Republican official, spent more than two decades under sentence of death in a political prison, suffering the psychological effects of that experience, during which fellow prisoners were executed daily. Others with Republican associations who were trapped inside Spain at war's end went into hiding, many remaining hidden under floorboards and in cellars and attics for decades. Some so-called *topos* (moles) emerged from the shadows only after the dictator's death nearly 40 years later—an extreme "service of darkness." One of the holiest liturgies of the Catholic Church, the *oficio de tinieblas* (office, service, or mass of darkness) refers to the Easter vigil, traditionally celebrated without light. In earlier times, this liturgy occupied three days representing the entire time Christ was dead, with dawn's light on Easter morning coinciding with the proclamation that "He is risen." As part of the religious culture of all Hispanic countries, the symbolically rich concept has been adapted for many purposes, often ironic, as in Cela's case. In *Oficio* the "service" does not lead to resurrection or end with a new day and new life; it leads to the opposite: it ends precisely at midnight, purportedly with the suicide of the narrative consciousness. This does not specifically indicate that Cela is subverting the mass, in spite of a litany in *Oficio* involving not names of Christ but of Satan. A curious footnote concerns the final words with which the author dates the novel's composition: "Palma de Mallorca, between the Day of the Dead, 1971, and Holy Week, 1973." These dates specifically link the act of writing with the liturgical calendar and bear upon death and resurrection.

In the absence of plot and other conventional structuring elements, structure is supplied by litanies (including parts of the canonical liturgy). Many forms of repetition exercise similar vertebrating functions. At least 14 obituary notices appear from monad 794 to the end; seven successive monads (778–84) summarize the deaths of apocryphal characters killed for eating excrement; another list involves 10 antique toilets in "your mother's boudoir" (785); monads 46 to 49 and 51 to 56 all refer to death or dying; and 62 to 67 all mention birds' eggs (a traditional Easter symbol of new life). Tag lines reiterated whenever a name or character is mentioned provide another case in point, as do their descriptions and formulaic actions. Sobejano lists several examples:

> They are extravagant caricatures from an abject underworld, monstrous snapshots of the lethargy of reason: "your father don't pronounce his name" (buried in the civil cemetery); "your granny" devourer of men; "yourcousin" prostrate in his "bed of frustrations"; "yourcousin's girlfriend"; the mother of "yourcousin"; the man dressed as Pierrot; ulpiano the stonecutter; the harelip boy; the baron with conjunctivitis and orange-colored mole; the superannuated Danish tourists visiting the

museums of Italy; the priest don iluminado . . . the buffoon; the woman dressed as a prussian colonel; the woman dressed in golden rags; and many other figures of the lugubrious carnival. These sinister mannequins reappear in nearly identical situations, with minuscule variations that stimulate no action. Numbered obituaries periodically announce the deaths of some of these puppets, thirteen of them, but it makes no difference that some die and others do not; all return again and again like fantastic, purely verbal supports that people the desert of boredom.[10]

The patently absurd blends with the meaningful; reiterated motifs and metaphors mimic poetic structure. Solitude is the major preoccupation of several lengthier monads, one (1146) meditating on the necessity for solitude to understand death. Another with considerable autobiographical substrata—a long interior monologue treating writing in existential isolation—repeats the insistent refrain, "solitude, solitude" (1149), recalling a theme of another prewar Cela associate, the philosopher María Zambrano.

Surrealist Aspects of *Oficio*

Literary variants of surrealism returned emphatically to visibility in Spain in 1970 with publication of the anthology *Nueve novísimos poetas españoles* and its introduction-manifesto by José María Castellet. Sobejano views Cela as a significant figure in the postwar development of surrealism in Spain, but Antolín Rato states flatly, "By no means is *Oficio* a Surrealist work. It perhaps belongs more to the expressionism of a Gombrowicz . . . not mainstream expressionism [like] Valle-Inclán's 'esperpento' . . . [but] an expressionism which . . . can only be called abstract" (Sobejano 1976, 36). Charlebois, however, believes that "*Oficio* is the narrative counterpart of Cela's two surrealistic dramatic works . . . [wherein] everything centers around public executions as a way of demonstrating the public's insatiable thirst for blood" (64). This is an important observation, as blood lust looms large in Cela's recent works, especially *Cristo versus Arizona, El asesinato del perdedor,* and *La cruz de San Andrés.* The resulting "emotionally charged scenarios" facilitate the "incorporation of quasiclassical choruses that . . . manifest society's complicity in . . . human depersonalization, a theme that surfaces with unparalleled vengeance . . . in *Oficio*" (64).

Man's inhumanity to man, a critically recognized leitmotiv of Cela's work, acquires heightened visibility in *Oficio* as well, thanks to the efficacy of surrealist elements.[11] For surrealist theorist André Bretón, poetic analogy was replaced by juxtaposing far-fetched chance encounters of two images (a frequent technique in *Oficio*). The result, usually absurdity, undermines distinctions between internal and external realities, subjective and objective existence, a crucial ingredient of the oneiric aspect of surrealist paintings. Cela's continuing involvement with surrealism is attested by his 1981 *Los vasos comunicantes,* whose title Cela borrowed from one of Bretón's major works, *Les vases communicants* (1932), a formulation of surrealist metaphysics fusing poetry and prose in a new philosophy of reality. Believing in the continuity of the state of consciousness and the dream, the lack of real separation between life and death, surrealists conceived of existence as a conciliation between apparent contradictions in form and phenomena (a principle repeatedly exemplified in *Oficio,* as is the concept of disorder). "Additionally, Apollinaire-like calligraphs are found, such as in monads 1042 and 1039 bis and 1156" (Charlebois, 67). Freudian influence and surrealist interest in the mentally deranged appear not only in *Oficio* but also in *El asesinato del perdedor* and *La cruz de San Andrés.*

Cela Conde describes the extremes to which Cela went to isolate and plunge himself in total darkness while writing *Oficio,* retreating for months to a "black box" from which he emerged only to eat and sleep (elsewhere he is described as working behind a black curtain). Monad 437 affirms that "man only sees clearly in darkness as he imagines the most beautiful and heroic happenings from the shadows" (*Oficio,* 66). Cela managed thereby to exclude or limit external stimuli, reducing concrete references to a particular reality (one reason there are almost no place names or geographic references in *Oficio,* as these would limit the novel to a particular country). The paucity of Spanish names, especially patronymics, contributes to the abstract effect achieved as Cela emphasizes the internal and subjective over the external and objective. Another lengthy monad concerns writing in isolation (1149), and the typewriter surrealistically reclaims its liberty even as the narrative consciousness/writer loosens his grip on reality (1170). Elsewhere, one of several voices advises that "from the contemplation of everything that has been said no effort should be made to derive general consequences" (853). Such immersion in the irrational evokes surrealist efforts to foster creative power by stimulating the unconscious to produce "automatic writing." Early surrealist theories demanded eliminating reason, taste, and conscious will from elaboration of the artistic work. Surrealism's quest for artistic freedom of expression makes it a logical mode for Cela's "purging of his heart," suiting the novel's bizarre gallery of fictional entities and experimental crossing of "the frontier where thought almost is no longer thought" (433).

Nevertheless, Cela does not repeat surrealism's "automatic writing" in *Oficio:* not all logical connections have been suppressed, and his language at times is quite academic except for the omission of capitalization and punctuation. The work abounds, however, in disjointed verbal images, iconoclasm, absurdity, challenges to bourgeois values, and irrationality (metamorphoses and mutations, for example). Specific surrealist principles are clearly exemplified, such as "Lautréamont's classical formulation of two or more elements of apparently opposing nature, upon a plane likewise opposed to those elements" (Ernst, 24–25). Surrealism originally appeared in Spain as a lyric mode, and Cela's own apprenticeship practice of surrealism was poetic, explaining abundant lyric techniques in *Oficio,* including parallelism, condensation, alliteration, and cadence. Gimferrer's review in *Destino* notes that rhythm is not lacking, although the rhythm inherent in Castilian phraseology is not "respiratory" in *Oficio* but "linked to the constant, bizarre verbal inventiveness" connecting the novel to Cela's earlier style.[12] Some monads recall the haiku: "Sobre el torrente el viento ha tendido una presa son las hojas rosas que no quiso nadie" [upon the torrent the wind has strung a dam with the rose-red leaves nobody wanted] (95). Other resemble a Vanguardist nonsense verse form associated with Lorca, the *jitanjáfora,* which relies heavily on onomatopoeia and evocative phonics, with the results often being whimsical, absurd, or simply incomprehensible; for example, "Creucobolo warriors mounted huge birds suffering indigestion from burnt butterflies great birds with perennial verbena mustard hemp in place of feathers" (126).[13] Zamora Vicente summarizes what Cela and other aspiring writers of the day discovered in Joyce's writing:

> the mixture of words from different languages [and] very strange sections which belonged to the special world of dreams. An unbridled subconsciousness mixing the entire life of humanity, contemporary history interwoven with ancient, blending peoples, races, heroes of all types. There was a mix of beliefs, of superstitions, . . . and absolute disintegration of language, without any respect whatever for traditional punctuation. Perceptible behind all that was something, perhaps absolutely unintelligible, but beautiful and fascinating for that very reason.[14]

Excepting for "absolute disintegration of language," this passage describes *Oficio.*

Autobiographical Substrata

As in *San Camilo,* the narrative consciousness shares Cela's approximate age and the fact that both are writers (cf. Monads 186, 308, 462). Both self-deprecating narrators suffer obsessive guilt, anger, and frustration, continually questioning whether they are alive or dead, and both novels abound in mentions of blood, problems of existential solitude, and facing oneself (as seen in their symbolic, repetitive mirror motifs). The life-death dichotomy, a major structuring polarity, inclines toward life at the end of *San Camilo* but is weighted toward death in *Oficio.* Although neither novel qualifies as autobiographical by Lejeune's criteria,[15] both have significant autobiographical substrata. In *Oficio,* this may include a reference to "floating on top of cadavers" (596), which has been deemed an allusion to Cela's military service (Charlebois, 69). Oblique references appear to the recent deaths of Cela's father (*Oficio,* 734), younger brother Ricardo (902), and cousin (1085). Journalist Luis Blanco Vila suggested that Ricardo's death weighed especially on Cela's mind during the writing of *Oficio* (quoted by Charlebois, 66). The narrative consciousness of *Oficio* shares his father's name, "Claudio" (458; Cela and his father similarly share the name Camilo); phonetic similarities between Claudio and Camilo are self-evident. Cela's memoirs and *San Camilo* reflect the writer's patronage of prostitutes (also mentioned in monad 647). In all three works, references occur to memorabilia collected by the narrative consciousness (cf. monad 594). As in *San Camilo* and in *Mazurca* (where "CJC" appears as a character), the *tú* is a writer (186, 308, 462, 591, 1149, 1170), and in all three novels, this persona indulges in *autocrítica* (self-critiques), self-conscious and self-referential commentaries. Like Cela, the narrative consciousness admires Picasso, whose death inspires a monad-elegy in the surrealistic mode (1057).

Sufficient evidence of autobiographical substrata exists to raise questions about the reference to "twenty-five years" that opens the novel and recurs periodically. Cela was twenty-five not in 1939 (when the civil war ended on 1 April) but in 1941, when he worked with the Franco censorship (an activity some would equate with obscurantism and metaphorical darkness). In that same year, he suffered a serious illness and believed he was dying. *Oficio* begins "it is comfortable to be defeated at twenty-five," and the second monad commences, "it isn't worth your undressing [exposing yourself], it's nobody's business." It would be erroneous to suggest that *Oficio* is confessional; Cela's literary beginnings under the aegis of Vanguardism and surrealism essentially preclude writing in the confessional mode, and his memoirs proclaim his refusal to write in that vein. Nonetheless surrealism (although hermetic) contains interpretive clues, and so does *Oficio,* especially when examined in the context of the writer's life and other works, as well as of textual clues, including repetitive themes and motifs. Although the novel, viewed in the context of Catholic sacraments, falls short of confession, it does constitute the prior step, "examination of conscience," during which Cela after more than three decades as a writer seeks the meaning of both his life and his works, notwithstanding textual contradictions such as the previously cited affirmation that "now it is too late to turn back and even to make an examination of conscience" (*Oficio,* 332). "Mistakes were made," this obsessive preoccupation suggests—mistakes that apparently continue to plague the writer.

Without mentioning any novel specifically, but in terms clearly applicable to *Oficio* (as well as to *Mazurca* and other later novels), Navajas affirms that Cela has

> elided all reference to the visible world and in its place appears a hermetic and self-sufficient world, beyond . . . premises of modernity. The unmasking of false reality and negation of principles of Classical Humanism's universalizing denial of difference are key factors defining aspects of Cela's epistemology. . . . His perspective is . . . a primordial pre-modern medium, before conventional time and history, a Ur-Chronos wherein the human being forms an integral part of Nature and has not yet fully separated from the original matrix. (123)

Navajas's appraisal applies more to form than (possible) content but helps to situate Cela's most perplexing work in the larger context of Western European literature and the ongoing evolution of modernism and postmodernism. The significance of *Oficio* in relation to Cela's other novels about the civil war, and his own understanding of how this experiment fits into the larger theoretical development of the novelistic genre, still need elucidation. His subsequent abandonment of this radical avenue of exploration and his reincorporation of more conventional elements suggest that (much like certain species that did not survive in the process of evolution), *Oficio* was doomed by inability to adapt its radical experimentalism.

Chapter Six
Dance of Death:
Mazurca para dos muertos

Following the decade of novelistic silence after the release of *Oficio,* and in light of the radical experimentation that the novel represented, readers could reasonably expect significant differences when Cela returned to the genre, including a retreat from extreme experimentalism or a reincorporation of more conventional elements in his long-awaited next novel. And differences there are in *Mazurca para dos muertos* (1983), including the resumption of conventional capitalization, punctuation, paragraphs, and standardized indication of dialogues. Traditional setting and language reappear—some functioning much like window dressing (anticipating similar use of "Old West" setting and toponymy in *Cristo versus Arizona*). Significant thematic links exist between *Mazurca* and such predecessors as *The Hive* (1951) and *San Camilo* (1969). Curiously, the specific, limited time frames treated in these novels—the outbreak of the civil war in the latter, and the initial postwar scarcity and fanaticism during the early 1940s in the former—resemble the temporal parameters set in *Mazurca,* as noted by the narrator: "There's a mazurka, *Ma petite Marianne,* which [was] played only twice, in November of 1936 when they killed Afouto, and in January of 1940, when Moucho was killed."[1] The victims symbolize the contending sides in Spain's civil war, with Afouto—of quasi-mythic proportions—representing "authentic," lusty Galicians, earthy and autochthonous, irrepressibly free. Afouto belongs to the same clan as the author (several Celas are mentioned, and the novelist makes cameo appearances as a writer, if not specifically as author of the novel in progress). Moucho, an "outsider" termed a "cobbler" *(zapatero),* minimized and marginalized, represents Fascist terrorists, cowardly perpetrators of political violence. The allegorical encounter between these two quasi-mythic antagonists reduces the national conflict to a personal dispute or clan feud, unequal because Moucho has allied himself with organized political oppression to accomplish his murder of Afouto and is ultimately linked with "ten or twelve" more assassinations.[2] The forces of totalitarian aggression win in the short term, but the novel's quasi-omniscient vision encapsulates long-term outcomes (i.e., the post-Franco return to democracy and recovery of regional autonomy) as the clan's vengeance wipes all trace of Moucho's remains from the earth. Cela received Spain's prestigious National Prize for Literature in 1984 for *Mazurca*.

Galicia: Reality and Fiction

Although some of Cela's stories (e.g., "El gallego y su cuadrilla," 1955)[3] and his travel book *Del Miño al Bidasoa* (1952) used Galicia as their setting, Galicia does not figure prominently in the novels of the writer's first four decades. Cela follows well-established patterns among modern Galician novelists in opting to write in Spain's official language instead of the regional vernacular: Emilia Pardo Bazán, Ramón del Valle-Inclán, and Gonzalo Torrente Ballester, among several eminent modern and contemporary novelists born and raised in Galicia, elected to use Castilian as their literary language. Galician literature evolved earlier than Castilian, acquiring such prestige that the Castilian monarch Alfonso X ("the Wise"), known for his contributions to learning and to the development of Castilian prose, nevertheless composed his own lyrics in *gallego-portugués*. By the sixteenth and seventeenth centuries, however, Castilian dominated politically and culturally. Weighty historical factors, dating from the fifteenth century, dictated the decline of other Peninsular tongues. Ferdinand and Isabel decreed Castilian Spain's official language, reducing Basque, Catalan, Galician, Aragonese, Leonese, and various other languages and dialects to second-class status. Spain's vernaculars have since been devalued, censored, ridiculed, and sometimes outlawed, suffering cultural marginalization and occasional political persecution, and such treatment explains the comparably few attempts by "mainstream" novelists to write in Galician and other regional languages. When Cela composed his "Galician novel," he looked not to the region's learned, literary past but to oral legend and folklore, which relied heavily on traditional matriarchal narrators of village tales. One of *Mazurca*'s narrators also obtains his materials orally from a pair of female storytellers.

Mazurca is Cela's first full-length novel set in his native Galicia, and his first long fiction in which Galician language and culture acquire heightened visibility (the Galician setting reappears in *La cruz de San Andrés* and in his long-awaited *Madera de boj*). Masoliver Ródenas affirms that Galicia "has an enormous influence on the conception [of *Mazurca*] which is . . . a heartfelt tribute to Galicia . . . [replete] with biographical resonances and autobiographical touches."[4] Commenting on Cela's "return to the Galician roots [which] implies a return to the [language] roots" (85), Masoliver suggests precedents in Cela's most relevant Galician forerunner, Ramón del Valle-Inclán, obliquely alluding to Valle's *Corte de amor* and Cela's use of verbs, expressions, and words in Gallego.[5] Cela's election to the Royal Galician Academy in 1980 strengthened ties with his family home in Iria Flavia and with Galicia. But Galician lexicon or other "bilingualism" at no time supplants Castilian as the basic narrative vehicle, and dialect forms pale beside stronger impacts achieved by the more pervasive Galician culture, climate, economy, folklore, legends, beliefs, and landscape. The atmosphere so created intensifies with proliferating regional patronymics and toponymics, local foods, drinks, customs, anecdotes, and superstitions, all rendering Galician settings especially conspicuous and magnifying differences with respect to Cela's earlier novels. But Galicia's highly visible presence does not equal what Masoliver deems a "heartfelt tribute," or an unmixed hymn of praise, even though the vision of rural Galicia (in wartime) proves less sordid, corrupt, and bloodied than that of wartime Madrid.

Galicia differs markedly from Spain as a whole, given its rainy climate, lush greenery, and quasi-feudal rural society surviving well into the twentieth century. This northwest corner of the Peninsula, bounded on two sides by the sea—and seldom far from salt water and the marine subculture, thanks to the *rías,* or Galician fjords—lacks cities (the largest towns being important seaports, Vigo and La Coruña). Galicia also differs racially from other regions of Spain, having been settled in prehistoric times by Celtic tribes whose modern descendants share cultural coincidences with Celtic peoples in Scotland and Ireland today, including the distinctive *gaita* (bagpipe), the almost identical remains of enormous monolithic shrines erected by heliocentric cults, and numerous parallel or converging legends and myths. Around the end of the first millennium, Galicia became Christendom's most important shrine, following Muslim capture of the Holy Land. Santiago de Compostela, putative burial site of the Apostle St. James, grew swiftly from an open field to a thriving cathedral and university town visited by thousands of pilgrims from all over Europe. But the remainder of Galicia, especially the mountainous interior, changed slowly; the twentieth century found most Galicians still living in semifeudal medieval villages or on tiny plots of land, so-called *minifundios* contrasting with latifundia (broad landed estates belonging to absentee landlords) characterizing much of

Spain and Latin America. Galicia's agricultural, shipbuilding, and fishing economy failed to keep pace with population growth, and the poverty-stricken region has long been a land of emigrants. Backwardness, illiteracy, and superstition abound among the rural poor, and in Galicia as in the Basque provinces, witchcraft has survived into the present; back-roads travelers on Saturday nights still report an occasional mountain *aquelarre* (witches' Sabbath). Local legends perpetuate beliefs in vampirelike creatures[6] and huge wolves or werewolves—relevant in *Mazurca,* as Afouto's brothers exploit the mountain people's superstition and credulity to wreak vengeance on his killer, Moucho (putative victim of a werewolf), at the juncture when Galician ambiance is most closely integrated with the plot.

Connections between *Mazurca* and Earlier Works

Notwithstanding *Mazurca*'s differences, many of Cela's constant motifs and preoccupations reappear, including eroticism, violence, aberration, retardation, mutilation, deformity, materialism, venality, cruelty, and death—motifs equally prominent in *The Hive* and *San Camilo.* As in these antecedents, *Mazurca* shows readers more of the inside of brothels and bedrooms than any other locale; characters engage more in sexual activities than any other. Cela's obsessive association of sexuality and death constitutes another constant in *Mazurca.* Other "constant" types reappear: the blind, the lame and crippled, the deformed and mutilated, the mad, idiot, tubercular, and invalid, the deviant and perverse. Characters lacking physical handicaps exhibit moral, social, or psychological blemishes, including alcoholism, pedophilia, sadism, criminality, prostitution, religious fanaticism, and hypocrisy. As one character observes, "the sick, the prisoners and even the dead are always the same" (*Mazurca,* 131). Illness and aberrations seem the norm, health and legitimacy a minority privilege, with admirable or exemplary characters being still more rare. Masoliver Ródenas may be correct in deeming *Mazurca* a "heartfelt tribute to Galicia," but Galician society's portrait contains no idealization, coinciding more with the worldview purveyed by Cela's previous novels than with most visions of Galicia.

The minority of more or less normal, judicious, and physically intact characters includes Raimundo el de los Casandulfes, a homespun philosopher, member of the same clan and companion of Cela's persona ("the artilleryman Camilo"), an occasional narrative voice, together with another of Cela's alter egos, Robin Lebozán (Castro de Cela), a principal narrative voice and primary amanuensis. Raimundo and Robin are both lovers of Ramona, who shares her favors impartially with her cousin Raimundo and with their relative, Robin. Robin and another Cela alter ego, a vague "don Camilo"—the clan intellectuals—carry the burden of the narrative. Raimundo narrates rather infrequently, with the other two citing his ideas and comments. Tío Claudio, the slightly grotesque uncle of "Camilito" (aka don Camilo or "the artilleryman Camilo"), another narrative perspective, sometimes appears to speak for the author. As already noted, Cela dedicated *San Camilo* "To the boys drafted in '37" and belonged to the cohort drafted that year (epigraph, *Pisando la dudosa luz del día*).[7] Formal and narratological divergences notwithstanding, *Mazurca* shares much with *San Camilo:* both demythologize the Spanish civil war, but *Mazurca* creates a countermyth. Nancy L. Dinneen observes that "blood is the predominant motif in both novels."[8] Blood and death are logical in wartime, but most deaths in *Mazurca* are not war related: they are freak accidents or murders. Death's presence is subliminally underscored by the fact that many women are widows, and Afouto's kinsmen refer to Moucho as "the dead man" long before his demise (as the clan has decreed his fate).

Sentiments expressed in *Mazurca* subvert the supposed glories of war in general and official Francoist versions of Spanish history and the civil war in particular. Raimundo, Camilo's cousin and companion, frequently proffers implied critiques: " 'Raimundo el de los Casandulfes thinks that we Spaniards have all gone insane.' 'Suddenly?' 'That I don't know; probably it started some time back' " (*Mazurca,* 169–70). Uncle Claudio echoes Raimundo's opposition to foreign intervention: "They're all just a bunch of adventurers, my boy, and . . . the bad thing is they're sowing death and destruction. Spain isn't a slaughterhouse, those phony [foreign] heroes are shitbags that just don't want to work" (193). Tío Evelio, "Xabarín," septuagenarian Moranes patriarch, offers his deprecating, demythologizing vision of the war: "This is a dispute between paupers, serious men don't kill each other capriciously, these guys are acting like Frenchmen, and what they're doing makes no more sense than trying to train goats, nobody but a gypsy would think of trying to train a goat" (212). Robin Lebozán, Cela's erstwhile mouthpiece, expresses this decidedly pacifist perspective: "Just review history from the Roman Empire to our days, killings fix nothing and they mess up everything for years, sometimes wars strangle two or more generations and they always sow hatred wherever they happen" (127).

Cela's subversive revision of the dictatorship's idealized version of the war is enhanced by portraying the war in miniature, from the vantage point of Galicia (mostly behind the lines, where no major battles occurred). Rather than emphasizing the war's international implications, Cela underscores the internal, provincial nature of events: "This will be a slaughter, nobody knows who will save his skin and who won't, this will be like burning Troy, there won't be anyone left, this is a fight between Spaniards" (149). Mocking official rhetoric, Cela satirizes Francoist propaganda: "The radio announces that the triumph of the uprising is inevitable: there's no more government in Madrid, the last bunch of fags and clowns that were selling us out fled by plane to Toulouse, ceding all power to the Communists. Their last act was burning and destroying the Prado Museum" (153). This bit of disinformation (actually broadcast by Falangists), distorting heroic Republican efforts to save the Prado's art treasures from Nazi bombings, prompts Raimundo's sneer, "The official news bulletin is worse than the war" (198). His internal monologue further parodies Francoist rhetoric:

> Ordering the destruction of pornographic, Marxist, atheist books (sicknesses of the soul are born of reading), co-education will be suppressed (promiscuity) . . . the worship of the Virgin is declared obligatory in the schools (the Roman [Fascist] salute should accompany the Ave Maria), there will be censorship of newspapers, books, theater, movies, and radio. (198–99)

Readers of *San Camilo* may detect resemblances between media representation in that novel and *Mazurca,* the unreliable information purveyed by both sides, with resulting confusion, doubt, and incomprehension among the populace. Governmental indecision, failures of modern technology to provide reliable information, and public disorientation and skepticism appear in both novels, and in each, Cela indiscriminately jumbles rumors, news, advertising, sporting events, speculation, gossip, grotesque sexuality, violent deaths, and tragedies unrelated to the political reality. By juxtaposing trivia with world news, military communiqués or proclamations with commercials promoting cures for urinary or sexual dysfunction, Cela devalues and subverts official historiographic mythification of Spain's civil conflict. The presentation of contradictory stories and insistent rewriting or unwriting likewise undermine accounts of the war—including his own. Cela further trivializes the war by associating the deaths of the emblematic protagonist and antagonist with a lively dance rhythm played on an accordion, not the chants of a funeral mass, much less a national anthem. Adega's blind brother Gaudencio, who plays the commemorative mazurka "My Little Marianne," resides and performs at La Parrocha's brothel.

Thanks to Cela's twenty-twenty hindsight, Robin and Raimundo occasionally speculate prophetically about events and attitudes half a century in the future, ironically enhancing authorial subversion of the victors' rhetoric exalting their rebellion against the legally constituted government. Cela minimizes the war by foregrounding the symbolic conflict between two mythic prototypes while reducing historical events to a distant echo.[9] *Mazurca* undermines accounts by allies of the triumphant Nationalists, questioning their motives (cf. 150, 163) and casting aspersions on the victors' versions of their own behavior (196). Memory's unreliability, often noted, extends the debunking of narratorial omniscience (and history *is* a narrative, as theorists of the New Historicism remind us). Confirming that authors of official "histories" are indeed targets, Raimundo observes, "When this is over, it will be the scribblers who are in command, you'll see, judicial scribes and those from the press and propaganda, the draft dodgers are well organized, and instead of going to brothels they spend the day planning what's in their interest . . . they'll be making money and being saved" (197).[10]

San Camilo emphasized the "war of the sexes" at the expense of military and political coverage, provoking adverse reaction to the perceived trivialization of historically significant events. Emphasizing the erotic was considered shockingly disrespectful of the values and principles involved, the millions of lives eventually sacrificed.[11] But Cela's context, three decades after Franco's triumph, necessarily incorporated more than the war and its moment in history: his perspective included decades of life under the Franco dictatorship and innumerable intervening events. Written while Franco's grip still held Spain, *San Camilo* suggests corrupt and venal leadership on both sides, unconcerned with principle; Cela's stance in 1969 recalls the biblical imprecation "a plague on both your houses." *Mazurca,* composed nearly 15 years later with the transition to democracy successfully negotiated, a Socialist government in place, and Cela a senator by royal decree, reflects further modifications: the narrative perspective openly favors liberty and democracy, caricaturing erstwhile totalitarian insurgents (although *Mazurca* still suggests that the primary human interaction is sexuality).

Cela and the War in Galicia

Readers unfamiliar with the war's varying effects in Spain's different regions should note that few similarities existed between the war as experienced by residents of Madrid and those of Galicia. Occupied by Franco forces early in the conflict and minimally affected by the fighting (most of which took place elsewhere), remote, rural Galicia underwent no sieges as did Madrid and Oviedo, no bombardments as did Madrid and Barcelona, and suffered comparably little hunger thanks to growing its food supply; wartime famine in Madrid, detailed in *Memorias,* is echoed in pervasive postwar hunger characterizing *The Hive.* Cela's memoirs emphasize abundance in Galician kitchens after months of scarcity, rationing, and near starvation in Madrid; even soldiers stationed in Galicia appeared well fed (he describes a four-course meal that astounded him the first night [*Memorias,* 176]). Backward, agrarian Galicia had little strategic value excepting its seaports, and Spain's civil war was not a naval conflict. In situating his mythic and symbolic drama of murder and revenge on a deceptively bucolic stage, Cela remains relatively faithful to historical facts: the civil war was but a distant echo in Galicia, which saw mainly behind-the-lines actings out of small-scale personal resentments and local conflicts. Cela spent most of the war as a noncombatant; as related in *Memorias,* he joined the Franco forces, was wounded shortly afterward (191), and spent several months recovering. Reporting again for active duty, he was hospitalized with tuberculosis (192–96), and upon being released as unfit for military service, he returned to Galicia, staying en route with relatives in León (202–10), where he dined in Rabelaisan abundance, gaining several pounds. *Mazurca*'s "behind-the-lines" perspective on war in Galicia thus reflects personal experience.[12] A real-life Galician "character" in Cela's memoirs is Papiano Grillo Pampín, the grandson of a maid of Cela's grandmother, a protective giant, "grande y fuerte como un oso" [huge and strong as a bear] (*Memorias,* 175), just released from jail because he had stuffed one of the cooks into the brigade's stew cauldron for making fun of Galicians. Papiano's unmistakable resemblance to members of the Gamuzos (Guxindes, Moranes) clan suggests a real-life source for characters and anecdotal materials in *Mazurca*'s secondary plots.

A passage in *Memorias* encapsulates Cela's vision of the civil war in Galicia, synthesizing its emblematic presentation in *Mazurca:*

> In Galicia, except for mourning the dead, the well-publicized mourning for the idealized fallen (Falangists), the shameful grief for the other dead, the minimized, obliterated, hidden dead along the roadside and outside the walls of the cemetery [Loyalist victims of Falangist terrorists], in Galicia everything was abundance . . . you couldn't go from one place to another without a safe-conduct, but on the other hand, those who wished

could appoint themselves judge, jury, jailer and executioner in the stinking process [of behind-the-lines vengeance]. (*Memorias,* 212)

Although *Mazurca* does not present an objective vision (impossible with protagonist and antagonist personifying heroism and abjection, respectively), elsewhere Cela's pronouncements on the war are more equitable: "I saw both sides of the coin and didn't find a single substantive difference, although [there were] several adjectival ones" (*Memorias,* 210–11). This recalls the "neutral" stance of *San Camilo,* and Cela reiterates his sense of identification with both sides:

> In the Spanish Civil War, one side was well fed, while the other endured extreme hunger; one side was whipped up by functionaries (ecclesiastic, civil and military) while the other was mired in the stentorian weeping of ineffective, romantic dreamers. . . . In one half of Spain, those assassinated were my companions from Jesuit [private] schools; in the other half, the assassins were my companions from Jesuit schools. (*Memorias,* 213–14)

During the winter of 1937 to 1938, Cela stayed with relatives in La Coruña, where "my life couldn't have been more pleasant and less heroic" (*Memorias,* 219). "Memory la Coruña" (216–224) rectifies minor details in *Mazurca;* for example, room numbers where "artilleryman Camilo" was hospitalized, and the names of hospital roommates.[13]

> In *Mazurca* I tell about a cousin of Raimundo el de los Casandulfes being kicked out of Mediateta's whorehouse for throwing a piano off the balcony; well, that was I and my unseemly action (of which I now repent) increased the common store . . . that's how legends and traditions are born. . . . Papagayo Street had the most trustworthy bordellos then, the houses of Mediateta, Apacha, Ferreña, and the Campanelas, with their clientele of village priests, bovine lust in filthy ecclesiastical skirts; now, since the pill, all that has disappeared. (*Memorias,* 222)

Reappearance of Conventional Narrative Elements

Unlike *Rest Home, Mrs. Caldwell, The Hive, Tobogán de hambrientos,* and *Oficio de tinieblas, Mazurca* features a clearly delineated protagonist and antagonist, plus a minimal plot, whose major events—murder and revenge—are causally linked. Novels preceding *Mazurca,* lacking sustained sequential action and plot, prove nearly impossible to summarize (the exception is *San Camilo,* where sequentiality inheres in the historical framework, re-creating historical events with reasonable fidelity to actual chronology). *Oficio de tinieblas* represented so radical an incursion into the antinovel, so extreme a transgression of genres, as to constitute a *non plus ultra*. In *Mazurca* not only does Cela retreat from the abstract, almost nonexistent setting of *Oficio*, but he replaces that novel's vague, shadowy outlines of skeletal personages—scarcely more than voices in the penumbra—with something closer to the opposite extreme, the overdetermined character on a heroic scale.

Mazurca must be termed a plotted novel, one that returns to "closed" form by contrast with several "open-ended" antecedents. Yet the narrative is by no means simple, given its multiplicity of characters and abundant interpolated anecdotes, condensed biographies, legends, and narrative digressions, disjointed and unrelated to the primary "plot" of murder and revenge that functions somewhat as a framing tale. The only perceptible links between numerous potential subplots and the primary action (or murder-revenge plot) are thematic coincidences: many involve deaths; others relate acts of cruelty and violence or recount incidents from the civil war, symbolically circumscribed by the two performances of the mazurka "Ma petite Marianne" and the two deaths that those performances commemorate. In the nuclear plot (a vignette periodically retold with minor variations), Moucho—a shunned outsider somewhere between pathetic and repulsive—is transformed by the war's outbreak from a fawning, servile tradesman to an influential, abusive political figure (comparable to Nazi collaborators in occupied France, for example). Although his motives are never explained, the narrative implies that envy, greed, and resentment over his neighbors' coldness fuel Moucho's vengeance. He denounces Afouto and "ten or twelve others" to Falangist death squads. Readers witness only Afouto's death: he refuses to kneel before his accuser and executioners, dying in silent dignity. The clan meets to pass sentence on Moucho, and responsibility for carrying out the verdict falls upon Afouto's eldest surviving brother, Tanis. This mighty hunter bides his time, stalking his prey until Moucho ventures into the mountains alone, enjoying false security following war's end and official cessation of hostilities. There Tanis looses his pack of huge dogs, which dismember the luckless Moucho in a death more animal than human (many victims in Cela's fiction die dehumanizing deaths, sometimes butchered as animals or suffering from animal diseases, etc.). In the interim, the clan refers to Moucho as nonhuman (the "cadaver"), and Adega's desecration of Moucho's remains ultimately denies him human burial.

Several secondary plotlines comprise a series of scenes or disparate fragments; anecdotes and bits of subplots interrupt like musical motifs, reappearing and fading. A majority involve erotic relationships; for example, the affair between Raimundo el de los Casandulfes and Señorita Ramona (and her relationship with Robin Lebozán) or Cabuxa Tola's enslavement by the repugnant villain Moucho. Cabuxa—one of this novel's several memorable females—clearly detests Moucho but submits to sexual blackmail, offering her own sacrificial prostitution to prevent his wreaking still greater havoc. Another subnarrative depicts the strange lifestyle and character of primitive Catuxa Bainte, a semi-feral female whose idea of fun is swimming nude in the millrace, to the delight of trout and other fauna—local yokels included.

Notwithstanding characters nearly as numerous as those of *La colmena,* the "lonely crowd" phenomenon does not reappear, nor does the reader encounter comparable alienation and existential solitude. Large groups in *Mazurca* share family and clan ties, and most know each other well, given the face-to-face relationships typical in rural areas. The Galician characters are better integrated than the similarly large cast of Madrid slum dwellers in *Tobogán de hambrientos,* whose connections are mediated by subterranean links (A knows B who knows C, who is the brother-in-law of D, the trash collector at the building where E lives, etc.). Degrees of acquaintance and duration of interaction between characters in *Mazurca* exceed those of any other of Cela's works (Pascual's lifelong conflictive relationship with his mother is but one instance; in *Mazurca* scores or hundreds of characters maintain lifelong interactions). Unlike the large cast of *The Hive,* disconnected except for being in the same place at the same time, characters in *Mazurca* belong largely either to the freedom-loving, lusty, vitality-filled autochthons (partisans of the heroic victim Afouto), or cowardly, Fascist partisans of Moucho (a "smaller than life" bully, whose ridiculous physiological defects and blemishes further demythologize the Franco invaders and their allies). Indigenous Galicians share a common culture, observing the *ley del monte* (law of the hills) that demands revenge, not merely an eye for an eye but total, exemplary vengeance.

Another subplot involves the primary narrative voice and the maid Benicia, nostalgically remembered for her culinary talents, storytelling skills, and perpetual readiness to join the narrator between the sheets for a rambunctious sexual romp. Characterization of women in *Mazurca* proves ambivalent: most are creatures of earthy sexuality and often boundless erotic energy but bear little resemblance to the "liberated" female. Uneducated, except for Ramona, nearly all are wives, widows, servants, or peasants, confined primarily to domestic spaces; none have careers or foresee a different, better future. Perhaps the most memorable woman in *Mazurca* is Adega, wife of another murder victim (Moucho persecuted the Guxindes clan; his second clan victim was Cidrán Segade, father of Benicia and late husband of Adega, the narrator's source of much genealogical data). Adega's passionate, unrelenting quest to avenge Cidrán's death defies extreme dangers to rescue his body and give it proper burial and ends only after Moucho's death, when she takes comparably extreme steps to desecrate his remains. Dismembered by huge black wolfhounds belonging to Tanis, Moucho's body was examined by government investigators, who ruled the death an accident: "As there is no evidence of human intervention or signs of struggle or human aggression, the cause of death, from the medico-legal viewpoint, must be deemed accidental," opines the coroner, in one of many spoofs of officialdom and its rhetoric (*Mazurca,* 256). Given Moucho's association with the victorious Nationalists, authorities buried the body. Adega disinters him with her bare hands by dark of night, feeding the remnants to the pigs.

Clan Structure and Related Subplots

The Guxindes clan comprises nine families, including that of Afouto and those of his brothers, the nine Marvises. Adega's paternal surname, Beira, is likewise that of her brother Gaudencio, the blind accordionist playing "Ma petite Marianne." Other clan families are the Celas, Farramiñás (Ramona's family), Portomouriscos, Requeixos, and Lebozáns (Robin Lebozán being a principal narrative voice). Raimundo el de los Casandulfes (implicitly identified as a cousin in *Memorias,* 222) also belongs to the clan, but his surname is never mentioned. Males of the clan, predominantly Celtic types, are large, heavy, and rawboned, some being veritable giants, often with reddish hair; another oft-mentioned clan characteristic is extraordinary genital development. Tribal myths deem the nine clan families descendants of the frog Liorta, of the legendary Antela Lagoon. As Dinneen notes, "the frog, symbol of sins of the flesh, is a fitting totem for the grotesque crowd of Guxindes" (73).

No other clan families are portrayed in such detail as the Marvises: most clan members have numerous legitimate offspring (and various illegitimate children as well). Clan names and relationships are complicated by another patronymic, Morán. The narrator's clarification is not too helpful: "People think that all of us Guxindes and Moranes are the same, but that's not it. . . . not all the Guxindes are Moranes, but it's true that all us Moranes are Guxindes. And also the Portomouriscos, Marvises, Celas and Faramiñás are Moranes; the others are relatives, but they're not Moranes" (*Mazurca,* 90). Masoliver Ródenas offers the following classification: (1) characters grouped around Adega and her brother, the blind Gaudencio; (2) uncles of the narrator(s); (3) characters grouped around Raimundo el de los Casandulfes; (4) characters grouped around the wretched Fabián Minguela (another name for Moucho); (5) characters grouped around Lázaro Codesal (killed years before in the civil war in Melilla) or around Afouto; (6) morons; (7) women whose lives revolve around sex; and (8) priests (90, 91, 93, 95, 98, 104). But these categories are neither exhaustive nor mutually exclusive; some "women whose lives revolve around sex" are morons, and some are "grouped around Adega," with others grouped around Raimundo el de los Casandulfes, and so forth. Masoliver's attempt at simplification indicates the clan's complexity—augmented by detailed family histories provided for most clan members. Navajas notes Cela's use of "micronarrations" in novels such as *The Hive* and *Mazurca,* observing that this minimalism constitutes the "preferred mode of the postmodern mentality in face of the macro-structures of totalizing discourse" (127). He also mentions the novelist's preference for minimal or self-enclosed spaces (such as the anonymous café in the earlier novel) or an abandoned region (Galicia, in *Mazurca*). Variations on this technique reappear in *Cristo versus Arizona.*

The numerous subplots, interpolated tales, and anecdotes involve a large supporting cast that would be sufficiently bewildering if all were clearly identified, but it becomes hopelessly confusing given Cela's practice (well developed in *La colmena*) of using multiple names and nicknames for many characters. Although Afouto—whose "real" name was Baldomero Marvis Ventela—belonged to the Guxindes clan, the nine Marvis brothers are also called Gamuzos; identification is further complicated by alternate last names, Afouto being known also as Baldomero Fernández. Similar situations apply with his eight brothers (but not necessarily the same variant names). The second patronymic of Cela's father was Fernández, and *La rosa* mentions another relative, Juan Jacobo Fernández, beatified in 1926 by Pope Pius XI, presumably the "Santo Fernández" mentioned in *Mazurca.* Compared with the women of Madrid who appear in *The Hive* and *San Camilo,* the Galicians seem more healthy and energetic, behave more spontaneously, and suffer fewer inhibitions, being simultaneously more lusty and less decadent. Although this typecasting falls short of fully rounded, realistic characterization, Cela's Galician females generally have more attractive personalities than their masculine counterparts. Most males (narrative voices included) are unabashed chauvinists, spokesmen for their *machista* culture.

Poetic Structure and Fugal Structure

Cela binds multiple narrative threads and characters together with reiterated motifs, the most significant referring to the rain—the only element deserving the name of leitmotiv. Masoliver affirms that "the most visible leitmotif is the nine signs of the bastard that appear in very few persons, one of whom is Fabián Minguela [Moucho]" (95). But the nine signs constitute a counterpart to the introductory presentation of the nine Gamuzos or Marvís brothers, interrupted by lengthy digressions (*Mazurca,* 16–91). These thematically important signs—all signifying lack or deficiency (e.g., Moucho's small, withered genitalia, dwarfed by the superendowed Gamuzos)—are not true leitmotivs, since this motif vanishes one-third of the way through the novel. The number nine has obvious cabalistic significance (nine signs, nine Gamuzos, nine families in the clan, etc.), but number symbolism remains implicit, playing no role in the developing action.

Time proves less simple than initially suggested by the reference to the two playings of the mazurka (November 1936 and January 1940). Although these dates fix the temporal parameters of the primary action (the murder-revenge plot), those chronological bounds—approximating the civil war's duration—fall decades before the novelistic present (i.e., when the memories and collected information of the several narrators are written or retold). The narration neither begins nor ends on these dates; two or three different temporal perspectives of the narrator(s) subsume the past, incorporate memory and oral history, and appropriate the knowledge of intervening events ("twenty-twenty hindsight") available at the time of writing. The opening paragraph refers to another, prior death or murder, when Lázaro Codesal (apparently a forefather of Afouto) was shot in the back by a Moor during Spain's war in Melilla—another civil conflict, inasmuch as Melilla was then a province of Spanish North Africa. Several references to the nineteenth-century Carlist (civil) wars also appear; for example, "In my family's home, for years and years, there were three white Carlist berets hanging around" (*Mazurca,*

104). Repeated references to the Moors in Spain (A.D. 711–1492) evoke another, more lengthy internecine conflict. Extending the time frame backward to accommodate various events whose common denominator is civil conflict insinuates that civil war is endemic in Spain and resembles a backwoods feud (as suggested by the environment and emblematic deaths of the title). Other repetitive references evoke happenings in the lives of grandparents and great-grandparents of the various narrators, especially the life of "Santo Fernández," born in 1808. Cela also extends the temporal plane forward by structuring the novel as a series of conversations between the several narrative voices years after the events in question, with multiple unidentified interlocutors. The only clue to dating the narrative present or time of these exchanges is that Benicia (a small child when her father died at Moucho's hand) is now a mature woman (apparently middle-aged); logically, some four decades have elapsed, placing the conversations at approximately Cela's time of writing.

Mazurca, a polyphonic composition with multiple themes, enunciated by several voices in turn, features a contrapuntal or fugal structure, with variations appearing in *El asesinato del perdedor* and *La cruz de San Andrés.* Themes appear, disappear, and reappear, being modified and reiterated by several narrators (without informing the reader of changes of narrator). Besides whole or partial reiterations of key events, usually incorporating variations on the theme, readers encounter repetitive descriptions of protagonist and antagonist, and of mythic antecedents (or parallel incidents in the lives of ancestors). Perhaps most visible of all such fugal themes, however, is the *orvallo,* or Galician mist, which, like biblical rain, falls on the just and the unjust. Regular, almost obsessive repetition of this motif provides a lyric structure or glue binding together multiple themes and variations, the multiplicity of narrators and characters, the proliferation of family histories, and intercalated stories and extraneous anecdotes. A final index, listing only three parts to the novel, subtly underscores the rain's prevalence and significance. The first part, "Llueve mansamente y sin parar" (It Rains Gently and Unceasingly) comprises the entire narrative per se: one long chapter, without internal subdivisions. Cela's use of rain here recalls its function in certain works of García Márquez, a lyric and symbolic precipitation with mythic overtones, a rain whose role transcends any possible reference to external reality. The other two parts listed comprise an "attachment" or "forensic report" (of the autopsy following Moucho's death), and a Galician-Castilian vocabulary.

The novel's initial paragraph is devoted almost entirely to the rain, described lyrically via triple repetitions: "The rains fall gently and unceasingly, raining unwillingly but with infinite patience, like life itself, falling upon the earth which is the same color as the sky, between soft green and soft ashen gray, and the outline of the mountain has long been blurred" (9). Much like a symphonic overture, these opening lines enunciate notes reiterated and recombined throughout the work. The rain's characteristics (gentle, unceasing, unenthused but infinitely patient), specific shades of green and gray, and the long-blurred outline of the mount, reappear frequently with variations. The motif of the mountain's blurred outline (or its mysterious disappearance) connects with the death in Africa of Lázaro Codesal and, via its recurrences, acquires attributes of an ill omen—the beginning of a series of apocalyptic woes for which no end appears in sight. After initial enunciation of the circumstances of Lázaro's demise, the narrative voice returns to the rain, whose duration exceeds the "forty days and forty nights" when Noah built the ark, suggesting for close readers that it should not be taken literally: "It has been raining slowly, unceasingly, for more than nine months upon the grass of the fields and the glass of my window-pane" (9). In later mentions, the rain falls on the waters of a river, associated with the feral, supposedly retarded Catuxa Bainte, and the villain Fabián Minguela, aka Moucho. Both characters are admonished for transgressions, Catuxa's apparently erotic, and Moucho's linked with homicides. The association between waters, rain, and death recurs throughout the novel; for example, the Fount of Miangueiro, whose clear waters are tainted by death, so that no one may drink, and the legendary Antela Lagoon, whose waters (known since Roman times) reputedly conceal the submerged city of Antioch.[14] Insistent links between water and eroticism are thoroughly Freudian, but more often the association is with death. Dinneen, however, considers the Galician rain "a symbol of life; it stops during the summer of 1936 . . . and this unusual change heralds the ascendancy of evil men who kill for pleasure. The rain does not reappear until the announcement of the end of the war, and . . . does not regain its old power until much later" (72). As part of the geographic and climatological reality of Galicia, the pervasive mist recreates ambience, being linked to peculiarly Galician landscape features, with Galician dialect forms enhancing lyricism.

The sound of falling raindrops metaphorically corresponds to the monotony and repetition of a litany, with Christian virtues attributed to the rain. Sobejano stresses the structural significance of litanies not only in *Mazurca* but also in *San Camilo, Oficio de tinieblas,* and Cristo *versus Arizona* (see Sobejano 1997). References to the rain constitute a primary fugal motif, restating ideas earlier associated with the rain, a litany merging with other water motifs (the Fount of Miangueiro, the Antela Lagoon; the river behind Ramona's house, specifically linked to death). Paradoxically, ever-present rain constitutes the norm, and its interruption spawns fear and dread, a prophetic foreboding or premonition of war's horrors; the lyric passages reappear only after the clan meets and decrees Moucho's death: "It rains like it rained all life long, I recall no other rain, no other color, nor other silence; it rains with slowness, with gentleness, with monotony, raining without beginning or end, they say the waters return to their source, but that isn't so" (*Mazurca,* 204). The sense of irreparable wrong or loss implicit in the final sentence alludes to Afouto's death and the war's horrors in the interim. Functionally comparable to reiterations of the nuclear murder and revenge, the falling rain provides a contrasting counterpoint to the horrors of war, an analogy between "history" and "intrahistory" (atypical, transitory, political conflict as opposed to nature's peace, which reigns when the guns fall silent). Rain is the most visibly lyrical motif of a quasi-lyrical structure, employing alliteration, cadence, repetition, metaphor, simile, and images. Lyric structuring devices acquire increasing significance in Cela's remaining novels.[15]

Linked to the rain is narratorial unreliability (a device of major significance for Cela's subsequent novels).[16] The narrator contradicts himself repeatedly concerning the rain, for example: "It rains without any mercy whatever, or perhaps it rains with a great deal of mercy" (*Mazurca,* 35); "The mist falls with faith, hope and charity upon the corn and rye . . . or perhaps it falls without faith, or hope, or charity, and nobody knows it" (61). The narrative voice waxes cynical concerning history ("History isn't always the witness of the ages, the light of truth, the life of memory, etc.; there's a lot of empty talk in it" [218]), echoing multiple assertions of the narrator's fallibility and that of his informants. Aware of lacunae, errors, contradictions, and falsehoods in official versions of the war, Cela refuses to replace them with myths of his own invention; the larger-than-life clan members of *Mazurca* fall short of classical heroic stature. Cela reclaims the civil war for Spain ("a disagreement between Spaniards"), ignoring historiographers' "myth of foreign intervention." At the same time, he demythologizes the war, undermining fictional as well as "historical" accounts, both marred by memory's failings, mistakes and fallacies of documentation, and human egotism. Cela's title for his 1993 autobiographical memoir (Memories, Understandings, and Wills) implicitly recognizes the subjective content in any retelling, fictional, autobiographical, or "historical": not only is memory itself fallible, but it is shaped by individual "understanding" or interpretation (subject to change over time), and by "will," or how one wishes to believe things happened. The fugal structure chosen by Cela in *Mazurca* and subsequent novels aptly imitates memory's intricacies, its doubling back on itself, its inability to grasp and fully recover. Memory is a key element for Sobejano, who affirms that "the compositional form of *Mazurca* is dictated by the process of a wandering memory, uncertain and interrupted, together with the rhythm of the all-encompassing rain" (141). Sobejano indicates that the date of the second playing of "Ma petite Marianne" is the day of San Andrés in 1939 (of interest because this saint reappears in *La cruz de San Andrés*). As does Knut Ahnlund, Sobejano stresses the novel's musical rhythm and elegiac character and the predominance of civil crime over warfare, terming it a "Galician elegy of dispersed memory, based upon the initial crime—the assassination of Baldomero Gamuzo" (150). Ahnlund emphasizes Cela's transformation of reality into poetry in *Mazurca,* with "audacious laconisms, Castillian-Galician hybrids, exorcisms and spells, Nature thronging with beings human, half-human and animal" (249). Ahnlund notes that although most action in *Mazurca* occurs during the time frame of the Spanish civil war, and that conflict is "discreetly mentioned," what really predominates is "the motif of civil violence; [the novelist] paints enmities, vendettas, hatreds, without it ever being known whether there is any political motive or not" (265). Nonetheless, violence seems less significant than the theme of victimization, central for Ahnlund in *Mazurca,* to which he attributes a "character of requiem, mass, elegy and canticle" (268). Thus *Mazurca,* the third novel of Cela's trilogy about the civil war, reiterates numerous notes sounded in *Oficio* and *San Camilo,* undermining prior attributions of grandeur, glory, and heroism and stressing the conflict's absurdity, human shortcomings, and needless suffering and loss. Rather than presuming to offer the final word on the civil war and its aftermath, however, *Mazurca* seems to enunciate the impossibility of any definitive pronouncement at the same time that it gropes toward closure.

Chapter Seven

A Trip to Arizona:
Cristo versus Arizona

Cela's most frequently used settings for his fiction, long or short, are Galicia and Madrid, two very different parts of Spain where his parents resided for many years and where he lived from infancy to adulthood. In novels of the first period, only two exceptions occur: Badajoz (Extremadura) in *Pascual Duarte,* and Venezuela in *La Catira*—the latter setting allegedly being a condition of Cela's contract with the Venezuelan government. Until 1988, *La Catira* constituted Cela's only novel set outside of Spain. In *Cristo versus Arizona* (1988),[1] Cela for the first time employs a setting almost totally beyond the Hispanic orbit:[2] Arizona—a stylized version of the "Old West" somewhat worse than Hollywood's worst, occupying a vaguely delineated chunk of desert stretching from the OK Corral and Tombstone down to the Mexican border somewhere south of Tucson. Cela supposedly wanted "his" Arizona to reflect something of the original, and two brief trips there were followed by a third when he had written part of the novel. His preface affirms that "in February of 1987, a few months before finishing this novel, I returned to Arizona to refresh my memory concerning certain people and landscapes." Similarly, Pedro Sorela's review of the novel states that as a result of that third trip, Cela changed parts of the novel, and that he brought back maps and a telephone book, from which he obtained some of the bizarre names for his characters.[3] Temporally, also, Cela moves from twentieth-century Spain to America's "Old West," treating an ill-defined period reaching approximately from 1880 to 1920,[4] making the novel his first to be set largely or entirely before his lifetime.

Although there is no assurance that the cover blurb was approved by Cela, it may be helpful to see the publisher's presentation:

> In Arizona, more or less between 1880 and 1920, and using the duel at the OK Corral as central axis, [Cela] relates, in a hallucinatory and hypnotic monologue, a succession of misadventures among an extensive list of characters, in a world dominated by brute force and the most ele-

mental instincts. This pessimistic, barbarous and epic tale does not exclude a certain poetry that springs in large part from the capacity of verbal fascination that the author possesses in the highest degree. A stunning example of expressive mastery and technical expertise, *Cristo versus Arizona* is a masterpiece. (*Cristo,* book jacket)

Although most of the foregoing affirmations are true, or defensible as authoritative opinion, they will not render a dark and difficult book more palatable for the squeamish reader.

Spatiotemporal Parameters

Historical (or geographic and temporal) accuracy can be deemed of little real concern despite references to Cela's trips to Arizona to document his sources. Various anachronisms appear; for example, a reference to the modern residential suburb of Green Valley between Tucson and the Mexican border town of Nogales—a winter retirement community whose existence probably dates from three or four decades after the end of the "present-tense" portion of the novel. Likewise, the narrator refers repeatedly to a "hospital for emergencies" (cf. 6, 30), unlikely to have existed in Tombstone or its environs. Within the text are numerous references to the gunfight at the OK Corral, "October 28, 1881" (14 and passim), and the cover photograph is identified as a street in Tombstone in 1881. Similarly, references appear to persons hanged in 1884 (195) and to 1887, when "John Doc Holliday died of TB" (78). More recent chronological allusions include 1905, when Wyatt Earp is said to have died (65), and 1917, "when the train full of sick Indians was derailed" (74). The narrator also mentions "San Luis Río Colorado, the city that Blas Yocupicio founded not long ago, around 1905 or 1906" (131). Turning his gaze toward the future, the narrator muses about "what this may become within a few years, in 1925, for example, or 1930" (131). Yet he mentions no specific date for the moment of the "action," that is, of rememoration, and he proves equally indefinite about his own life, age, date of birth, vital statistics, name, and the identity of his parents. From chronological clues, readers may deduce that the novelistic present—sometime after 1917 and before 1925—covers approximately 1920 to 1922. In that case, yet another anachronism appears when the uneducated narrator mentions the death of D. H. Lawrence (which occurred in 1930), alluding to his grave nearby.

Numerous references to Tombstone might suggest that it is the principal site of the "action," or that Cela's change of locale will be reflected in essential shifts in characters and events. Neither is true—notwithstanding the oft-mentioned nuclear events of the legendary shoot-out, the nature of the narrative is such that location matters little, although the desert (with its primitive barrenness and violence) functions to enhance or intensify brutality. Yet so much is memory, digression, or repetition that "action" is largely internal, subjective, or retroactive: *Cristo versus Arizona* offers nothing resembling plot, no sustained action, no narrative continuity, no protagonist in the usual sense, because there is no primary "present-tense" conflict (the past-tense shoot-out at the OK Corral is in no way central, constituting a painted theatrical backdrop reinforcing the theme of ongoing, senseless violence throughout). One may more precisely speak of acts of remembering, moments of writing the text, since the setting-down of discourse acquires high visibility; nevertheless, much is conjecture, secondhand stories or twice-told tales, self-correction.

The narrative voice belongs to a memorialist or autobiographical chronicler struggling to recall and arrange his recollections; for example, "this shouldn't go here, but I'm going to write it down anyway before I forget" (109). He repeatedly forgets, however, continually changing not only narrative details but even his own name: "surely the reader of this chronicle already knows that my name is Wendell Liverpool Espana or Span or Aspen" (111); "before learning who had been my father and mother, I was called Craig Tiger Brewer, my name is Craig Teresa and the following pages are mine, I wrote them in my own hand" (152–53). Among multiple names, one combination, with its variants, appears most often, and the narrative voice affirming that identity also speaks of essential veracity (albeit mixed with lies) in his account: "Now I'll get on with the story line, my name is Wendell Liverpool Espana or Span or Aspen and whatever has been said heretofore I wrote in my own hand, there's a lot of truth in it although I put a few lies in for decoration" (124). Readers can form impressions of the character to which the narrative voice belongs: "Wendell" is rustic, unsophisticated, with a rudimentary education, apparently a naive ranch hand or day laborer, with few possessions. He seems comparably "better" than most characters teeming in his narrative (and in this he resembles Pascual Duarte). Wendell has no criminal record, and his early years in a church-related orphanage in New Mexico apparently provided him basic grounding in Christian morality, especially the concepts of sin and punishment (a formation that does not prevent his persisting in incest but torments his conscience, leading him to see potential chastisement in otherwise normal phenomena). Wendell is something of a loner, having never lived with family or relatives, and has few long-time friends, which may explain his reflective bent. At times he seems a homespun philosopher (and his reflections on the human condition, interspersed with deadpan narratives of atrocities, constitute another parallel between this novel and *Pascual Duarte*). In both, as in the picaresque tradition, a pseudoinnocent, seemingly unaware autobiographical narrator comments deadpan on inequities, injustice, and abuse as though these were perfectly "normal."

Truth, Memory, and the Unreliable Narrator

"Wendell's" affirmations cite undocumented and unsubstantiated accounts—oral history or legend, gossip, campfire stories, even conjecture—filtered through memory (his own and that of others), with all of memory's failures and shortcomings. Indeed, the fallibility of memory constitutes a minor leitmotiv, along with the (doubtful) veracity of witnesses: "Well, no, I didn't see it, but I heard it from some men who seemed to be truthful" (130); "life is woven with the memories of everyone, and it does no good to try to flee from memory" (69); "no one can assure this [is true], because it could be a lie, people tell a lot of lies hoping that somebody will regard the liar with a bit of charity" (147). Not only does the decidedly nonomniscient narrator affirm general human tendencies to prevaricate, but he casts a skeptical eye on historiographers: "The fight at the OK Corral is usually explained according to the version told by Wyatt Earp, the Lion of Tombstone, who was the last to die, and then nobody could contradict him; . . . [I think] he sometimes added things on his own, or he imagined the details" (163).

Despite some vague historical background (the legendary characters and events of the shoot-out at the OK Corral) whose repetitive partial reiteration (at least 15 reappearances, according to one critic's count) exercises a structuring function in the absence of plot, that legendary background or framing narrative is no more essential to (or integrated with) the "present-tense" action than painted scenic backdrops for a ballet. Rather than "history," what the fundamentally flawed and unreliable narrator presents is history's impossibility: a narrative based on recollections—confused, deficient, adorned, or skeptically edited—of things said by others with equally defective memories, doubtful veracity, and questionable motivations. Whether or not Cela read any New Historians, *Cristo versus Arizona* demonstrates their dictum that history is a fiction.[5] And regardless of whether he read Lejeune or other theoreticians of autobiography, this text (whether or not it is a novel) likewise demonstrates that autobiography, too, is a fiction. With its retelling, unwriting, gainsaying, contradictions, and self-subversion, the discourse of *Cristo versus Arizona* proves fully postmodern, with ontological groundings continually destabilized. Few "facts" emerge, and few actions can be affirmed unequivocally to have occurred, or to have done so when, where, and in the manner stated (and variously restated), although "historical" background includes accounts of the Mexican Revolution and tales of Pancho Villa as well as versions of the Tombstone shoot-out, the Earp-Clanton chronicle, and America's westward expansion, with the settlement of the "last frontier." Much in the manner of medieval Spanish chroniclers who included everything in their "histories" (biblical materials, myths, epic poems, popular legends, folktales, genealogies, etc.), Wendell sets down everything he hears, thinks, and witnesses. Unlike the early chroniclers, however, he seems doubt filled, qualifying, rectifying, contradicting, or unwriting passages repeatedly. The rhythm of the narrative (like that of *Mazurca*) is largely the rhythm of memory, accounting for the chronological breaks, fragmentation of anecdotes, overlaps, and repetitions.

Perhaps Wendell's reiterated affirmations of his manuscript's limitations and shortcomings explain his decision to delay publication: "Now that the litany is ending and I should put the final period at the end of my chronicle, I ask that these papers not be published until everyone [mentioned] has died . . . the written word can do a lot of harm to people" (238). Even in the mouth of an unreliable narrator, the affirmation of the harm that words can do rings true, suggesting that historiography, Francoist or otherwise, may indeed be a conscious target. This seems all the more likely in light of Cela's having written two "historical" novels in the two preceding decades: *San Camilo* (1969) and *Mazurca para dos muertos* (1983) offer subjective and mythical interpretations, not "factual" or conventionally "historical" accounts of Spain's civil conflict; they constitute earlier rejections by Cela of "history" according to the dictatorship. Stephen Miller similarly believes that "demythification, deconstruction and historical revisionism . . . [and] broader understanding of the marginalized and minorities of all kinds"—very much a part of the intellectual climate of the times—account for a certain suspicion and mistrust of whites in *Cristo versus Arizona*.[6]

Narrative Devices and Antecedents

Cristo versus Arizona is first and foremost metaliterary, a novel centered around the writing of a "chronicle," and like many metanovels, it is both self-conscious and self-reflective. The narrator frequently refers to the act of writing, to the literariness of situations, to his own role as author or narrator, to characters as literary entities (instead of affirming their "reality"). Lacking plot, protagonist (and hence antagonist), and sequential or coherent action, *Cristo versus Arizona* features several characteristics of the antinovel. Cela's most populous novel, it qualifies as a work of collective protagonist (like *The Hive* and *San Camilo*) and logically contains preoccupations of the "social novel," including heightened social conscience. As in earlier works, readers find the same division of society into exploiters and the exploited, the same preoccupation with social injustice and man's inhumanity to man, but *Cristo versus Arizona* presents a new dimension, largely absent from Cela's earlier novels: racial and ethnic discrimination and persecution. Although ethnically diverse Spain is more homogeneous racially, Jews were persecuted in the sixteenth and seventeenth centuries, for example; gypsies appear as an oppressed minority in the works of García Lorca and such postwar novelists as Ignacio Aldecoa; and Moroccan immigrants have been the target of recent riots in southern Spain. But racial diversity in quality or quantity is slight in Spain compared to the United States, and in Cela's Arizona, even the present demographic variations have been exaggerated. Mexicans and others of Spanish descent, Native Americans, and considerable numbers of Chinese and blacks throng the novelistic desert. Citing 1880, 1890, 1900, and 1910 census data, Miller indicates that the population at the time of the narrative was far less dense than the novel suggests; Cela presents a "demographic deformation" of the historical Arizona territory (78), inverting the proportions of whites and nonwhites (Indians, Mexicans, mestizos, Chinese, blacks, and mulattoes), as whites then numbered more than 50 percent but appear in much smaller numbers in the novel. Cela was not portraying demographic reality, however, but creating an allegory of humanity.

Sobejano groups the first 4 of Cela's 11 novels under the classification of "confession," the next 3 under the rubric of "chronicle," and the next 4 (including *Cristo versus Arizona* as the 11th) as "litanies," which he defines as a mode combining the individual confession and vast collective chronicle (Sobejano 1997). Wendell's "mournful confession" is part of a "terrible chronicle" of the "mass of ills of an inhuman or subhuman

world of misery, violence, cruelty, and aberrations" (140), and the narrative voice continually accumulates anecdotes—nearly all sadistic or
cruel—while having recourse "every three or four pages to the Litany of
Our Lady, from the *kyrie eleison* on page 11 to the *Agnus Dei qui tollis pec-
cata mundi: Miserere nobis* of the final page" (142). The "Litanies," characterized by repetitive rhythm and elegiac tone, feature a plaintive confessional voice, begging mercy for himself and the merciless world that
emerges from his soliloquy. The 61 verses of the Litany of the Virgin are
recited parodically by a minor character, an adulterous woman who uses
the beads of the rosary to remember the men with whom she has slept
at least three times. In the first half of the novel, Wendell enunciates the
verses one at a time, demanding the reader's response. In the second half
(beginning on page 114), he informs readers that hereafter they will
recite two verses at a time. Some lyricism results from interpolated litanies, as well as passages such as the following, whose colloquialism and
simple imagery fit the untutored narrative consciousness as they evoke
the "Western" environment: "before God our Lord one must appear on
foot and hat in hand, with great humility and good manners. . . . Christ
is God, nobody should forget that, Christ is the strongest of all creation,
stronger than a thousand bisons, or the sandstorm which sweeps the
desert from side to side, north to south, and east to west" (*Cristo,* 93).

Lyric interludes are interspersed between cruel deaths, rapes, torture,
and other horrors, providing moments of philosophical meditation,
much like the pattern of alternating violent action and reflexive meditation in *Pascual Duarte.* Sobejano concludes that the only possible meaning in Wendell's reciting the litany while "fornicating with his mother
and reciting a string of brutal events . . . seems to be to remind Man of
his uncertain place of perdition, between child and monster" (144).
Wendell, in his "culpable innocence, or innocent guilt, in his solitude
before evil and the evils of the world, as well as in his subliminal
appetites, exhibits traces of Pascual Duarte" (154). Pascual (as his name
indicates) is a Paschal Lamb, implicitly a Christ figure, a sacrificial
scapegoat executed for society's sins. By no coincidence, the final lines of
Cristo versus Arizona invoke the Lamb of God.

Various details connect *Cristo versus Arizona* with earlier novels:
Tobogán de hambrientos and *Oficio de tinieblas* exhibit similar lack of plot,
protagonist, sustained action or continuity, "real" (as opposed to abstract
or stylized) setting or landscapes, and character development, alongside
a large number of undefined personages. Cela returns to lyric structures,
seen previously in *Mrs. Caldwell,* in *Oficio,* and especially in *Mazurca*

(refrains appear in earlier novels, beginning with the repeated motif of the gardener's wheelbarrow in *Pabellón de reposo*). The novelist recognized his combination of lyric structures with grotesque incidents in his prologue to the 1957 edition of *Pabellón de reposo:* "If we were to have to split hairs, it might be as much a novel as a prose poem." José María Castellet observes lyric aspects of *La Catira:* "The huge poetic vein, that tremendous torrent of poetry that Cela's works contain. In reality, the conflict between novelist and poet coexisting in the literary personality of Camilo José leads to works difficult to classify in any literary genre."[7] Cela's most significant lyric device is repetition: reiteration of motifs, conversations, phrases, incidents, words, rhetorical parallelisms, and variations on a theme. Other repetitive techniques such as interpolations, variations on numerous condensed biographies, frequent digressions, and extraneous anecdotes intensify the lyric effect, sense of polyphony, and fugal structure (another function of the fragmentary creation myths cited earlier).

Obvious differences notwithstanding, important similarities and coincidences exist between *Cristo versus Arizona* and *Mazurca*. Both feature significant lyric devices, looming larger in *Mazurca,* with its tag lines evoking the green Galician landscape and persistent *orvallo* (fine rain), contrasting with the burning Arizona desert. Both abound in repetitions of conversations, motifs, incidents, tag lines, and phrases. Similar elements in both create environment, whether regional or territorial, employing peculiar names and patronymics, toponymy, bits of local folklore, legends and superstitions from the area, local beliefs, drinks, customs, objects. Both novels exhibit an accumulation of strange and horrifying deaths, degrading and grotesque killings, suicides, accidents and executions, vengeances and betrayals. Death by natural causes is the exception (if by "natural" one means old age or illness). Allusions to the Dance of Death are less specific in *Cristo versus Arizona* than in *Mazurca,* but ritual aspects of death echo that motif in both. Each intercalates music and bits of song, and parts of Mexican *corridos* recur in *Cristo versus Arizona*. Common to the two also is the theme of xenophobia: a character in *Mazurca* observes that "the Carroupos aren't from around here, it really took a lot for us not to run them out of town" (39), and the narrator of *Cristo versus Arizona* comments that "there's no need to let foreigners talk, when a man leaves the land where he was born, it's a sign there's something wrong" (79). Other contemporary Spanish novelists, including Miguel Delibes, have identified xenophobia as a national ill, especially in the small towns and villages. In the Arizona Territory 130 years ago, everyone (possibly excepting Indians and perhaps some Hispanics) would have been "foreigners," newly arrived "pioneers," adventurers, soldiers of fortune, outlaws, and fugitives; such affirmations thinly disguise prejudice and intolerance. The "foreigner" is the pariah or social outcast, persecuted for whatever reason: "the whole world knows it's bad and even dangerous to be a foreigner" (*Cristo,* 120).

The "found manuscript" device or "legacy" of a dead man, published almost by accident an indefinite time later, provides another tenuous connection between *Cristo versus Arizona* and Cela's first novel, and in both *Cristo* and *Pascual Duarte,* the novelist employs first-person, autobiographical perspectives, together with abundant picaresque details and the pseudoinnocent tone of a mature narrator gazing backward to more youthful, less skeptical times. "Family values" are demythologized, presenting parents who are neither models to imitate nor authorities to respect, whose offspring are neglected or abandoned, left to fend for themselves. Pascual's mother, a filthy, drunken, witchlike adulteress and procuress, eventually suffers the protagonist's matricidal fury; the narrator's mother in *Cristo versus Arizona*—a comparably kindly prostitute—continues providing the son her professional services after revealing their consanguinity. The putative fathers are lazy, irresponsible criminal types whose deaths elicit no grief. Like *The Hive, Cristo versus Arizona* involves a huge cast, but little structure or vertebration; similarly, it avoids sequentiality, narratological or chronological. "It's a novel that lacks a plot, lacks a protagonist, has more than 500 characters and takes place in a continual narrative flow interrupted solely by commas and a single final period which marks the end of the book."[8]

Masoliver Ródenas did not mention that instead of straightforward chronological sequence, narrative discourse moves constantly backward and forward in time, lacking connectedness, cohesion, and closure. Nevertheless, by following the tangled musings of the narrator (whose predominant mode is the internal monologue), readers can reconstruct parts of an autobiographical narrative, piecing together a logical, if fragmentary, sequence of biographical events, perhaps even a family chronicle. Sketchy data appear concerning the life of Wendell's maternal grandmother, his mother's life before and after the narrator's birth, and events in the lives of two half brothers subsequently discovered on his mother's side. Disconnected details concerning his father's life provide contradictory versions of the father's death (thrown into the sea from different boats in different oceans, eaten alive, or killed by sharks [*Cristo,* 144], even a death from natural causes: "according to the photographer, my father died on dry land, and not too far from where he had always lived" [145]). Varying accounts relate the death of "Zuro Millor, the shit-bag Indian," killed by the narrator's father, a murder prompting the progenitor's flight. Nothing explains how Wendell obtained this information; he confesses more than once to including lies, although his principal informant seems to be his mother, whose function parallels that of women storytellers in *Mazurca,* including one narrator's erstwhile lover.

Cela essentially agrees with Pío Baroja, novelistic model and mentor, that the novel is a "sack in which anything (and everything) fits." *Cristo versus Arizona* contains not only myths, legends, and ballads (Mexican *corridos*) but also fragments of drama. Charlebois notes the presence of theatrical passages depicting sexual abuse where narrative gives way to dialogue, with men's names indicated parenthetically (see *Cristo,* 146 – 47), "using terminology such as *scenes, protagonists, main characters,* and *puppets*" (see *Cristo,* 127), which infuses the narrative with a "stage-like quality that converts both narrator and reader into spectators rather than mere passive readers" (Charlebois, 89; italics in original).[9] At least two more narrative threads are not of Cela's invention. The first is the shoot-out at the OK Corral, retold in more or less chronological order, albeit suspended and resumed many times. The second alludes to American Indian mythology concerning a meeting of talking animals endowed with magical powers, a chorus of primitive gods. The narrative of the shoot-out, interruptions and delays notwithstanding, is eventually completed, even following principal survivors from the climactic encounter to their respective deaths. But the Native American cosmogony remains incomplete. Miller distinguishes two such creation myths, one purely Indian, the other a mixture revealing Christian influence, plus an overlay of a third, the "Christian myth of sin and absolution" (79). The purely indigenous cosmogony relates a meeting of animals to create Man. Miller detects emphasis on the "continuity between persons and animals, the bestial part of human beings" (82), citing numerous images of animalization and pervasive bestiality. Important both in the context of Christian myths of sin and redemption and in animal cosmogony is the serpent (traditionally associated with wisdom in various pagan mythologies, and biblically with seduction, treachery, and the Fall). The serpent's major role in both narrative lines makes it another repetitive motif.[10]

These quasi-mythic materials are not the primary stuff of Wendell's narrative, a kind of mosaic comprising innumerable tiny shards, ranging from tales of people he knew who were cured with snake oil to accounts of abuse of recent (nonwhite) immigrants by *blancos* (whites), numerous hangings and other executions exemplifying frontier "justice," and Mexican *corridos* recounting loves and deaths along the border, together with countless individual tales of horror. One such fragmentary narrative concerns the narrator's father, Cecil Lambert Espana, and his bilingual pet alligator Jefferson (who not only spoke English and Spanish but recited poetry and did horse imitations). These accomplishments were belittled by the half-breed Zuro Millor, leading to his murder by Cecil Espana. Wendell's chronicle documents every imaginable form of depravity, brutality, and degradation. Examples include missionaries, supposedly religious laypeople, priests, and nuns who abused orphans and transmitted sexual diseases to populations being proselytized. Abuse of women is rampant, perhaps the most horrifying example being that "the Indian woman Azotea's husband turned her into salt pork or bacon, he buried her [alive] up to the neck in a roadside salt-flat" (*Cristo,* 98). Instances of cannibalism also are repeatedly alleged.

Wendell's Life

A key year in the narrator's life is 1917, and specifically 20 September, the day he learned the identity of his parents: "I had lived without knowing who I was, from whence I came, that is, who my mother and father were, up to the age of twenty or twenty-two [until] being recognized by my mother, who was working as a whore in Tombstone" (7), an incident repeatedly evoked (cf. 221). Thanks to this discovery, Wendell fixes the date of his birth around 1895: "the mark branded on your butt [she told me] was made by your father to celebrate the arrival of the new century when you had your fifth birthday and were old enough for the branding iron" (7). Wendell's father leaves him in the orphanage of a distant city (Portales, New Mexico [66]), denying the mother all information about the son's whereabouts; he repeatedly modifies accounts of learning his identity and origin. This incident figures among many about which his memory falters: "maybe this date is incorrect" (7). Obsessive returns to this moment of epiphany, together with other repetitive motifs, exercise structuring functions in the absence of plot, a kind of lyric structure, as in *Mazurca.*

Wendell's discovery of his "roots" communicates much about the novel's climate and other significant characters: the prostitute the narrator patronizes each Saturday reveals that she is his mother, having recognized him because his father had branded the same mark on their 12 offspring—Wendell and 11 brothers. The mother's place of business is Tombstone: "my mother had her 'love shop' to the east of Sixth Street, she reached Tombstone ahead of the decent women and first worked in the bawdy-house of the Hungarian Kate Elder, Big Nose Kate, the sweetheart of John Doc Holliday, one of those who fought at the OK Corral" (*Cristo*, 8). This passage links Wendell's family chronicle with the background narrative of the legendary shoot-out—providing more explicit connection than with the truncated Indian myth, which shares only the desert geography, while offering a more idyllic world in contrast to the violence and sordidness of other story lines.

Wendell's mother does not immediately inform him of her discovery: "I didn't want to say anything in case you might not visit me any more, you realize I have to make a living, but now I see it doesn't bother you, so I'll be able to tell you lots of things" (9). He knows nothing about his progenitor other than what his mother tells him (his putative father is long dead), but the man reportedly was a murderer, thief, sadist, and abuser of Wendell's mother and all their children (one of his favorite amusements was to force the mother to have intercourse with his pet alligator—who seemed more human and cultured than the father). Wendell calculates that "my father must have been born around 1865 or maybe before in Alamosa, on the banks of the Rio Grande" (11; cf., "my father was from Alamosa, Colorado, most likely that's where he was from, my mother says this city is on the banks of the Rio Grande, I don't know because I was never there" [74–75]). His mother was born "on the Mexican border, in a village called Sasabe, with one foot on either side of the border" (12). Without emotion, he summarizes his mother's difficult early years: "she didn't know her father, although she did find out who he was, they told her when she was ten and had her first communion, and Buffalo Chamberino got her drunk and took her to bed, and he told her, they hanged your daddy in Pitiquito" (13). The deflowering of Wendell's mother figures among the novel's most frequently repeated motifs: retold with variations, half anecdote, half lyric refrain, it too structures the work in the absence of a plot.

Despite repeating details about his progenitors, Wendell shows little filial piety: "my mother really gets me excited, she's a bitch that knows how to pleasure a man" (19). He worries, however, when the "flower" (or scar where his father branded him) oozes pus, fearing it is "a cancer God has sent to punish me for going to bed with my mother after knowing about it" (19). He changes his relationship with his mother only in that (after learning their identities) he grants her request that "whenever you're satisfied, put on your pants and kiss me on the forehead" (14). Cela previously insinuated the theme of mother-son incest, which appears (at least as desire) in *Mrs. Caldwell,* possibly a modern Jocasta (mother-wife of Oedipus). Jocasta hanged herself upon realizing she had committed incest with her son, a mythic antecedent contrasting violently with the matter-of-fact reactions by Wendell and his variously named mother. Occasionally he comments positively; for example, "My mother was sixteen years older than I, not yet old although she looked it, and she was pleasant and kind" (59)—no obstacle to his hitting the road to Tombstone each weekend with his friend and fellow worker Gerard Ospino to "take turns in my mother's bed—me first, of course" (51). Although little concerned about incest, he seems aware that some disapprove of prostitution: "I wasn't ashamed of my mother's trade, there are worse ones" (74). Wendell passively accepts almost everything: "His experience with humanity in Arizona has expunged his beliefs in the macro-myths of our civilization. There are no ideals, no principles, only word-games and instinctual actions" (Miller, 86). But Wendell offers occasional telling criticisms and protests.

Echoes of Other Works

Although the novelistic time and space of *Cristo versus Arizona* have no precedents in Cela's repertoire, readers will recognize constants: emphasis on eroticism, sexual deviation, violence, death, cruelty, mutilation, madness, illness, deformities, retardation, greed, lust, and corruption. Cela's extensive sexual lexicon emerges uninhibited along with virtuoso expressions of the scatological and shocking; for example, the following description of another victim of senseless violence:

> She passed the time delighting in the sounds of her abdomen and other noisy cavities of the body, it would have been better had she died at the hands of the revolutionaries, the only things she ever managed were automatic reflexes and physical or chemical reactions, growing to maturity getting fatter each day, breathing, belching, farting, eating, drinking, pissing, shitting, sleeping and hearing her heartbeat. (213)

Just as the novel presents no "good" characters (the narrator and his mother being among the least objectionable), neither are there healthy ones: idiots, cripples, and the blind and tubercular abound, as do sadists, criminals, drunks, and drug addicts. Numerous scenes involve (other) prostitutes and bordellos, and pimps and other exploiters of the weak and of weaknesses. Torrente Ballester's comment nearly five decades ago concerning *The Hive* also describes *Cristo versus Arizona:* "The motor driving these [hundreds of] characters is fundamentally sex, and . . . coitus, whether achieved or frustrated, is the climax of their lives."[11] Cela's well-known narrative world has moved intact from Spain to a stereotyped movie set version of the Old West identified as Arizona.

Cela's discourse constantly includes the use of multiple names and patronymics, tag lines, and nicknames for numerous characters—a nomenclature frequently satiric or ironic, as well as dehumanizing: Pato (the Duck) Macario, Erskine Aardvark Carlow (alias the Anteater), Cam Coyote Gonzales, Buffalo Chamberio, Macario the Skull Davis, Guillermo Codfish Sunspot, Bill Hyena Quijotoa, Nickie Marrana (the last name means Sow), Adorno Frog Allomoore, Frank Banana, Esmeralda Rawhide, Frank Sapito ("the Toad"), and many more. Some obviously evoke a "Western" atmosphere (Rawhide, Coyote, Buffalo), but African animals also appear (Hyena, Anteater), as well as others associated with aquatic environments, though water is nowhere to be found. The names' dehumanizing function outweighs verisimilitude and atmosphere.

Cela's use of multiple names for certain characters here goes to greater extremes, implicitly including all humanity in the portrait of depravity. Some characters' names are so frequently multiplied or rectified as to imperil any and all individuality, for example, the narrator's mother: "Her name was Matilda, but she had various other names, before I was born she was called Mariana, which sounds a little foreign, and also Sheila, and some called her Cissie, and Bonita, and some said Bonnie" (124; cf. 192). The narrator harbors comparable doubts concerning his own name: "My name is Wendell Espana, Wendell Liverpool Espana, maybe not Espana but Span, or Aspen, I never really knew" (5; cf. 75); "for a while I was called Wendell Liverpool Lochiel but afterwards things got straightened out" (111). Craig Teresa or Craig Tiger Brewer were other aliases (152–53). Similar confusion exists regarding his father's name: "My father's name was Cecil Espana, Cecil Lambert Espana, maybe it wasn't Espana but Span or Aspen, I never saw it in writing, and I never found out" (11). Nothing explains Wendell's certainty concerning his progenitor's identity, considering his mother had been a prostitute from the age of 10. Doubtful identities affect others: "Taco Peres, some call him Taco Lopes and others Taco Mendes, actually almost nobody calls him Taco Peres" (34; cf. 5, 16). Sometimes multiple names may be reasonably explained, as with this escaped convict:

"Almost certainly Bill Hyena is now far away, maybe now he's called Mike San Pedro, nobody will ever know" (41; cf. 158). Understandable reasons also underlie certain nicknames: "There were three brothers, all three homosexuals, Don, Ted, and Bob, nicknamed Jessie, Nancy and Pansy" (11). Other explanations prove less reasonable, although perfectly postmodern: "Guillermo Codfish Sunspot was also known as Marco Saragosa Toyahvale, obviously to create confusion" (40).

Narrative "unwriting" or rewriting and erasure of identities, characteristic of much postmodern discourse, transcends nomenclature. The narrator frequently confesses ignorance; Cela's earlier works present limited, nonomniscient, and fallible narrators who verbalize doubts, contradicting and correcting themselves, arguing with other characters, disputing their versions of events, and forgetting what has been said before. Such narratorial shortcomings loom large in *San Camilo* and in *Mazurca;* similar lapses in *Cristo versus Arizona* merely add to Cela's demythification of narrative authority.[12] Wendell repeatedly confesses his lack of details or personal knowledge, and like the other characters, he exhibits neither clear identity nor personality. Scarcely even caricatures, these shadowy figures are but the sum of their actions—almost unvarying and usually bad—plus their defects and vices. Cela's fictional division of humanity into victims and executioners seems less sharply differentiated than in early works such as *La colmena:* some executioners later become victims in turn. Cela dehumanized early characters, although to a lesser extent, employing animalistic imagery and methods such as illnesses (often diseases of animals), and manner of death (slaughtered like sheep, butchered like hogs, their necks wrung like chickens, etc.). Similar dehumanizing motifs reappear in *Cristo versus Arizona,* especially disrespectful treatment of the dead:

> and my father, when he got smallpox, the captain of the freighter Fool's Wedding ordered him thrown overboard, the sharks didn't eat him alive, they ate him dead. (18)

> Teodulfo Zapata drowned in the Colorado River . . . the fish ate his eyes, and somebody cut off his private parts, the cadaver had the privates sawed off. (40)

> the dead they grind into flour to feed a flock of noisy, aggressive geese. (54)

> Fermincito Guanajato was shot in the throat, they stuffed his Adam's Apple inside, he swallowed it, they didn't pull it out through his neck because it broke in a hundred pieces. (55)

the negress Patricia was hung from the same tree as the drug dealer
Sunspot for beheading children, she made magical potions with their
fresh blood and their body fat. (73)

it's a village which has neither cemetery nor whorehouse, they take the
dead and mash them up and kind of grind them to meal. (79)

it was rumored that Wong from the Chinese restaurant prepared his
Happiness Dumplings with cadavers, especially the bodies of little children, it was true, but nobody could prove it. (100)

Other characters are no better: "Anteater" collects the skulls of Indians,
keeping them in a cage in the tavern bathroom; another collects human
eyes in a bottle, and so on, ad nauseum. What the reader almost never
finds are comfortable deaths and normal burials (infrequent "proper"
burials are often followed by grave robbing or other profanations).

"Reality" and Fiction

Gruesome deaths may evoke the American West for some acquainted
only with paraliterary imitations in pulp fiction or B movies, but it
seems unlikely that Cela attempted an accurate portrayal of Arizona or
expected Spanish readers to accept it as such. Instead, he creates a paradigm of lawlessness, a kind of no-man's-land (and certainly no
woman's), a cruel and violent wilderness where nothing is prohibited.
Nonetheless, Cela's trips to Arizona really occurred, according to the
versified account by Miguel Méndez (although they were no prerequisite
for writing *Cristo versus Arizona*).[13] The putative setting—if it ever
existed beyond the silver screen—vanished long since (excepting the
geography), as did the legendary characters of Tombstone. Nor did Cela
intend chronological accuracy, judging by the number of anachronisms.
Charlebois (153–54 n. 8) observes that Wendell mentions the Hearst
fortune and the late-1980s Louisiana politician David Duke. The novel
makes numerous references to taverns, gunmen, and revolvers, brands
of weapons and of tobacco (cf. 149, 153, 202, 203) possibly calculated
to provide specificity, but the result is simply a caricature or parody of
the Old West as purveyed by Hollywood. Some toponymy is authentic
(but could have come from maps or tourist guides); other place names
are not in the atlas and may be apocryphal. The clichéd, stylized, and
wooden environment is merely a backdrop for the characters, following
usual models in Cela's fiction. Cela's earlier novels abound in sexuality

and death, usually abnormal, shocking, violent, and cruel. These traits have merely intensified. The painful vision of human beings as puppets controlled by hunger, lust, and greed, essential to Cela's novels from *La colmena* onward—starkly visible in its nakedness—remains, unrelieved by charity or tenderness. "Wendell repeats one of the most moving ethical statements of the novel: 'nobody should live without being loved a little, even though it is almost next to nothing' " (quoted in Charlebois, 96).

Location in Arizona probably need not suggest that Cela views this state as more evil than the rest of the country. Indeed, "Literally hundreds of places are mentioned, including Colorado, New Mexico, Texas, South Carolina, Louisiana, California, Wyoming, West Virginia, Nebraska, Utah, Pennsylvania, Arkansas and Iowa" (Charlebois, 154), as well as "names of towns, streets, deserts, mountains, rivers, business establishments, cemeteries, banks, national wonders and parks, stage-coach routes, Indian reservations, ranches and farms, and historic places" (155). This list certainly constitutes a representative sampling of the United States. Cela merely expands on his negative vision of Spain in earlier works to include the rest of the world, humanity everywhere, as witness the numerous races in *Cristo versus Arizona:* blacks, Chinese, Indians, mestizos, half-breeds, Caucasians, and Hispanics. Arizona could have been chosen as the setting because of its cinematographic association with lawlessness and violence, but Cela's geography symbolizes man's inhumanity to man: he could have selected Auschwitz or Hiroshima. Cela's "Arizona" symbolizes mercilessness, sins against humanity: "Christ goes towards Arizona and wherever, New York, San Francisco, Europe, Africa, because that's why he's the Son of God . . . the devil also goes incessantly, eternally, from one place to another" (*Cristo,* 228). "Arizona" would thus include the entire world. Sobejano's suggestion that the novel is a "chronicle of collective sinfulness" fits well within the broader context (Sobejano 1997, 158). This critic also perceptively suggests that the Arizona desert may represent the "moral wasteland of vice, impiety, tedium and rage which inundate the frontier territory" (151). Wendell's branding "to celebrate the new century" evokes by association the impending millennium and millennial associations with Christ's return. The vision presented has much of the apocalyptic (and notes of apocalypse reappear in *La cruz de San Andrés*). Aspects of the world portrayed evoke paintings of Hieronymus Bosch, with all their earthly excess and hellish torments, a vision already noted in *Oficio.*

Subtexts and Authorial Attitude

Wendell, a "voice crying in the wilderness," calls repeatedly for an examination of conscience (*Cristo,* 230), the step preceding confession. Preparing to confess his own sins, Wendell declares, "I don't believe in eternal condemnation but in the infinite mercy of God" (231), possibly explaining the litanies, which critics heretofore have seen as important but have not managed to elucidate. The title's invocation of Christ (a name synonymous with charity, altruism, and goodness) must be considered in the context of Cela's fiction and the selfishness and abuses proliferating therein. Christ's name, when linked with Arizona—historically associated with tales of violence, brute force, and animal instinct—evokes the millennial conflict between good and evil; the symbolic space "Arizona" represents the Antichrist, the epitome of humanity's inherent evil, violence, and sin, the lack of mercy and charity so prominent in Cela's somber paintings of Spain. Other passages expand on the title allusion: "Christ doesn't wear spurs, because he commands Death" (22). Several refer to a trial: "Do you know if it's true that Christ was charged in a lawsuit in Arizona?" (32). Apparently there was no trial, after all:

> Nobody could have brought suit against Christ because he's God and God always wins. (32)

> Christ is tougher than Arizona and the whole border put together, sinners betrayed Him many times but you can't litigate against Him because He's as clean and hard as diamonds. (52)

> maybe it was the other way around and Christ wants to sue Arizona, at the end of the world He's got to be fed up with sinners because they always did bad things to Him, Christ is God and you can't bring Him to trial because he is infinite and omnipotent. (137)

And finally, "it's not true that there was a trial against Christ in Arizona, nor is the opposite true" (176). Further clarifying "Arizona's" status as allegorical space is the following affirmation: "No one should forget that Christ is God and He is not against man in spite of the fact that man would deserve it if He were, here in Arizona and across the River there in Sonora and in Chihuahua there is neither more virtue or vice than anywhere else" (103). The borders of the symbolic desert are thus indefinitely expandable, and its inhabitants represent the races of the earth.

This makes it less surprising that Cela's "Paschal Lamb" Pascual Duarte reappears in his next novel.

Cristo versus Arizona protests humanity's inhumanity by pleading for tolerance: "Here we're all against everybody, because we fit so badly, we hardly fit at all, *veritatis simplex oratio est,* but in the final analysis the whole world is confused, Hispanics, Jews, Indians, Blacks and Chinese, we're all against everybody" (226). In this novel, "Cela comes closer to Freudian-Marcusian analysis of our civilization and its ills than in any other novel" (Miller, 87); there is no "message," only the narrator's impassive observance of what people do, with the resulting "patent contradiction between Judeo-Christian ideals and actions determined by the overwhelming force of a misdirected Eros" (87). Faced with Christians' lack of charity, Cela's narrator appeals to reason: "Here we are pushing against each other, it's true, but we can all fit, we fit badly but we fit, so far nobody has fallen off the earth" (*Cristo,* 224–25). He seemingly appeals also to popular religious beliefs: "Before God our Lord it won't work to try to play *macho* and break things and try to give orders, because with just a glance He could melt us, Christ is God and the only way to get to Him is through mercy" (233)—and mercy is among the rarest qualities in Cela's novelistic world, a world that unfortunately contains too little fantasy or fiction. The litany, a repetitive prayer for mercy, suggests via its parallel structures humanity's positive and negative sides, striving to oppose to the persistent negative litany of atrocities a positive counterpoint, *Ora pro nobis.*

Chapter Eight

The Return of Pascual Duarte: *El asesinato del perdedor*

Upon winning the Nobel Prize in 1989, Cela had reportedly been work-ing for some time on *Madera de boj,* a novel dealing with seafaring Gali-cians. Despite repeated announcements of its imminent appearance, *Madera de boj* was delayed until late 1999. Instead, Cela published two very different novels, both in 1994, neither treating Galician seafarers (though *La cruz de San Andrés* is set in a Galician seaport, location has minimal impact on plot, characters, and themes—unlike those of *Mazurca,* which are more significantly shaped by their Galician setting). Shortly before *La cruz*'s publication, *El asesinato del perdedor* (1994), Cela's first work of long fiction since winning the Nobel Prize, appeared, closing a six-year novelistic hiatus (following *Cristo versus Arizona*). Con-trasts are immediately evident: Cela returns to Spain and contemporary time, and—rather than vast frescoes with dozens, even hundreds of crimes and ghastly demises—he focuses on the miscarriage of justice concerning a single "crime," a minor misdemeanor of "public inde-cency," that is, the "loser's" allegedly fondling his girlfriend in public. Public affection, prohibited under Franco, was still criminalized in an outdated legal code, zealously enforced by certain fanatic judges. Incar-ceration by the primitive criminal justice system proves so traumatic and destructive as to provoke the suicide of the "offender," Mateo Rue-cas, who was raped and brutalized in prison. Accounts of police or mili-tary brutality provide relevant contexts for readers, although Cela's satirical commentary targets the judge. Relevant essays (in *Vuelta de hoja* and *¡A bote pronto!* [1998; Quick! To the Lifeboats!]) treat the need for clear, equitable laws providing justice for all and demand reform of the penal code.

Cela and "Criminal Justice"

Mateo "the Loser" was punished less for amorous effusiveness than for showing "disrespect" to His Honor. Cela's ironic statements concern judges generally; for example, "you can't be disrespectful to judges because they've got the skillet by the handle; in theory no, but in practice they're the ones who classify conduct and make disposal of liberties and that's very dangerous, especially if they believe they're backed by the Holy Spirit."[1] Wendell (the narrator of *Cristo versus Arizona*) comments sarcastically (concerning the dismissal of charges against the Tombstone aggressors) that "the decisions of judges should not be disputed by anybody," affirming shortly afterward that "judges' decisions should be accepted by everybody" (*Cristo*, 215). In both instances, Cela's narrator denounces miscarriage of justice, as judges acted neither impartially nor in the spirit of the law. *El asesinato* indicts the authoritarian nature of a judicial establishment that rarely brooks criticism despite its fallibility in innumerable rulings. A diatribe denouncing Don Cosme's judicial incompetence stresses that "it's dangerous for judges to be young and gullible, judges should be serene, very old and skeptical, as justice's mission is not to fix the world but rather to avoid its deteriorating further" (*El asesinato*, 8). The cover blurb of *El asesinato* terms the nuclear anecdote the "sordid and pathetic history of a helpless being impelled to suicide by hypocritical and brutal social repression of amorous expression." References to Judge Cosme Naranjo Tena's supposedly privileged relationship with the Holy Spirit satirize the fanaticism of religious conservatives and their "unholy alliance" with the politico-legal establishment. Challenge to authority is hardly new, as seen in the legend of William Tell, where it provokes repressive retaliation, but Tell was not a "loser." Mateo, besides being a loser, lacks judgment concerning those moments when "discretion is the better part of valor." As explained by the letter in the epilogue,

> things happened thus: February 2 of last year, several young couples were watching television in a bar. One couple was kissing and an unknown gentleman (Judge Cosme) approached and said that that shouldn't be done in public. Mateo replied "with my girlfriend I'll do whatever I fucking please" and imagine his surprise when that man called the police and ordered his arrest, accusing them of public indecency and disrespect for authority, because he was the judge. (*El asesinato*, 235)

Twenty-year-old Mateo and his 16-year-old girlfriend Soledad, both from humble backgrounds, have rudimentary educations and no prior contact with the law. Their court-appointed lawyer, awed by the judge, bungles the defense, and Mateo and Soledad receive excessive fines and sentences. Following eight days in jail during which Mateo is raped, sodomized, and otherwise abused, Mateo is sentenced to five months in prison, fined PTA 30,000, and disqualified from publicly funded positions for seven years. Although subsequently granted probation as a first offender, Mateo suffers paranoia, depression, and a sense of degradation resulting from the rapes. Fearing return to prison, the Loser hangs himself from the lintel of his family's stable. Unrest and resentment among the enraged townspeople provoke threats against the judge, and Mateo's friends smear feces on Don Cosme's door.

The romantic paradigm pitting the individual against society in an unequal and ultimately doomed struggle is replicated in twentieth-century literature's portrayals of numerous characters alienated and existentially isolated by society's growing dehumanization. Such individuals, generally antiheroes (as is Mateo), lack the larger-than-life dimensions of romantic heroes (and their struggle similarly lacks grandeur). Mateo's antagonists include the Spanish legal establishment and civil code plus reactionary, prudish codes of public conduct under the Franco regime, whereby even publicly kissing one's spouse on the cheek in greeting could be fined. This background sociohistorical context produced a real-life incident inspiring *El asesinato*. Several factors conspired against the Loser. Judge Cosme, enraged at the lack of respect for "His Honor," is said to have summoned Mateo from jail to appear before him in the absence of counsel at all hours. "Convincing" the Loser to dismiss his public defender and defense witnesses, as they "would only complicate things and irritate the judges," Don Cosme insinuated to Mateo what he must say. Mateo can only for the sake of convention be termed the protagonist: he acts very little, and his dubious accomplishments are antiheroic, reducible to public indecency and unwitting disrespect for authority. The Loser (a Cela archetype) is crushed in the unequal struggle against an overwhelming antagonist, symbolically represented by Don Cosme, who incarnates society's most repressive structures. Despite brief initial macho posturing, Mateo is feminized, most notably when repeatedly raped in jail. His feminization permeates his pathetic suicide note expressing guilt resulting from the rapes: "From the time I was jailed I suffered a lot and since I got out my conscience hasn't quit bothering me day and night and sometimes I can't sleep. I ask God to forgive me and all those that knew me" (*El asesinato,* 94). Mateo's role is largely passive, consisting mainly in being a bewildered victim of harassment, abuse, and violence, as well as deliberate obfuscation and misadministration of "justice."

Connections with Other Works

The imprisoned protagonist constitutes one link with *Pascual Duarte,* although *El asesinato* features multiple narrators and begins with third-person commentary. Other narrative devices repeated from Cela's first novel include the use of letters: *El asesinato*'s nuclear anecdote is summarized in a final letter suggesting that the historical incident has already provoked much interest and discussion. As in *Pascual Duarte,* the letter represents correspondence between the author and a putative interlocutor who has alleged further knowledge of events. In the final "Letter of Advice," a first-person speaker claims to have learned certain facts thanks to a priest's letter: "Literary history [often employs] false manuscripts, documents, letters or confessions as the origin of a tale, a procedure already used [by Cela] in several works: the memoirs, *Pascual Duarte,* the 'Addendum' with the coroner's report in *Mazurca.*"[2] Cela uses variants of the Cervantine "found manuscript" device to suggest that he is neither author nor inventor of a fiction but merely the transcriber of events already recorded by another historian. Even more significant connections with *Pascual Duarte* involve a narrative voice identified as Esteban Ojeda, a death-row prisoner where Mateo was incarcerated. Intertextual evidence later reveals Esteban as none other than Pascual: "I was famous some years ago when I wrote some pages that began thus: 'Sir, I am not bad, although I don't lack reasons for being so, etc.' " (*El asesinato,* 101). These opening words from *Pascual Duarte,* later prefaced by references to society's pro rata of guilt in the acts of criminals formed by that society, identify Esteban as a persona or mask of Cela, identical with the first-person autobiographical narrator of *Pascual Duarte.*

The same authorial "mask" comments obliquely on Cela's fondness for first-person narratives, linking Pascual Duarte and the protagonist of *El asesinato,* both antiheroes and victims of Spain's criminal justice system: "Esteban Ojeda likes to write in first person, it's always easier. It's as if I were Mateo Ruecas, I close my eyes and I feel like Mateo Ruecas, the loser mentioned in this true history" (*El asesinato,* 116). Even more than Pascual, Mateo is accurately described by Pascual's prison chaplain: "a gentle lamb, frightened and corralled by the justice system." Implied metamorphosis (Pascual/Esteban/Mateo) creates a multilayered narrative discourse that fluctuates as each identity predominates, obscuring narratorial outlines and the identities of the voices in dialogue. This device facilitates authorial intervention; although the author infrequently speaks directly (e.g., "I copy-edited . . ." [234]), the technique distances him from the narrative by making him seem little more than another reader, albeit an active and informed one—exactly the kind of reader that *El asesinato* demands. It requires special effort and complicity to reconstruct the fragmented sequences and determine who is speaking and about what. As in *Pascual Duarte,* social inequality is an underlying cause, but Cela's focus is the de facto lack of equality of all citizens before the law, and the fact that punishment too often varies according to the rank of the accused. Cela's father had insisted on his studying law, and although he never completed the degree, the future novelist spent enough time studying the subject to become well versed and to formulate informed opinions concerning the civil code and its shortcomings. *El asesinato* alludes to the principle that ignorance of the law is no defense and especially criticizes legal jargon and the handing down of unintelligible rulings (as with Mateo Ruecas and Soledad Navares). To figure out that they would not be sent to the penitentiary because they were first offenders, Mateo and Soledad had to read the decree "a thousand times." The narrative voice, speaking from Mateo's perspective, muses that when words cease to be intelligible, they become "venomous pus" and end by "poisoning and annihilating the soul" (220).

As in *Mazurca* and *Pascual Duarte,* the protagonist's death, known to readers from the outset, provides the unifying axis around which other events converge and revolve, together with fragmentary and sometimes contradictory information about circumstances leading to that death. In Cela's later works, progressively more extraneous characters, anecdotes, and fragments of dialogues or stories are introduced (as opposed to the unitary, autobiographical format of *Pascual Duarte*). *El asesinato* lacks plot in the traditional sense of sustained, connected action, susceptible of summary, although frequent amplifications of the nuclear anecdote provide vertebration. *Mazurca* constitutes the most significant structural antecedent for *El asesinato,* with recurrent lyric devices or repetitive motifs recalling musical forms. Just as certain nuclear incidents are repeated with variations in *Mazurca* (and in *Cristo versus Arizona*), so too are they repeated in *El asesinato.* Structure in the three novels constitutes an amalgam of the fugue and variations on a theme. In *Pascual Duarte, Mazurca,* and *El asesinato,* the outcome (or protagonist's death), known to readers from the opening pages, seemingly mimics the detective or mystery novels that begin with the discovery of a crime, devoting the narrative to discovering causes, motives, circumstances, and specifics. Cela's novels, however, see the perpetrator in society as a whole, focusing not so much on "who done it" as on what it all means.

Recalling litanies in *Oficio* and *Cristo* are some 50 variant titles suggested for *El asesinato,* formulaic reiterations following this pattern: "This book should have been entitled ———— but that was not to be [because] . . . " Reasons for discarding the alternative titles vary, as do the suggested titles. The explanation frequently involves a non sequitur; for example, "This book should have been entitled 'Chronicle Which Narrates How the New Judge Washes his Condoms in the Baptismal Font of Saint Stanislaus Parish,' but that couldn't be, it would have brought great unpopularity to Montesquieu" (*El asesinato,* 50). "This book should have been titled 'Notions of Algebra and Trigonometry for War Orphans' or else 'The Economic Theory of the Location of Railways,' but that couldn't be; both forms were prohibited by the UN" (61). Two alternative titles imply another authorial identity: "This book should have been titled 'Doubts About Solitude' but it couldn't be because its ill-intentioned author, Miss Mary Tavistock, threatened to publish the erotic correspondence between a certain judge and a certain military chaplain" (91–92). This subversive reason for rejection implicitly ridicules the religious and military establishments and the legal system via a tightly condensed conceit in the expressionist or *Esperpento* mode (a grotesque caricature inverting values). Allusion to another author, theoretically compatible with Cela's use of the "found manuscript" device in *Pascual Duarte* and elsewhere, interests especially because of suggested cross-gender authorship (an echo of *Mrs. Caldwell*)—anticipating the enigma of authorship central to *La cruz de San Andrés.*

An early review by Ana María Platas Tasende notes the narrative's origin in "tragically real events that happened in a small town in Spain in 1987";[3] similarly, Cela terms it "this true story" (*El asesinato,* 116). Platas, writing in Gallego, does not identify the setting as Galician, but Charlebois affirms that the events in question took place "in a small Galician town" (102).[4] Platas and Iglesias state that the events occurred in the province of Badajoz and were played up in the press, as a result of which the young man, "victim of the judge's excessive zeal, committed suicide 6 January 1987" (606). Mention of Badajoz provides another link to *Pascual Duarte,* Cela's only prior novel set in that province. Identification of the town merely as "N" and the absence of details of dialect, geography, climate, food, and other regional specifics prevent linking the "murder" with a specific locale, thereby generalizing and endowing the case with symbolic or allegorical proportions. Similar effects are achieved by imprecision regarding names, and one primary narrative voice proclaims that "almost all [the names] . . . are false" (*El asesinato*, 167). Likewise nameless is the bar where the "crime" occurred (although once it is identified as "Celestino's," the name of the "other bar" in *La colmena*). Cela repeats several names of shadowy, insubstantial characters from other novels, especially *Cristo versus Arizona*.

The protagonist of *Mazurca* is endowed with quasi-mythic proportions; unbowed in life and noble in death, he is definitively avenged, thereby achieving a symbolic postmortem victory that is denied the Loser (his friends' painting the judge's door with feces is clearly a loser's "revenge"). *El asesinato* also resembles *Mazurca* in using multiple narrative voices, one or more being specifically identified with Cela as author, and another of which is his mask or spokesman. The two novels' contrasting treatment of sexuality merits noting: whereas eroticism in *Mazurca* is earthy, liberated, and lusty, *El asesinato* abounds in grotesque, aberrant sexuality whose participants—secondary characters unrelated to the nuclear event—exemplify extremes of age, abnormality, deformity, ugliness, and bizarre complications. Examples include the marathon fornications by Claudina and "the fiancé of her sister-in-law Estefanía Yellowbilled," the presumably sinful and hypocritical affair of Pamela Pleshette and the Bishop of Restricted Beach (Florida), the sado-masochistic relationship between the Bandit and "Blind Countess" (whose eyes he gouged out), the repugnant geriatric affair of "venerable Zaccheus Nicomediano, in his orthopedic chair" with the aging harpy Waldetruda, and the confused, overlapping, bigamous conjugal relations of "Norbert and his two wives, Elsa and Gertrude, and Elsa and her two husbands, Norbert and Raul" (69). Charlebois adds to this list

> distinguished men whom the narrator has unscrupulously dubbed members of a "club" of homosexuals which includes high-ranking (fictitious) church and government officials . . . [and] men whose sexual appetite is so insatiable that Cela uses it to defile further the pomp and circumstance of aristocracy and at the same time underscore the commonality of basic human needs. (104)

Sociocultural Context

Illicit and aberrant sexuality has been prominent in Cela's novels from *La colmena* hence, but in *El asesinato,* contrast has been carefully orchestrated between the "normal" youthful couple arrested and persecuted for public indecency and the numerous older, presumably wiser, clearly more worldly, influential, wealthy, and hypocritical characters whose conduct is far more flagrant and offensive. These figures are tolerated and protected by the establishment (which is the essence of the message). The novelistic discourse accumulates examples of other public erotic behavior—including all conceivable deviation—protected by the veneer of respectability. The Franco regime's innumerable repressive, moralistic controls and penalties were selectively applied. Cela shows from *La colmena* onward that such codes were systematically flouted, as reflected by the multitude of highly visible prostitutes peopling his works, or the numerous "respectable" bourgeois characters in *The Hive* visiting houses of assignation.

Prostitutes abound in *El asesinato* and are constantly mentioned by other characters; the majority of these unfortunate women meet horrifying ends in circumstances evoking the Inquisition, often via the gallows or other forms of public execution, eagerly attended by characters such as Dame Waldetruda and several of the novel's grotesque sexual partners. Cela uses these prostitutes not to portray sexual activity, "normal" or deviant, but to symbolize exploitation and victimization, as shown by many examples in Umbral's study of "illicit love" in Cela's fiction. Prostitutes, lacking legal protection from abuses by their customers, are doubly vulnerable because of the criminalization of their jobs. Exemplary incidents include the hanging of a "Portuguese prostitute" (*El asesinato*, 11) and a "docile Moorish prostitute" (125), enthusiastically cheered and applauded by attendees. Among numerous similar occasions (whose victims are all women) is the execution of a "little grandmother" who draws her last breath amid the spectators' guffaws (147); elsewhere, the narrative voice qualifies as breathtaking the spectacle of an old woman's naked cadaver (146). Public executions, repeatedly cited in *Oficio* and numerous in *Cristo versus Arizona*, symbolize society's blood lust, alluding to Cela's opposition to the death penalty (enunciated in *Oficio*). Public appetites for violence and death (ably exploited by the entertainment industry) accompany the emphasis on sexuality, echoing Cela's characteristic combination of eroticism and death. Adding to the bizarre carnival atmosphere of executions (and repeating the device of the chorus from *Oficio*) is a "choral mass" of beggars who perform amid ridicule and abuse by spectators. Reinforcing suggestions of theatricality and farce are various degenerations of the commedia dell'arte masks seen in *Oficio,* Punch and Judy puppets who (as in some of Lorca's theater)[5] intermingle with "human" characters, although no one seems to notice.

Thematically, *El asesinato* most closely resembles Cela's *La insólita y gloriosa hazaña del Cipote de Archidona* (The Uncommon and Glorious Feat of the Archidona Stud).[6] This tongue-in-cheek bit of vulgar erotica is indirectly cited via an intertextual allusion proposing an alternative title for *El asesinato:* "This book should have been titled 'Exposition of Skins and Painted Leathers in Admiration and Homage for the Archidona Stud' " (*El asesinato,* 209). Both works inscribe themselves in the documentary genre, as Cela presents them in the guise of nonfiction, evoking the similar accusations of public indecency on which the respective works are based: "In Archidona something similar happened and people took it as a joke on the judges, the bad thing is that here somebody died" (26). That fatality motivates Cela's change of tone: ribald humor and macho complacency in the former give way to gravity, sarcasm, and underlying anger in the latter. *El Cipote* also incorporates the letter device, with putative correspondence between Cela and one Alfonso Canales in the possibly apocryphal context of epistolary dialogue involving members of Spain's Royal Academy, Málaga's provincial government, the scientific community, and the general public. Both works display Cela's mastery of esoteric variants of vulgarity and obscenity, recalling Cela Conde's attribution of a "new literary genre inaugurated by my father, subterranean erudition or . . . obscene scholarship" (220). Cela transcends the limits of erudite vocabulary in his representations of the lewd, lascivious, obscene, and pornographic in *El asesinato,* incorporating innuendo, euphemism, slang, and vulgarity, and translating certain obscenities to French (cf. 218).

Another antecedent is Cela's 1964 text for the photographic documentary of pitiable, aging, hopeless prostitutes working Barcelona's *barrio chino* (red-light district), entitled *Izas, rabizas, y colipoterras: Drama con acompañamiento de cachondeo y dolor de corazón.*[7] Cela identifies secondary characters in *El asesinato* as "the *iza* [bawd] Virtudes," the "*rabiza* [slattern] Inmaculada," and "*colipoterra* [whore] Encarnita" (178). Ironically, their given names imply the opposite: Virtudes equals Virtues, Inmaculada refers to the Inmaculate Conception, and Encarnita to the Holy Incarnation. David W. Foster's examination of *Izas* links "countercultural discourse" and the erotic to a subversive, demythologizing intent in multiple Cela novels and the *Diccionario secreto,*[8] alleging an implicit attack on the "hypocrisy and self-serving blindness of the morally righteous"— words that also aptly encapsulate the thrust of *El asesinato,* wherein the "morally righteous" are incarnated in a neophyte judge whose intolerance is compounded by youthful inexperience and self-importance.

The incident inspiring *El Cipote* allegedly occurred in 1972 (some 15 years before that prompting Cela to write *El asesinato*) in a small-town movie theater in the province of Málaga. In both instances, unmarried couples take advantage of the darkened locale, others present take offense, and the offenders are hauled away to face charges. Both texts parody official rhetoric, combining legal terminology with pompous circumlocution and prudish euphemisms, lampooning pedantry and pretentiousness with vulgar colloquiality. *El asesinato* advances Cela's plumbing of the hidden interstices of language begun in the *Diccionario secreto,* continued in the *Enciclopedia del Erotismo,* and embodied in a dialectical poetics of obscenity and euphemism characterizing major novels such as *San Camilo, Oficio, Mazurca,* and *Cristo versus Arizona* to varying degrees. *El asesinato,* some five times longer than *El Cipote* and more solemn and accusatory, incorporates experimental narrative techniques and structures absent in the antecedent. The death of the Loser, rather than typical murder, involves a crime of omission—perhaps negligent homicide. Javier Gómez de Liaño, an expert on jurisprudence and author of a lengthy essay on the role of justice in Cela's work, salutes the novelist's legal expertise,[9] noting Cela's preoccupation with the principles of liberty, equality, and justice (Gómez de Liaño, 359–60) and his commitment to democracy and the principle of majority rule (361), and cites the "Chronicle of Political Thought" contained in Cela's essay collection *Vuelta de hoja.* Cela believes that chemically, physically, and psychically, human beings are equal, but "before the law, that part about equality isn't usually believed by anybody, or almost anyone" (*El asesinato,* 363).

This applies to the legal abuse inspiring *El asesinato,* which leads Cela to comment that "it's easier and less risky to hunt down prostitutes, persecute gypsies, punish conscientious objectors, and lock up bandits . . . than to take seriously the dangerous premise that the law is equal for all and to put a marquis in jail, or accuse a financier, although both may have done plenty to be sentenced."[10] Gómez de Liaño stresses that Cela believes justice should be coolheaded, never administered in anger: "Hot-headed justice ceases to be just and becomes a contradiction of its own essence" (367). Acting in the flush of self-righteous anger at the perceived affront to his dignity, Judge Cosme incarnates this principle. Another principle that Cela upholds in *El asesinato* (and in *La cruz de San Andrés*) is that nobody has a monopoly on truth; no one is an exclusive interpreter of the law (or of religious dogma).

Chronology

Treatments of time contain numerous contradictions. The opening lines apparently situate the action toward the end of the eighteenth century: "One Ash Wednesday many years ago, at least 200, the knight Michael Percival the Crouching faced his own silhouette" (*El asesinato,* 7). The Percival allusion evokes quest romances and chivalric novels, as do references to the Knights Templars. Instead of rescuing maidens, however, the knights commit gang rape, and Percival's actions have nothing of the heroic: "Ash Wednesdays every year for at least 200 years, Hussars Captain Michael Percival the Crouching commits some stupidity" (82). His apparent immortality notwithstanding, Percival's insignificance precludes meaningful conclusions regarding him. He belongs with numerous secondary characters functioning to subvert concepts of valor, virtue, and nobility, thereby reinforcing themes of negative heroism in the "hero" (or Loser), and negative justice in Justice's representative, Judge Cosme. Percival's recurring marginal presence confuses an already ambiguous chronology including references to such temporally incompatible phenomena as AIDS (161); obscure or apocryphal episodes of nineteenth-century Spanish history ("We've not seen each other since [1870s] King Amadeo's first trip to Zaragoza," 85); a recently televised soccer match between Spain and Ireland; conversations between Dido and her sister concerning Aeneas (202); and scenes from the home life of Archimedes (61). Obvious anachronisms when juxtaposed to contemporary scenes from the Loser's life, these passages, plus repeated use of medieval titles and the *vosotros* form of address with singular interlocutors (obsolete since the Middle Ages), convey Cela's subtext, that the injustice perpetrated on the Loser belongs to all time, not just a single moment—"Many years ago, at least 100, maybe even before the Spanish Civil War" (125).

Time not only fluctuates but exhibits no reliable connection with birth dates: "The monk Basterot was a Goliard born 500 or 600 years too late, his talent for playing the accordion and singing medieval love ballads never interfered with his powers of discernment" (210). Among the few affirmations about time susceptible to being accepted at face value is this one: "nobody can measure Time because it was created at the same time as the world" (54). The "historical" event inspiring *El asesinato* is dated with notable inexactness: "More or less on Saint Gaston's Day one of these years, Mateo Ruecas turned up hanged" (233).

Chronological indefiniteness concerning Mateo constitutes the norm and is exacerbated by dispersion of relevant sections at various intervals throughout the novel, interspersed in a complex network of anecdotal fragments and narrative voices proceeding from a plurality of perspectives. "Given Cela's proclivity for obliterating factual objectivity regarding the Ruecas case, chronology is not of the essence" (Charlebois, 103). He makes an "obvious effort to distort sequential chronology and the correspondence between characters and historical context" (Platas and Iglesias, 612). Augmenting textual complications are mentions of places as varied as Singapore, Barcelona, Mt. Athos, Hamburg, Bratislava, the Congo, New Orleans, London/Soho, Paraguay, Soria, Lesbos, Bosnia, Heaven, Hell, Paradise, and Iria Flavia (612 n. 9).

One sober, isolated mention of socioeconomic injustice implies an indefinite, contemporary chronological perspective: "The Twentieth Century is ending, but in this century thus far nearly 600 boxers died because of blows received" (El asesinato, 175). This motif reiterates Cela's preoccupation with exploitation of the economically weak and disadvantaged (prostitutes, budding bullfighters, and those risking their lives in the ring). These people too are losers —regardless of epoch—and many are "murdered." Such references abet Cela's generalizing of his denunciation of abuses of power to other times and places. Even though a concrete historical incident inspired Cela to write El asesinato, readers should realize that abuses of the "justice" system are wrong, regardless of when or where they happen or who commits them. Thus Judge Cosme's treatment of Mateo before the Loser's trial is a "model of what the interrogation of the accused should never be, confusing, disorienting, and overwhelming him, without letting him breathe. The account of how Mateo was [mis]informed of his rights is shocking for anyone involved with the law" (Gómez de Liaño, 373).

Structuring Devices, Unwriting, and the Unreliable Narrator

The narrative discourse, characterized by biting irony and black humor, was deemed by an early reviewer to be a "surrealistic version of Quevedo's humor," as well as a hallucinatory carnival.[11] Additionally, it is a "Pandora's box of narrative devices (multiple narrators, points of view, and narratees) which expand beyond readerly tolerance the traditional boundaries between literary genres" (Charlebois, 101). In addition to polyphonic techniques (numerous voices in conversation, multiple nar-

rators of the nuclear incident, independent anecdotes, and story fragments), various speakers interrupt, fall silent, digress, or resume their discourse, blending their voices with others, offering self-conscious critiques,
or repeating earlier narration. Counterpoint, efforts at simultaneity, and
the interweaving of voices with written media (letters, legal documents,
and intertextual allusion) add to the confusion, as do innumerable regis-
ters of discourse inferred from the varied dialogues, some rapid, humorous, and colloquial, others slow, ponderous, and grandiloquent in tone,
still others of recurring symmetrical forms suggesting liturgical origins.
As with narrative passages per se, time and space, continual digressions,
and dialogues may not be indicated by visible signs or typographic conventions or arranged thematically or logically.

The concept of art as reiteration provides the basis for both structure
and style in *El asesinato* (Platas and Iglesias, 611), and thus Mateo's story
is retold by several secondary character-narrators—his friends and relatives—who add their reflections, judgments, and unrelated materials,
creating an appearance of disorder (which is nonetheless far from chaos).
Because the outcome is known from the beginning, Cela seeks not to
interest readers in the intrigue or plot-related conundrums but to
attract appreciation for stylistic and structural virtuosity. Reader attention is deliberately drawn to repetitions; for example, "almost everything must be said several times so people learn it" (*El asesinato*, 25), or
"Don't you agree that the simplest and most quintessential art is likewise reiteration?" (148). Conte detects a confluence of *El asesinato* and its
successor, *La cruz de San Andrés*, in a

> single narrative mold, that of extended, cumulative verbosity which con-
> fuses divers episodes. . . . But perhaps their coincidences are more formal
> than real, as the earlier one revolves around an injustice, largely a judicial
> error, while the second treats a collective error of metaphysical or spiri-
> tual nature, madness of religiosity or superstition.[12] (68)

This important observation draws attention to another significant
resemblance between two narratives composed almost simultaneously.
Platas and Iglesias point out that voices in *El asesinato* belong not only to
the living but also to the dead (*El asesinato* 13, 14, 34, 46, 58, 73, 92,
124, 181–83, etc.); animals, demons, puppets, St. Peter, God, Lucifer,
and human consciences likewise contribute to the incessant cacophony
(Platas and Iglesisa, 613). "Everything has its voice or could have one"
(613 n. 13). Echoes sound in *La cruz*, where demons and "divine" voices
are heard by some characters. Contrasting with the excess of speech in

El asesinato, description is minimal; spaces (as in *Oficio*) are abstract and lack details, and the characters' generic nature renders their appearance moot.

Abundant apocryphal citations undermine the authority of the text, which abounds in unkept promises by the narrator (e.g., "everything will become clear in due time" [71]). The only fulfilled promise states, "Toward the end or slightly before, this premise will be repeated for consolation of the dying," an apocryphal and contextually absurd reference repeated twice "toward the end" (228, 233). Newly deceased personages absurdly refuse to lie down and play dead, insisting on behaving like the living. Another repetitive motif involves reiterated demands for the execution of prostitutes (combined with the depiction of mass blood lust at public executions). Many conversations turn upon death, funerals, and the ravages of the aging process. Another recurring theme involves displays of authorial or narratorial ignorance:

> Somebody arrived late, I don't know who, nobody knows who or what, but somebody arrived late, life, death, the wrath of God, the poisonous benevolence of the devil, fortune—the truth is that almost always something was arriving late, probably a confused man, a confused theorem, an executioner looking bored, not frightfully bored or irrevocably bored, just somewhat bored, hardly at all. (9)

References to arriving late connect with a similar repetitive motif in *Oficio.* The implicit equation of opposites (life, death) and paradoxical and antithetical dualities (God's wrath, the devil's benevolence) via apposition and juxtaposition suggests rampant amorality belonging logically not to the narrative perspective but to the social or legal establishment that the various anonymous voices represent.

Cela repeatedly demonstrates the fallibility of language, deflating clichés, popular sayings, and official rhetoric. As in *San Camilo* and *Mazurca,* the novelist implicitly indicates the unreliability of history and hence of officially sanctified accounts of collective events. History, after all, is written by the winners, and in the case of the Loser's "murder," the clear winner is His Honor, Judge Cosme. One of the narrator's more temperate judgments of Mateo's antagonist terms Cosme a hothead, then quotes his self-justification with respect to Mateo's suicide: "Judge Cosme says eight days in jail can't mark anybody, well, they definitely marked Mateo Ruecas, Cosme crushed him with his pressuring" (*El asesinato,* 79). A series of dehumanizing similes and metaphors in the next two pages consistently likens Mateo to insects and inanimate objects. Even worse than Cosme's error in judgment is his refusal to admit his mistake: "Judge Cosme thinks very highly of the principle of authority and would do what he did again without thinking twice" (87). Cela changes the judge's name, thereby generalizing his traits to other judges (cf. 195); to ensure that readers notice, the narrator points out that "I call the judge by different names, Cosme, Constantine, Ephrahim, this really doesn't matter. . . . I also call Avelino one thing one time and something else the next" (167). Cosme's behavior provides an ironic gloss on the tongue-in-cheek comments by Wendell (the narrator of *Cristo versus Arizona*) concerning judicial infallibility (*Cristo*, 215). Gómez de Liaño identifies two types of crimes that Cela attacks as especially reprehensible, terrorism and corruption (374), with the latter defined as "utilizing a public position for self-enrichment" (375); by extension, this would logically include other abuses of power for personal benefit, such as Cosme's personal revenge against Mateo.

Cosme as "every judge" acquires enhanced significance as the narrative voice refuses to consider judicial ignorance (of penal conditions) a defense—appropriate inasmuch as Cosme never considered Mateo's ignorance of the judge's identity an extenuating factor. Cosme's subjective overreaction to a perceived slight involved retaliation using resources of the penal system that his profession placed at his disposal, for which reason justice per se suffers scorn, and critiques of judges and "justice" are numerous (*El asesinato,* 92, 94, 98, 101, 112, 129, 184, 190, 199, 201, 210, 226). Cela juxtaposes reflections on the shortcomings of jurists and historians, subtly reminding readers that legal transactions and records are part of history, for which reason Cosme should set the record straight. Injustice is compounded when evildoing is concealed by alleging the perpetrator's rightful behavior, and thus Cela writes:

> The worst thing about corruption is that it becomes monotonous and boring. . . . The law is neither flexible nor intelligent; its application is picturesque and sometimes irrational and paradoxical, with a triple result: institutions and their representatives lose prestige, people turn their backs on politics and politicians, and democracy begins to falter.[13]

Cosme's persecution of Mateo allegorically parallels innumerable imprisonments and executions justified by the "Glorious National Crusade" in Francoist historiography (indirectly indicted in *San Camilo* and *Mazurca*), suggesting Cela's reason for calling Mateo "loser" rather than victim or scapegoat.

Much of the text consists of speculations, qualified, rejected, modified, and reduced to absurdity. Many conversations display similar ignorance, or depict abrupt, illogical reversals whose underlying premise is
equally absurd:

> — Do you want to die?
> — No, not yet.
> — When are you going to want to die?
> — I don't know, I always have too many doubts. Not now, no; maybe
> the end of October, when dogs turn yellow and constipation plugs up fat
> ladies torturing them cruelly, that's the plot for the farce. . . . Toward the
> end of October is a good time to die; rent on the cemetery niches
> increases, but that doesn't worry us dead people. (*El asesinato,* 9)

The number of deaths in *El asesinato* is small by comparison with
Mazurca and *Cristo versus Arizona,* but some characters discuss death at
length, and others imply ontological or metaphysical preoccupations
heretofore unprecedented in Cela's works. The text comprises a
palimpsest of intertexts, with the discourse incorporating ossified language, litanies involving questions and answers, ritual phrases, and formulaic conversations—an allegorical representation of moral codes and
legal discourse whose petrification is exposed via the empty exchanges.
Works and writers ancient and modern, Spanish and international,
appear among the intertexts, which allude indirectly to Valle-Inclán (*El
asesinato,* 101), cite Goethe (13), mention the Pythagorean theorem
(55), recall myths of the Amazons, Dracula, and the Minotaur (41), satirize the Beatitudes (179), and repeatedly allude to Gil Blas de Santil-
lana (54, 85, 99, 172, 212). Famous lovers mentioned include Anthony
and Cleopatra, Daphnis and Chloë, and Abelard and Eloise (173).

Cela's significant auto-intertextuality (besides allusions to *Pascual
Duarte*) includes passing reference to Marco Polo followed by parenthet-
ical indication that more relevant information appears "in the novel
Madera de boj, still being detained by the censors" (69). Governmental
censorship was formally abolished on 31 December 1978, following the
country's first democratic elections in 40 years. Thus although problems
with the censorship were real enough in Cela's early years, blaming the
supposedly nonexistent censors for delaying the long-awaited novel is
another of Cela's jokes. If a manuscript of Cela's were now retained by
censorship, it could immediately appear in a dozen different countries
where having been "censored" in Spain would simply enhance its salabil-

ity. Reference to censorship interests for another reason, however, one directly related to a major theme in *El asesinato:* the tragedies caused by the media (including an unfettered and untrammeled press) in unprincipled pursuit of "all the news that's fit to print," as well as much that is neither particularly newsworthy nor deserving of publication. Although it is comparably rare for the Spanish press to carry persecution of celebrities to extremes such as those surrounding the death of Princess Diana, Cela himself, with his heightened notoriety following his receipt of the Nobel Prize, undoubtedly had occasion to feel his privacy invaded, and he clearly includes the media among his indictments of those responsible for Mateo's death: "War correspondents aren't usually dangerous, but commentators, editorialists and rear-guard interpreters tend to confuse things and that way nobody writes chronicles with the necessary objectivity" (179).

The novel's subtext warns that history and those who blindly accept its judgments or write the winner's version cannot be trusted: "History is always a science subject to revision" (197), and many would-be chroniclers pass off their own moral judgments as "fact." Mindful of the fallibility of sources and historians, Cela unmistakably indicts history in *El asesinato,* even if less visibly than in *San Camilo* and *Mazurca.* A perceptive recent commentator on history and the Spanish civil war observes, "There is no such thing in history as a standard method, as there might be in an exact science."[14] The lack of scientific exactitude in historiography does not elude the narrator of *El asesinato,* who affirms that "History is written in huge slices and abysmal gaps and the philosophy of history is still in diapers, still in the dawn of knowledge" (220). British Hispanist Jo Labanyi contended that Cela in *San Camilo* "is concerned not with demythifying specific official accounts of Spanish history, but with rejecting all accepted accounts,"[15] and this affirmation applies equally to *El asesinato.* Cela aims at the "party line" or voice of authority everywhere, ridiculing official accounts whether legal, religious, or historical, including sensationalism purveyed by the mass media, and expressing his cynicism without modifiers or overt protest.[16] Recalling Cela's prologue to *La colmena* ("life isn't good; mankind isn't either"), the narrative voice in *El asesinato* observes that "the world isn't just, truly it isn't just, but you can't demand rigor of chance" (184). This ironic commentary reveals another facet of Cela's subtext: justice should not be governed by chance or history. Neither should the personal errors and personal agendas of justices and historians masquerade as justice and history.

Chapter Nine

Death and Disintegration in Galicia: *La cruz de San Andrés*

La cruz de San Andrés (1994) appeared some six months after *El asesinato del perdedor.* Controversy swirled around the announcement of *La cruz* as winner of the Planeta Prize,[1] the most heavily endowed of Spain's commercial literary prizes. Postwar prizes so proliferated that overabundance reduced their prestige, and Cela commented with apparent satisfaction to interviewers during those years that he had never received prizes: most were considered politically motivated or promotional ploys. Although Cela won several major prizes in later years, they were awarded without his having to enter himself into competition. His decision to compete for the Planeta Prize was unexpected, therefore, and as Iglesias Feijoo observes, Cela's receipt of this "polemical prize did produce commentaries that were less than benevolent" (164).[2] The Planeta Prize is the only one for which Cela competed, and he apparently decided to enter as a personal challenge—to test his own ability to appeal to a mass market. Although literary purists might consider this unbecoming for a Nobel prize winner, Cela is not the only recent experimental novelist to attempt a less "serious" form. Juan Benet, another leader of the postmodern "New Novel," accepted the challenge with *El aire de un crimen,* allegedly to prove that he could write successful detective fiction. Reactions to Cela's competing have been mixed. Cela responded that adverse criticism of his Nobel selection had made him abandon thoughts of retirement (see Iglesias Feijoo, 163); that decision produced two novels in 1994.[3] *La cruz* contains several self-conscious metafictional references to the manuscript's being prepared to meet publishing deadlines, together with humorous, ironic metaliterary comments on demands made by editors and publishers.

La cruz, like *Mazurca,* is set in Galicia but differs in its largely urban landscape, primarily the large seaports and shipbuilding centers of La Coruña and El Ferrol. Gone are *Mazurca*'s larger-than-life characters, mythic conflict, and the sense of purpose that conflict provided. Characters in *La cruz* seem smaller than life, many of them desperately seeking purpose and meaning. If *Mazurca* narrated what was in some sense the beginning of the end (of old ways of life in Galicia), what *La cruz* presents is the end of that process, the collapse of a family or dynasty, possibly symbolizing the larger social fabric. In the novel's opening lines, the narrative voice terms the work in progress a "chronicle of disintegration";[4] this is Cela's most apocalyptic work—only partly because several characters die in the mass suicide of an apocalyptic sect. An enormous sense of futility and absurdity pervades the novel, periodically underscored by the narrator's affirmation of writing on rolls of toilet paper. The mass suicide is not apocalyptic in a biblical or science fictional sense, being less than cataclysmic, and there is no new beginning. The characters' "world ends / not with a bang but a whimper," as T. S. Eliot put it. Charlebois sees *La cruz* as "an intentionally apocalyptic deconstruction of certain narrative and literary theatrical devices" (116).

Based on the narrator's remark ("Today is the sixty-third anniversary of the Second Republic [declared in 1931]," [*La cruz,* 16]), 1994—the year of the novel's publication—is the probable narrative present (i.e., time of the author or narrator's writing). As in *San Camilo,* interpolated world news, local advertising, snatches of conversations, and headlines suggest current events during moments of the retrospective (reconstructed) "action"; for example, "Israeli commandos leave half of Egypt without electricity" (16), an allusion to the late-1960s conflict. A paragraph summarizing the family history of the López Santanas (during at least a generation) notes that "in July of 1969, man reached the Moon and expanded still further the range of his stupidity, man doesn't know how to govern, nor pacify, nor feed the Earth, nor . . . how to cure or prevent cancer or AIDS, they still didn't have AIDS then, but found the way to the Moon" (24). The citation illustrates the narrator's multiple chronological perspectives and tendency to combine and compress time periods. Confusion of times and dates presumably reflects the narrator's disordered memory (a structuring principle of the novel, as in *Mazurca* and *Cristo versus Arizona*), recalling various past moments while writing near the time of publication. Narrative flow is governed, as is memory, by free association rather than orderly, linear chronology.

Antecedents for Structure and Form

Cela's experiments with novelistic structure, varying or eliminating conventional plot and other elements, date from his early career. Consequently *La cruz* presents largely (re)combinations of formal elements in different proportions, changed setting, new characters, and an unprecedented focal incident. *Pabellón de reposo* (1944) reflected experiments with multiple perspectives, presenting the final months of four men and three women terminally ill with tuberculosis, and contained minimal action, narrated in the first person. Cela's prologue to the second edition (1952) termed it a "poem in prose."[5] Sudden, cinematographic shifts (parodied in *La cruz*) suggest motion in an otherwise passive, anonymous, enigmatic painting of suffering and slow deaths. Perspectives in an intervening interlude or intermission are those of an unidentified narrator, and of Cela as author, who offers various notes referring to alleged criticisms of the novel in hand (parodying an episode in the second half of *Don Quixote* where Cervantes has the characters react to reception of their "history"). Distinct echoes resound in *La cruz,* as do lyric devices used in *Pabellón:* parallel structures, refrains, surrealist imagery, antithesis, anaphora, cadence, and "idea rhyme" (regular recurrence or echoes of ideas such as quiet desperation and indifference of the strong toward the weak).

Antecedents from *La colmena* reappearing in *La cruz* include the absence of a protagonist (a collective protagonist), absence of plot, and use of nonlinear chronology and occasional simultaneity. *La colmena* abandoned conventional chapter divisions for five major parts, and the same kind of divisions recur in *La cruz.* Poetic structures and techniques (important in other "later" novels) scarcely appear, however. From *Mrs. Caldwell* (1953), *La cruz* draws surrealist imagery, together with repetitive motifs of the sea, shipwrecks, and sailors (logical for both novels, given the latter's seaport setting and the drowning of Mrs. Caldwell's son). A female narrative consciousness, with obsessions bordering on madness, likewise appears in both. Linear chronology is nonexistent, although Cela deemed this novel a "homage to order" and his "tribute to logical rigor."[6] The motif of the novelist as editor or transcriber of another's manuscript also recurs. Mrs. Caldwell, an eccentric, arbitrary, apparently unbalanced female narrator, is an obvious antecedent for Matilde Verdú in *La cruz.* Cela purports to have met Mrs. Caldwell, who emerges as a self-conscious metaliterary narrator reading him portions of her work in progress and discussing alternative titles (a major structuring motif in *El asesinato*). Mrs. Caldwell's affirmations are often absurd, as are Matilde Verdú's.

Chapter divisions and traditional textual markers (paragraphs, conventional punctuation, etc.) are absent in *San Camilo* and *Oficio de tinieblas,* given radical variants of stream-of-consciousness techniques. Paragraphs and punctuation reappear in *Mazurca,* and again in *La cruz.*

These novels (which share Galician settings with the 1999 *Madera de boj*) offer vastly different visions of Galicia and of Galician characters. *Mazurca*'s nuclear "plot" (periodically repeated, with minor variations, as in *El asesinato*) becomes more diffuse in *La cruz*. Certain situations are insistently repeated: the act of writing, interrogation or trial of the narrator, the alleged crucifixion, scenes from the lives of members of the López Santana family. As in *Mazurca*, polyvalent versions are superimposed, and somewhat divergent versions of the nuclear anecdote or key incidents create a kind of palimpsest, a multivoiced and polyphonic whole that Mikhail Bakhtin terms "heteroglossia."[7] Much as rhythmically recurring references to the rain, mountains, and obscured horizon provided lyric interludes in *Mazurca,* in *La cruz* frequent mentions of wind and waves and the "Tower of Hercules" (a legendary Roman lighthouse near La Coruña) remind readers of geographic setting while interweaving contrapuntal glimpses of nature in an intensely subjective text. Given the urban setting and more contemporary time frame, however, nature occupies much less space than in *Mazurca,* as do folklore, superstition, atavism, and mythic elements.

La cruz's major legacy from *Cristo versus Arizona* is an unreliable author/narrator/character who exhibits considerable metafictional self-consciousness, continually retouching and rewriting. *Cristo versus Arizona* also contains a brief dramatic episode (146–47), comprising dialogue with typographical indications of the speakers' names and stage directions. "Cela has regularly woven references to drama and theater into his narratives [and] herein lies the genesis of *La cruz de San Andrés*" (Charlebois, 153 n. 7). Parodically, drama acquires visibility in *La cruz,* although readers may find little more of classical tragedy here than of the thesis novel in *Oficio. El asesinato del perdedor,* like *Mazurca,* contains a nuclear anecdote repeated frequently (with minor variations) and employs lyric structures, numerous unrelated interpolations, and multiple narrative voices, two or more identifiable with Cela or his authorial masks—as in *La cruz.* These novels deal with fatal errors by interpreters of law or dogma, exhibiting skepticism concerning history and the media. Both feature varying perspectives and narratees, and the shifting ontology characteristic of the postmodern.

La cruz reintroduces formal divisions or chapters (albeit parodically), producing a deceptively conventional appearance, perhaps because the novel was written to compete for a prize catering to the mass market. Five internal divisions allude openly to theatrical contexts, recalling five-act classical plays: "Dramatis Personae" (introducing the characters),

"Plot," "Exposition," "Crux," and "Dénouement, Final Coda, and Inter-
ring of the Last Puppets." Reinforcing suggestions of drama, references
to Shakespeare appear throughout and in two of four epigraphs. Cela's
transgression of conventional genre boundaries (his incorporation of
poetry, lyric techniques, and poetic structures) here echoes *El asesinato,*
with its insistence on the theatrical (*La cruz* alludes to farce, mime, and
puppetry). Cela's two 1994 novels abound in postmodern attributes,
according to Jean François Lyotard's definition,[8] reflecting iconoclastic
attitudes characteristic of postmodernism, and sounding an aggressive
challenge to canonical ideas and norms of the cultural, social, and political establishment. Their lyric structure, depending largely on repetition,
parallelisms, cadence, symbols, refrains or litanies, and metaphors,
repeats formulas used in *Mazurca* and *Cristo versus Arizona,* numerous
differences notwithstanding. Narrative unreliability increases significantly in the latest three novels, and doubts concerning narratorial identity multiply in the two from 1994, with the enigma of authorial identity becoming a central problem in *La cruz.*

Questions concerning the Narrator

The late Torrente Ballester, in a seminal study of *Don Quijote* applicable
to many metafictional novels,[9] affirmed that the essential question is
"Who narrates?" This question proves all but impossible to answer in *La
cruz,* as Cela deliberately obfuscates and contradicts, rewriting or
unwriting in fully postmodern fashion. In *El asesinato,* external historical
referents reinforce one of many successive versions-with-variations of the
nuclear anecdote, helping readers to identify the "factual" version. No
such "objective" history assists readers of *La cruz,* given the absence of
clues indicating a privileged or "truthful" perspective. The narrator frequently admits ignorance; for example, "nobody knows that, you can't
put your hand in the fire for such things" (*La cruz,* 20); "I don't believe
it, that's always very mysterious" (23); and "Would you put your hand
in the fire for those things you're telling? — No, never, I already told
you no, your hand should never be put in the fire for anything or anybody, much less in these cases where it's so easy to invent and deny"
(23–24). The narrator repeatedly admits lying, advising a horrified
interlocutor not to be credulous: "It's awful to admit that what you're
saying could be true. — Then defend yourself by not believing it" (27).

The female narrative voice, despite aggressively reminding readers of
"her" feminine condition, differs little from masculine narrators in *Cristo*

versus Arizona and *El asesinato*. This voice is amoral, hedonistic, skeptical, and ironic, lacking in attributes that might reaffirm femininity or distinguish the feminine gender. "She" speaks several times in plural ("we ordinary women don't have history" [10]; "that happens to all us mothers" [26]; "we ordinary women are also wounded" [58]) but shows no solidarity with other women and discusses no distinctively feminist issues. Narrative perspective varies as this voice sometimes refers to her putative identity in third person: "Then Matilde Verdú received orders to continue with the thread of the story" (37); "Matilde Verdú called the judge aside and whispered in his ear" (39); "Matilde Verdú, the circumspect narrator of this chronicle of events" (53). The narrative perspective apparently compresses several narrative planes and varies from a form of omniscience (e.g., "Both will die of cancer, but they don't know it yet" [33]) to confusion ("We ordinary women have as much history as those who aren't [ordinary], but what happens is that we usually forget or confuse it" [45]). And frequently the narrative conscience simply renounces knowledge: "the luminous desires of gaining control of my mind have sunk forever. . . . I don't know what I'm saying" (55).

Iglesias Feijoo considers narrative identity central to *La cruz* and especially to understanding its "most complex level" (173). From the opening lines, which mention writing on toilet paper with a ballpoint pen, an obsessive first-person monologue alternates with third-person commentary. References to qualities and defects of several toilet paper brands for writing purposes provide one structuring motif. So regular are these reiterations that the narrator terms her discourse a "monotonous melopeya" (*La cruz*, 213), or a rhythmic monotone chant. Other frequently repeated motifs are metaliterary, concerning the act of writing itself, or comprise literary and theatrical allusions. Likewise significant is Saint Andrew's Cross (an X-shaped cross) and the narrator's alleged crucifixion thereon (47, 63, 64, 85–86, 115, 123, 181–82).[10] This event is never narrated, although tenses mentioning crucifixion vary from past to present to future. According to the initial citation, "They crucified me and my husband naked and like St. Andrew on a windmill-shaped cross" (12; cf. 85). Later, however, "they're going to take our lives nailing us on St. Andrew's Cross" (99; cf. 208); and another passage exemplifies the ambiguity of tenses: "the same thing happened to my husband and me, that is they also crucified us, they're going to crucify us" (163).

Readers may wonder how Matilde survived her crucifixion to write the chronicle; or realize that the site of crucifixion changes from Punta Herminia (64), to somewhere between Punta Herminia and Cabalo de

Pradeiras (181–82), to "Parrote Beach" (208). Such contradictions would subvert narratorial reliability, if the narrator herself had not already done so by forgetting, confessing ignorance ("I don't know where to begin" [14]), and modifying events already narrated. Frequently self-corrections involve changing from hyperbole and exaggeration to insignificance, or unwriting places, persons, and objects previously described. These mechanisms of subversion of textual or narratological authority typify postmodernism.[11] The author-narrator eventually revokes the existence of this work in progress, expressing disenchantment with the experiment and disbelief in the concept of the character as authorial mask. As in Torrente Ballester's *Fragmentos de apocalipsis*,[12] the character is absorbed by the text, lost in the verbal space projected, the "heterotopia," in Bakhtin's terminology.

Matilde the narrator—one of three entities with that name—identifies herself as an inspector of primary schools, although her professional life has no relationship with the narration. The cover blurb terms her the protagonist, but she scarcely acts, functioning as putative author, spectator, and commentator. Readers never see her do anything; presumably she inscribes the narrative allegedly being composed on toilet paper—judging from her comments on different brands, her auto-criticism, and references to the deadline (1 September [17]). Similar inferences are suggested by metanarrative declarations such as "One must write things down when they come to mind" (21–22), or commentary on literature, "Life doesn't have a plot. . . . life is usually very habitual and monotonous, the logic of a plot follows a different path" (54). This declaration points to Cela (who believes that life has no plot). Matilde's numerous self-descriptions seem generally disillusioned and somewhat self-pitying; for example, "I'm nothing but a bitter woman . . . a disappointed woman who is not resigned, a woman who takes refuge in love of a dog" (54), or "I'm only a woman who's no longer young, and in bad health, very bad health" (15).

The narrator states that her mother was also named Matilde Verdú; shortly afterward, she mentions that she is the daughter of a single mother, noting that her mother was fond of literature, and attributing to her progenitor "biographies for schoolchildren of St. Teresa and St. John of the Cross [that] had considerable success, especially the second" (11). Iglesias provides information that in 1948, Librería y Casa Editorial Hernando in Madrid published a book of 163 pages titled *San Juan de la Cruz* and signed by Matilde Verdú, with "mediocre sketches by Rivas; today it's a rarity. . . . What isn't so well known is that 'Matilde Verdú' was a pseudonym of Cela" (184).[13] Conte reiterates that Cela published a "biographical essay" on *San Juan de la Cruz,* using the pseudonym of Matilde Verdú; however, Conte gives a considerably earlier date, 1941 (50).[14] Cela's choice of this pseudonym for the author-narrator of his latest novel parallels his transferring similar functions to Pascual Duarte in *El asesinato.* Blurring boundaries between literary and extraliterary worlds, it recalls the dialogue between Unamuno as author and his character Augusto in *Niebla;* both place the creature on equal ontological footing with the creator. Postmodern ontological obfuscation frequently depicts the extraliterary author-creator occupying or trapped within the same "reality" as his creation. Narratologically, as Iglesias notes, complexity increases in the case of *La cruz,* for the voice that speaks of Matilde in third person apparently belongs to another, more powerful narrator. That voice terms her the *relatora* (storyteller) and describes her movements and voice while writing, adding that "this about the gestures and tone is merely a subterfuge" (*La cruz,* 37–38). Matilde is unreliable, forgetful, inclined to making mistakes, and she repeatedly contradicts herself. She mentions her grandfather's death in the war while he was serving in the infantry (11), the cavalry (62), and the artillery corps (126), confessing that "sometimes I don't have the strength to keep from lying" (62).

Matilde's unreliability affects her treatment of names: "Clara, her real name is Ermitas, she prefers to be called Clara, she'd also like to be called Lucia, but she wasn't lucky" (19); "Mary Carmen—her real name is Vicenta—is a nymphomaniac, well, half nymphomaniac" (20). Similarly, "the oldest son Diego, or rather Pichi, and the two girls Marta and Claudia, that is Matty and Betty Boop, are married; the other son Paquito or Fran is still single" (25). As in *Cristo versus Arizona,* names sometimes have multiple variants, and thus don Jacobo is Santiaguito but also Diego (22). Don Nicolás Iglesias Blázquez is called Jules Verne (43). One of many dialogues with an unknown interlocutor parodies the name game:

> Was her name Mary Berriedale?
> I don't know. Why would her name be Mary Berriedale?
> I don't know.
> If this were a novel, couldn't we arrange it so that she could be called Mary Berriedale?
> I don't know that, either; maybe so. (32)

A much briefer interpolated exchange goes thus: "Will you permit me to call you Fifi? — Why Fifi? Oh, well, whatever you like" (34). Such conversations suggest that the answer to "What's in a name?" is "Nothing much." More serious narratological consequences accrue from Matilde's sudden revelation "My name is Matilde Lens, Matilde Meizoso, Matilde Verdú" (125). All three could be the same person, or perhaps three configurations of a first-person narrative voice, as Iglesias suggests (186). But later the narrative voice declares, "My name is not Matilde Verdú, I say that in order to confuse" (189–90). Creating similar effects are the names of seven (or more) devils representing incarnations of Satan apparently peculiar to Galicia, who occupy equal social and ontological footing with the other characters, working at various trades while also tempting and seducing. The resulting tropological world suggests postmodern allegory, given several potentially allegorical elements (e.g., the title). Consciousness by characters of their own fictive condition, typical of postmodern fiction, forms part of the metafictional game wherein the "fictitious" character (created by a fictional entity) seems to achieve autonomy, only to be annihilated in what Gerard Genette calls *metalepsis,* creating varying ontological levels comparable to concentric circles. Such description characteristically repeats, bifurcates, and contradicts itself; lines cancel one another out in "narrative erasure."

La cruz presents constant stylistic characteristics associated with Cela. Conte observes that the two 1994 novels "exhibit the same powerful prose, popular and Expressionistic, precise and offensive . . . [as if] insisting on following a single model, [old] yet new. . . . But perhaps their coincidences are more formal than real" (68). Language per se acquires special importance, not merely because Cela has always carefully selected his words but also because language's possibilities and limitations are part of contemporary literary theorizing. *La cruz* demonstrates that there is no necessary correspondence between "words" and reality, between signs and the "real" objects they supposedly designate. As with other postmodern novels, Cela creates a verbal construct where things simultaneously exist and are erased, are narrated and canceled. The contemporary renaissance of allegory springing from the postmodern poetics of ontology is based on dual levels, "real" and metaphorical, producing elusive variants that lack the unequivocal force of traditional allegory. Brian McHale explains:

> Some practitioners of postmodern allegory . . . seem to solicit allegorical interpretation, but withhold indication of specifical allegorical content.
> . . . These are *overdetermined* allegories: they have *too many* interpretations

... and this indeterminacy has profound ontological consequences ... indeterminate allegory is a means of inducing an ontological oscillation. (142; italics in original)

Iglesias groups *El asesinato* and *La cruz* apart from Cela's other novels, in a category termed "novels of indeterminacy":

The reader confronts an edifice of words before which he feels insecure, unable to affirm with certainty what is happening, or to whom, nor what are the conditions of time and space in which these things seem to occur. ... on the level of discourse, Cela's last two novels form a group apart within his work that could be called "novels of indeterminacy" in which data assimilated may be altered, corrected, or negated a few pages later. (169–70)

In *El asesinato* and *La cruz,* these traits are unavoidably manifest, much as in *Cristo versus Arizona*—it is simply a matter of degree.

Characters and Events

The narrative concerns an apparently random succession of stories involving the López Santana family (a couple with five children), their relatives, friends and acquaintances, business associates, and sweethearts and lovers. Several are converted by the cult precipitating the final tragedy, the "School of Gamma-Delta-Pi Dawn" (Community of the Daybreak of Jesus Christ). "Schoolmaster" Julián Santiso uses hypnotic techniques to convert followers, especially immature individuals, those who are not too intelligent or suffer from emotional problems (e.g., the sexually insatiable and perennially disappointed "Betty Boop," lonely widows, and frustrated housewives), and a family riddled by congenital mental instability. Although the numerous characters seem initially unrelated, successive anecdotes provide linkages and explanations of relationships, tying together disparate characters, themes, and narrative threads. The chronicle traces the López Santanas from grandmothers to grandchildren, revealing a congenital family madness (perhaps explaining the narrator's seemingly irrational assertions). Augmenting ambiguities created by multiple names, the cult requires that recruits adopt new names as evidence of breaking with the past (*La cruz,* 153); Fran (the youngest López Santana) becomes Simon Peter (158), sister Claudia/ Betty Boop becomes Mary Magdalene (203), and sister Matty becomes Marta (160). Betty Boop and Matty are allegedly the narrator's best friends; she indicates that Matty is approaching her 38th birthday. The narrator's obsession with St. Andrew's Cross may reflect the cult's emphasis on the symbolic adoption of saints' identities; perhaps the cult's ritual name changing foments this practice in her narrative.

Matilde, like a good surrealist, transgresses many sexual and social taboos and challenges orthodox Catholicism. She mentions reincarnation (195), claiming to have received secret messages (a "paper" referring to tremendous hidden powers possessed by chosen human beings [86]). Her husband (who never appears) seemingly opposes the government, perhaps explaining Matilde's references to their victimization and persecution (intermittent protestations of virtue notwithstanding). Several López Santana family members and relatives are associated with strange events, bizarre deaths, countless seductions and adulterous affairs, and ominous behavior. Given the narrator's numerous self-corrections and contradictions, it is unclear whether such happenings have any "objective" existence or whether they are simply part of Matilde's self-confessed lies, hallucinations, or fantasies. Some apparently exist beyond the narrator's mind and are related to the "objective" mental instability of López Santana family members, or cult activities. Cumulative enigmatic acts and anecdotes rise to a dramatic climax at the end of part 5 with the ritualistic suicides of several cult members, including three López Santana offspring—Betty Boop, Matty, and Fran—plus others from their social circle whose personal failures, disastrous marriages, and meaningless lives make them easy marks for the charismatic sect leader.

Interwoven with the chronicle of dynastic decadence and disintegration are such sacred motifs as the Crucifixion and celebration of the holy sacrament of mass. Religious motifs multiply in Cela's novels following *San Camilo,* with its title references to vespers, feast, and octave (or novena); *Oficio de tinieblas,* whose title denotes a high mass; and *Cristo versus Arizona.* Dangerous topics under the dictatorship concerned secret organizations (e.g., the sect in *La cruz*) and the Freemasons—apparently considered diabolical by Franco. Charlebois (159 n. 9) notes allusions to Masonic beliefs or practices in *La cruz,* including messages from the "Supreme Architect" traced on paper by Julián Santiso as directed by the "will of God" (*La cruz,* 65); calling the cult leader Amancio Jambrina "the apex of the triangle" (125); and describing the cult as a "pyramidal organization" (174). Although the triangle and pyramid have been symbolically associated with Masonry since biblical times, this is not the only "occult" organization suggested; besides the numerous references to devils already noted, the novel's first pages announce the sound of trumpets signaling the "black Mass of confusion" (9), described as a "solemn academic ceremony" wherein priests and priestesses in blood-red, gold-embossed "military uniforms" assemble to eat "filthy pork" and meditate upon the image of an unshaven dead man appearing on their towels (perhaps alluding either to the Shroud of Turin— allegedly the face cloth for Christ's burial—or to Christ's encounter with St. Veronica en route to Calvary, when she gave him a cloth to wipe his face). Sacred processionals and religious pageantry suffer parodic defor- mation, and the sound of bells may bring good news or "sound out death according to the phases of the moon" (9), implicitly evoking witchcraft, druids, or similar pagan rituals. The same paragraph men- tions storytelling by the fire, the staging of farce, and throwing "rotten entrails, lungs, hearts, intestines to the hyenas." Placing these elements in the context of "black mass" invites attributions of sacrilege. Recalling the narrator's comments about Christ in *Cristo versus Arizona,* one can reasonably assume that Cela does not intend sacrilege or offense to sin- cere believers, despite his intermittent iconoclastic pronouncements and activities since his early associations with surrealism. In *La cruz,* Cela foregrounds problems of blind fanaticism, whether perpetrated by the Inquisition, tyrannical cults, or extreme traditionalists. Targeting cults (not a widespread problem in Spain) suggests that the real object of con- cern is something deeper, a more profound social malaise of which cults are merely a symptom. The unique constitutional status of the Spanish Catholic Church (until recently) conferred a sort of monopoly, and cults are thus something of a novelty in Spain. Precisely because few Spaniards have experience concerning cults, however, they do threaten vulnerable psyches. Nevertheless, it seems improbable that Cela views cults themselves as the menace. A larger menace, and one with centuries of history, is fanaticism—a more likely target. Conte, noting another parallel between *La cruz* and *El asesinato,* observes that the latter con- cerns a miscarriage of justice and the former is presented as a judicial interrogatory (68)—an interrogation occasionally seeming to evoke echoes of the Inquisition. Blind obedience to dogma, and by extension to any leader's interpretation of that dogma (which in *La cruz* leads to the cult members' mass suicide), is the real problem.

Chronicle and History

As in *El asesinato del perdedor,* Cela implies profound skepticism concern- ing the possibility of history, a topic first enunciated in *San Camilo* by demonstrating that eyewitnesses not only are fallible but often fail to comprehend what they are seeing. Multiple variants on nuclear anecdotes in *Mazurca, Cristo versus Arizona,* and Cela's last two novels demonstrate that witnesses of the same event do not necessarily see the same thing, and the vagaries of the several narrators further illustrate the fallibility of memory. Writing is not an "innocent" act, regardless of genre, but especially with "history." By no coincidence, Matilde repeatedly terms her narrative *historia* and chronicle, rather than novel, narration, or story, several times confessing that she has fabricated untruths. For example,

> when I mention the two López Santana sisters [Betty Boop and Matty] and myself and our adventures, I am lying. I was never involved in those goings-on nor would I want to be . . . but I'm telling the truth, sometimes I write in the first person to satisfy my agent and my editor. (94)

Ironically, Matilde's interlocutor is supposedly her confessor, and confession suggests another motive for the unreliability of history; namely, to satisfy others, be it the regime in power, "schools" of history, public opinion, or the adherents of a particular ideology. Matilde's receptiveness to suggestions about organizing her chronicle and the variance between her version and those of other narrative voices also bear upon the questionable content of "historical" documents and the biases of historiography. Even stopping the narrative at a given point appears arbitrary in Matilde's case, occurring as she exhausts the toilet paper (237), perhaps silencing significant parts of the chronicle, or (by constituting closure), conferring undue emphasis on moments that would lack significance within a complete narration of all relevant events. Cela's subversion of history (including formerly sacrosanct Franco historiography) appears in the following exchange, presumably Matilde's testimony during the official inquiry suggested in the opening pages:

> History is based on history books, on rules established for history books, and it's nothing but literary fallacies. . . . may I please have a glass of water? . . . yes, may I continue? With your permission. The worst thing about ordinary women isn't that we have no history, that's the last of our concerns, the worst thing is that history submerges us in vulgarity, monotony and routine. (200)

The tautological nature of this enterprise is evident in the affirmation that "History is based on history books," a process whereby the blind

leading the blind acquires official sanction and becomes institutionalized.

What is omitted or deliberately silenced might clarify or radically
change the meaning of a historical account, as seen in Matilde's han-
dling of her chronicle concerning the religious sect. Upon meeting
Julián Santiso (64), she did not trust the cult (65); nevertheless, she too
falls under his influence, eventually recognizing the authority of the
sect's leader, Amancio Jambrina, and even changing her name: "I will
be called from this moment on and forever Adoración Cordero Chousa"
(214). Her conversion to the cult gives readers yet another reason to
mistrust her narration, in addition to her confessed lies, contradictions,
and apparent self-deceptions or hallucinations. Cult membership obviously constitutes a particular bias in her account of happenings, imply-
ing less objectivity in her chronicling of the tragic events precipitated by
the leader she belatedly admits she follows. This context suggests that
strategic and rhetorical reasons may underlie her metanarrative reflections, as Matilde discusses questions of placement in the overall narrative, order, and authorship of certain sections by others (considerations
that may impact how the narrative is read, how it affects readers, and
how it is interpreted). Seemingly casual "technicalities" such as where
something appears in the "true history" and in what context can determine or modify "meaning." Contextualizing events is never an innocent
exercise, for context has much to do with motivation, ethics, and morality: an action that might be heroic in one context can be criminal—or
simply absurd—in another. Cela thus deconstructs historiography,
memoir, eyewitness accounts, and similar "documentary" genres as
being no more reliable than their patently unreliable narrators. Readers
must decide whether the chronicler is sane, to what extent her account is
motivated and influenced by the cult or other ideologies, and whether
anything believable remains in this (or any) "true" account.

Chapter Ten

Summary and Conclusions

Cela affirms that he has experimented with novelistic form throughout his career, even though certain earlier novels would not be deemed experimental by twentieth-century European standards, nor the forms seen as innovative. Cela, however, consistently stresses that each of his novels differs from those that have gone before; he has not used the same format twice. Each novel thus represents a new challenge with distinct forms and techniques to master, whether recombining traditional Spanish materials (as in *Pascual Duarte* and the *"Nuevo Lazarillo"*) or "importing" formats and devices of European modernism and postmodernism adapted to the Spanish context (as in *Pabellón de reposo, La colmena,* and *Mrs. Caldwell* in his early period). These anticipate later experimentation, more radical in Cela's second period; in extreme cases (especially *Oficio de tinieblas*), the medium nearly devours the message.

Cela's evolution as a novelist may be envisioned as a striptease, divesting himself of unnecessary elements—plot, protagonist, sequential action and chronology, narrative per se, recognizable characters, setting, and more—until reaching a *non plus ultra* (i.e., *Oficio de tinieblas*) where essentially nothing remains of the novel as genre but language. When he returns to the novel years after *Oficio,* the process of discarding is reversed as he reincorporates heterogeneous materials in varying degrees and proportions, experimenting with different combinations. The result—more conventional packaging—is deceptive, for novelistic ontology has been destabilized.

When *San Camilo* is judged by future generations, it may emerge as Cela's masterpiece, not for what he achieved on the formal level but for what he attempted in human terms—even more than sociopolitical ones—on the level of the collective psyche. Three decades after the Spanish civil war, when *San Camilo* appeared, wounds were healing, but painful scars remained. Three decades after *San Camilo,* neither Spanish nor international novelists have yet managed to treat Spain's civil conflict with the equanimity of Tolstoy in *War and Peace* (Bertrand de Muñoz put the number of Spanish civil war novels at 1,300 in 1997). Few have managed to write in a spirit of impartiality and conciliation, and Cela's generation has produced only two significant, impartial novels of war that reach toward peace, *San Camilo* and Miguel Delibes's *378-A, Madera de héroe* (1987). *San Camilo* attempted catharsis with its Dantesque vision of Madrid entering war—an infernal, Boschian carnival where each side was as wrong as the other. *San Camilo* should not be measured by whether that attempted catharsis failed: Spain was not ready in 1969. *San Camilo* initiates Cela's meditation on the impossibility of history, a major theme in several later novels. While constituting antihistory (as Polt suggests), and an exercise in *intrahistoria, San Camilo* also demonstrates history's limitations (i.e., of witnesses' comprehension, of memory, of insufficient or corrupt documentation, and of bias), undermining history's "scientific" pretensions and dooming it as an art.

Oficio occupies a pivotal position. As Cela's most fragmented novel, it "narrates" the least, preceding several unplotted, essentially nonnarrative "discourse" novels—enchained repetitive incidents without progression—essentially poetic in structure. They depend on repetition of themes, motifs, scenes, and incidents, juxtaposition, cadence, and metaphor, more than anything approaching sequential action. *Oficio* is not presentational (descriptive), narrative, or analytical. In the absence of essentially all traditional ingredients save language, theme, and artifice, *Oficio* retains little of the novelistic prototype beyond the label. Despite its surrealist and nightmarish atmosphere, *Oficio* is seldom surrealistic at the level of language, which remains academic, clear, and often within the bounds of propriety, as well, communicating on the "cellular level." A narrative apocalypse, *Oficio* presents bits and pieces of Cela's narrative world after its destruction, a subhuman world of inhuman cruelty, aberrations, violence, and unspeakable misery and suffering, compounded by absurdity, despair, and self-loathing. Unlike the Catholic liturgy to which the title alludes, no day of resurrection follows.

Having gone to the edge of the novelistic universe, Cela had changed when he returned, reintroducing elements suggesting relatively conventional or traditional narration at first glance, although *Mazurca*—by no means a conventional novel—transgresses genre boundaries, with much of the epic and lyric, and much of music and myth. Despite dealing with war, murder and revenge, violence and death, *Mazurca* presents a world of primitive vitality, earthy, lusty, and occasionally exuberant. Nature's visibility contributes to feelings of life, lulled by the rhythm of the rain. Much of *Mazurca* depicts hedonistic enjoyment of life's pleasures, despite the war, relegated to the background. The war is viewed more serenely than in *San Camilo,* but less impartially, given the prevailing countermythologization. Seemingly less "serious," *Mazurca* proved more palatable to Spanish readers than *San Camilo*—as much an accident of timing as resulting from the novel's nature. Relying on repetitions and parallelisms, alliteration and cadence, poetic refrains and musicality, *Mazurca* experiments with lyric structures—structures repeatedly used thereafter. *Mazurca*'s singularity among Cela's novels results from several larger-than-life characters, enhancing its mythic and epic dimensions.

The uniqueness of *Cristo versus Arizona* resides only superficially in its setting, number of characters, and step backward in time. On a deeper level, beneath pained ironies, and via the voice of a most unlikely spokesman—the most unreliable of postmodernism's doubtful, deceptive narrators—Cela formulates his clearest articulation of why crimes against humanity (individual or collective) diminish us all. Amid almost inconceivable cruelty, abjection, and mindless violence, the narrator invokes the power of love incarnate, eternal mystery, and last hope. Excepting specifically postmodern narratological aspects, *Cristo versus Arizona* repeats techniques and structures already essayed in *Mazurca* (reappearing in *El asesinato*). *Cristo versus Arizona*'s paradoxical novelty is precisely the presence of something so old-fashioned as a "message"—a traditional one at that—in a radically experimental vehicle.

El asesinato, perhaps the most straightforward of Cela's later works, provides fewer problems of interpretation than any except his first three or four novels, the fluctuating chronological planes, ongoing narrative erasure, and biting irony notwithstanding. Knowledge of the specific current event inspiring *El asesinato* is helpful but not essential, and few readers could miss Cela's sarcastic critique of the legal and judicial systems. His position in *El asesinato* approaches that of Francisco Ayala in *Los usurpadores* (1949; *Usurpers,* 1987): any power exercised by one man over another is usurpation. The generally corrupt and repulsive mass of secondary characters (identified with the Establishment and eager backers of its sentences) suggest another biblical judgment: Let him who is without sin cast the first stone. Cela's resuscitated Pascual Duarte fuses at times into Mateo—for good reason: not merely authorial masks, both are scapegoats, condemned by the judicial system for crimes the novelist attributes equally (if not predominantly) to society.

The resuscitation of Mrs. Caldwell in *La cruz de San Andrés* (logical enough in light of both novels' unbalanced, unreliable feminine narrators) highlights conundrums of narratological theory: relationships between the author (and his alter egos and masks), the narrator, the character(s), and the reader. *La cruz* contains Cela's most prolonged meditations to date on the act of literary creation and on the nature of history. Although less visible than anecdotal events related to cult members' suicides, the importance of these themes transcends the covers of *La cruz,* as both appear elsewhere (the impossibility of history, for example, in *Memorias* and *El perdedor*). The novelty of style, techniques, and other formal aspects of *La cruz* is relative: Cela simply recombines ingredients used before in different proportions. Considered on the macro level of thematics, the cult suicides are but a pretext or metaphor for more ancient ills: fanaticism, intolerance, zealots' claims to monopoly on the truth—control of human minds and beliefs by any totalitarian authority. The apocalyptic ending proves an apt metaphor for the consequences of perennial human failings.

Cela's later novels grow logically out of earlier ones, with differences involving form more than content, and structure more than themes, characters, and worldview. Cela was never an "easy author" in the sense that his works created shock and discomfort from the beginning, but his early novels posed few problems of comprehension (readers had little difficulty understanding "what happened" and interpreting "what it meant"). Beginning with *San Camilo,* reader disorientation and bewilderment increase (as evinced by the breadth and depth of early critical disagreements). The later novels, more complex and hermetic, move increasingly farther from familiar, recognizable, quotidian "reality," presenting hallucinatory, nightmarish worlds. Postmodern in theory and spirit, they confound casual readers and resist "experts." Yet Cela's characteristic techniques and style persist (albeit in different guise), so that classic analyses of his early novels can fruitfully be applied to later works as well. Earlier observations concerning characters and themes still help in understanding the novels studied here. One conclusion that must be drawn involves revalidation of numerous earlier conclusions.

Changes and experimentalism notwithstanding, Cela's essential themes remain the same, perhaps having become more intense, with their dark tints even darker. Primitivism and violence, cruelty and exploitation, alienation and solitude, sexuality and death—obsessive themes from the outset—continue to be starkly visible in the later novels. Much the same applies to those techniques, literary devices, and stylistic characteristics that critics have most insistently associated with Cela: caricature, dehumanization, black humor, exaggeration, irony, expressionistic deformation, parody, repetition, impassive understatement, tag lines and refrains, popular sayings and clichés, vulgarities and obscenities, colloquial flavor and academic correctness of syntax. Division of society into victims and executioners, man's inhumanity to man, the world's indifference, the wall of metaphysical silence—such early scholarly clichés have stood the test of time, reflecting constants of Cela's fiction in both early and later periods with little variation beyond differences of degree. Just as constant are certain lacks or absences: Cela does not portray "beautiful people," and the rare personages who might qualify as "normal" or healthy are scarce and often unintelligent. The happy or good are a small minority, and the loving couple (of any configuration) is as rare as altruism and charity. Cela's fiction has no heroes, only antiheroes, victims, and criminals; no saints or martyrs, only sinners and the fallen. His protagonists are collective, or they are almost exclusively spectators, passive *agonistas*. Such absences create eloquent silences, likewise characterizing Cela's fiction.

Time does not pass in vain, and important changes have occurred in Spain, its literary scene, and Cela's writing. Significantly differentiating early and later novels is the presence of postmodern ontology in the later period. In *San Camilo,* not yet full-blown, that ontology is insinuated by oneiric and hallucinatory episodes, fantasies, and especially the shifting narrative identity (from *tú* to first-person viewpoints and third-person quasi omniscience). Together with the obsessive internal monologue, these contribute to displacing and destabilizing the recognizable neorealistic, neo-naturalistic environment, undermining the reader's sense of reality. Several later novels situate characters and events in vague, bizarre, or unrecognizable environments—no longer twentieth-century Madrid or mimetic facsimiles of Badajoz and Venezuela, for example. Even identifiable Spanish locales (e.g., La Coruña in *La cruz de San Andrés*) are comparably unreal, stylized, with a carnival air, evocative of theatrical backdrops. These environments, as though built on quicksand, can vanish without a trace (as in *El asesinato del perdedor).* It is difficult to ascertain where much action—exclusive of the repetitive nuclear anecdote—occurs, when it occurs, to whom, and why. Many characters are carnivalesque, and others are literary types, heightening their air of unreality. Character identities are thoroughly destabilized, as well, with unexplained metamorphoses, anonymity, and multiple heteronyms complicating their identification.

Constant experimentation, apparent throughout Cela's novelistic career, is not simply a pastime or intellectual exercise but part of how he sees both his obligation as a writer and the novel per se. "The novel is something yet to be defined . . . a proteic genre where everything fits, including essays, poetry, etc.," he affirms (echoing Baroja). Cela has stated that "a novel has no business expressly defending anything, absolutely anything at all. . . . those novels which are known to be, before they are opened, intent on defending this or that, are devoid of any importance whatsoever."[1] It matters little whether Cela's poetics of the novel grew out of postwar totalitarianism and censorship, as an extension of making an aesthetic virtue of necessity, or whether that credo was formulated earlier. Obfuscations abound in his "creative" writings, so that his nonfiction works remain the best hope of clarification, contradictions notwithstanding. Scholars should beware the dangers not only of contradictions and Cela's camouflaging what he attacks or defends but also of misinterpreting an increasingly difficult writer by forgetting or overlooking his ludic vein and deep-seated love of contradiction. Seriousness is there as well, and Navajas perceptively observes that "Cela's work is a reflection upon Spain as cultural entity, which may be judged among the most acute and painful of modern literature" (140). Cela's investigations of the concept of nation, specifically in regard to Spain, are ranked with those of the Generation of 1898 (Unamuno, Valle-Inclán, Baroja), Ortega y Gasset, and Juan Goytisolo, among writers for whom the "consideration of Spain is central" in numerous texts. Cela's meditation on national identity, like that of Ganivet and other writers of 1898, finds the collective *yo* (ego) problematic. Uncle Jerónimo in *San Camilo* affirms that Spaniards feel "ashamed of their present and expect to be ashamed of their future, and therefore they believe in fire above all, having a Torquemada in their hearts, Spaniards don't believe in God but in fire" (327). Reading these words in light of Cela's Nobel acceptance speech, *Elogio de la fábula* (In Praise of Fabulation), which stressed the need for ethical content in literature, helps readers understand Cela's later works as postmodern allegory, directed at Spaniards who believe "not in God but in fire." Cela's painful vision of his homeland links him to Unamuno ("me duele España," [Spain hurts me]), further identifying Cela's literary forebears and those with whom history (in which he believes so little) may one day situate him.

Notes and References

Chapter One

1. Lucile Charlebois, *Understanding Camilo José Cela* (Columbia: University of South Carolina Press, 1998), 2; hereafter cited in text.

2. *Madera de boj* (1999), published when the present volume was in press, also treats Galician themes and locales. It constitutes the third part of a Galician triad or trilogy, the first novel treating the countryside, mountains, and villages *(Mazurca);* the second depicting contemporary urban Galicia *(La cruz);* and the third evoking mystic, millennial, maritime Galicia, its coastline strewn with the wrecks of centuries, the history of invasions and Viking raids, memories of the dead, and legends of ghosts and demons.

3. For more pre-1968 biographical data, see D. W. McPheeters, *Camilo José Cela* (New York: Twayne Publishers, 1969); hereafter cited in text.

4. Camilo José Cela, *Memorias, entendimientos y voluntades* (Barcelona: Plaza Y Janés, 1993); hereafter cited in text as *Memorias;* all translations mine.

5. See José Luis Giménez Frontín, *Camilo José Cela: Texto y contexto* (Madrid: Montesinos, 1985), 10; translations mine.

6. Camilo José Cela Conde, *Cela, mi padre* (Madrid: Ediciones Temas de hoy, 1989); hereafter cited in text; translations mine.

7. In addition to McPheeters (15–30), Charlebois (2–10), and Cela Conde, these include statements by Cela in prologues to his works, short pieces in *Papeles de Son Armadans,* various interviews, and a sketch compiled by Cela using materials from previous biographies *(Revista Hispánica Moderna,* vol. 28 [1962]). Several books treat Cela or aspects of his life, including Gabriel Ferret and Fernando González, *Cela en Mallorca;* Arsenio Muñoz de la Peña, *Los viajes de CJC por Extremadura;* and José María R. Tejerino's three medically oriented pamphlets, *CJC y la medicina, Historia clínica del niño CJC Trulock,* and *Nuevos ensayos sobre CJC y la medicina.* Others combine biographical notes with journalistic interviews: Eduardo Trives, *Una semana con CJC;* Marino Gómez Santos, *Camilo José Cela;* Joaquín Arozamena, *Cela;* Porfirio Díaz Machicao, *Camilo José Cela;* Jacinto Luis Guereña, *Retrato de Camilo José Cela;* et cetera.

8. Alonso Zamora Vicente, "Camilo José Cela, cincuenta años después," *El Extramundi* 9 (Spring 1997): 27; hereafter cited in text as Zamora Vicente 1997.

9. Charlebois states, "It was not until he was transferred out of Republican-held Madrid and to Nationalist Valencia that he was drafted, on 4 December 1938, as a soldier on the side of the insurgents" (3). This conflicts with *Memorias.* Cela mentions 4 December 1938 in recalling a certificate from

his captain when he left the regiment at war's end (316), reflecting his final service with that regiment, not his initial induction. Charlebois reports that Cela was "down to skin and bones," whereas Cela's recollections of Valencia (314–16) state that the soldiers were well fed.

10.   Camilo José Cela, interview by Michael Friedrich, *El País*, reprinted in *Prólogo* 5 (October–December 1989): 20; hereafter cited in text as interview 1989.

11.   See Darío Villanueva, "Leer los manuscritos de Cela," *El Extramundi* 9 (Spring 1997): 63–92; hereafter cited in text.

Chapter Two

1.   For example, Gareth Thomas, in *The Novel of the Spanish Civil War (1936–1975)* (New York: Cambridge University Press, 1990), reprinted a 1977 photocopy published by *Fuerza Nueva* purporting to be Cela's application to the Nationalist regime (March 1938) for a position with the "Corps of Investigation and Vigilance" alleging that he "believed he could provide information on people and their conduct, which could be of use" to the regime (588).

2.   See Phillipe Lejeune, *Le pacte autobiographique* (Paris: Seuil, 1975), and *On Autobiography,* trans. Katherine Leary (Minneapolis: University of Minnesota Press, 1989). Also see Lejeune, *Moi aussi* (Paris: Editions du Seuil, 1986); hereafter cited in text as Lejeune 1986.

3.   Roger Fowler, ed., *A Dictionary of Modern Critical Terms* (London: Routledge and Kegan Paul, 1973), 24; hereafter cited in text.

4.   *Tremendista* is a reference to the neo-naturalistic violence, shocking events, and characters in Cela's early novels.

5.   Francisco Umbral, "Cela y el mal amor," *El Extramundi* 9 (Spring 1997): 52; hereafter cited in text.

6.   Examination of poetry in Cela's fiction appears in Janet Díaz (with Ricardo Landeira), "The Novelist as Poet: A Key to the Literary Evolution of Camilo José Cela," *Anales de la Narrativa Española Contemporánea* 4 (1979): 30–52.

7.   Víctor García de la Concha, "La poesía de Camilo José Cela," *El Extramundi* 9 (Spring 1997): 216; translation mine. Hereafter cited in text.

8.   Villanueva cites Cela's statement that "literature is nothing but an ongoing struggle against literariness" (Villanueva, 67) at the postpublication reception of *Oficio.*

9.   See Martin Nozick, *Miguel de Unamuno* (New York: Twayne, 1971); and Beatrice Patt, *Pío Baroja* (New York: Twayne, 1971).

10.   For more on this (with Cela among the authors examined), see Janet Pérez, "Functions of the Rhetoric of Silence in Contemporary Spanish Literature," *South Central Review* 1, no.1 (1984): 108–30; "Techniques in the Rhetoric of Literary Dissent," in *Selected Proceedings, Third Louisiana Conference on Hispanic Languages and Literatures* (Baton Rouge: Louisiana State University Press,

1984), 216–30; and "The Game of the Possible: Francoist Censorship and Techniques of Dissent," *Review of Contemporary Fiction* 4, no. 3 (Fall 1984): 22–30.

11. Camilo José Cela, "Elogio de la fábula," *El Extramundi* 1, no. 1 (1995): 145; hereafter cited in text as "Elogio."

Chapter Three

1. See Verity Smith, *Ramón María del Valle-Inclán* (New York: Twayne, 1973).

2. Gonzalo Sobejano, "*Cristo versus Arizona*: Confesión, crónica, letanía," *El Extramundi* 9 (Spring 1997): 139–62; hereafter cited in text.

3. See Fernando Cabo Aseguinolaza, "Cela y la picaresca (apócrifa): Temporalidad literaria y referente genérico en *Pascual Duarte* y el *Nuevo Lazarillo*," *El Extramundi* 12 (Winter 1997): 151–88; hereafter cited in text.

4. Camilo José Cela, "Sobre las artes de novelar," *Correo Literario*, 1 May 1952, 6; reprinted in *La rueda de los ocios,* 3d ed. (Madrid and Barcelona: Alfaguara, 1972). Several other Cela articles amplify his ideas on the novel. See "Nota sobre la herramienta literaria," *Papeles de Son Armadans* 72 (March 1962): 23–46; "Hacia una revalorización del idioma," in *Obras completas,* vol. 9 (Barcelona: Destino, 1970), 93–95; "Addenda," in *Obras completas,* vol. 2 (Barcelona: Destino, 1964), 530–40; "De algo, no de alguien," in *Al servicio de algo* (Madrid and Barcelona: Alfaguara, 1969), 9–12; "La comba de la novea," *Papeles de Son Armadans* 117 (December 1965): 272–321.

5. J. S. Bernstein, introduction to *Mrs. Caldwell Speaks to Her Son,* by Camilo José Cela (Ithaca, N.Y.: Cornell University Press, 1968), xx–xxi.

6. The deliberately enigmatic title of *Cristo versus Arizona* (Barcelona: Seix Barral, 1988) involves wordplay, as the "versus" does not mean "against" but "toward."

7. Luis Iglesias Feijoo, "*La cruz de San Andrés,* última novela de Cela," *El Extramundi* 9 (Spring 1997): 163–95; hereafter cited in text. See especially pp. 186–87 n. 11 concerning "melopeya." Also see Sobejano 1997, 139–40 (work cited in n. 2).

8. Guillermo de Torre, "Vagabundeos críticos por el mundo de Cela," *Revista Hispánica Moderna* 18, nos. 2–4 (April–October 1962): 152; hereafter cited in text; translations mine.

Chapter Four

1. Camilo José Cela, *Vísperas, festividad y octava de San Camilo del año 1936 en Madrid* (Madrid: Alfaguara, 1969); hereafter cited in text as *San Camilo;* all translations mine.

2. Representative are the following: Joaquín Marco, "El retorno de Camilo José Cela," *Destino,* 31 January 1970; Andrés Amorós, "*San Camilo,*

1936," *Revista de Occidente,* July 1970; Santos Sanz Villanueva, "La esperada novela de Camilo José Cela," *Hogar y pueblo,* 20 March 1970; Guillermo Díaz Plaja, "*San Camilo, 1936,*" *ABC,* 8 January 1970; Fernando Pérez Olmo, "Cela en la guerra," *Diario de Navarra,* 11 January 1970; Tomás Zamarriego, "*San Camilo, 1936,*" *Reseña,* February 1970; Domingo Pérez Minik, "*San Camilo, 1936* de Camilo José Cela," *El día,* 8 February 1970; Ignacio Iglesias, "*San Camilo, 1936,* la última novela de Cela," *Mundo Nuevo* (Paris), July 1970; Antonio Iglesias Laguna, "La guerra y el placer," *La Estafeta Literaria,* February 1970; Antonio Valencia, "El episodio nacional de Cela," *Arriba,* 11 January 1970.

3.   In *Understanding Camilo José Cela,* Charlebois's footnote 3 (p. 142) lists several commentators as "most critical" and others who "praise" *San Camilo 1936*—although I would describe several of the latter as balanced.

4.   Paul Ilie, "The Politics of Obscenity in *San Camilo, 1936,*" *Anales de la Novela de Postguerra* 1 (1976): 25–63 (characterized by Charlebois as a "pernicious rhetorical attack on Cela's *irresponsibility*" 174; Ilie's italics).

5.   Jo Labanyi, "Fiction as Release: *San Camilo, 1936,* Reivindicación del conde Don Julián, La Saga/fuga de J.B.," in *Myth and History in the Contemporary Spanish Novel* (New York and London: Cambridge University Press, 1989), 178–246; hereafter cited in text.

6.   Maryse Bertrand de Múñoz, "Cela se enfrenta con la guerra civil," in *Camilo José Cela: Homage to a Nobel Prize,* ed. Joaquín Roy (Coral Gables, Fla.: University of Miami Press, 1991), 76–82; hereafter cited in text. Bertrand's additional studies include "El estatuo del narrador en *San Camilo, 1936,*" in *Crítica semiológica de textos literarios hispánicos,* ed. Miguel Angel Garrido Gallardo (Madrid: CSIC, 1986), 579–89; "Estudio de la 'voz' en *San Camilo, 1936,*" in *Actas del VIII Congreso de la Asociación Internacional de Hispanistas,* ed. A. David Kossoff et al. (Madrid: Ediciones Istmo, 1986), 211–20; "Novelas de la guerra: *San Camilo, 1936,*" *Insula* 517–18 (February–March 1990): 10–11; and "*San Camilo, 1936:* Encrucijada en la novelística de Camilo José Cela," *El Extramundi* 12 (Winter 1997): 211–44.

7.   Olga Prjevalinsky studied Cela's reiterations in *El sistema estético de Camilo José Cela: Estructura y expresividad* (Madrid: Editorial Castalia, 1960), with particular reference to *La Catira.* Systematic repetition constitutes a standard device in later novels.

8.   See Mariano Antolín Rato, "Cela: Writing about Death," trans. Lois Parkinson Zamora, *Review of Contemporary Fiction* (Fall 1984): 34; hereafter cited in text.

9.   The title's "eve, fiesta, and octave" presumably indicated 17, 18, and 25 July (the same weekday one week later). Events in *San Camilo* actually begin 12 July.

10.   Santos Sanz Villanueva, *Tendencias de la novela española actual* (Madrid: Cuadernos para el Diálogo, 1972), esp. 63–69.

11.   Genaro J. Pérez, "Fondo y forma en *San Camilo, 1936* de Camilo José Cela," *Antípodas* 4, no. 2 (December 1992): 43; hereafter cited in text.

12. Camilo José Cela, interview by Stephen Miller, *Antípodas* 4, no. 2 (December 1992): 12; hereafter cited in text as interview 1992.

13. Mikhail Bakhtin, *Problems of Dostoevsky's Poetics,* trans. R. William Rotel (n.p.: Ardis, 1973), 163.

14. See, for example, José Domingo, "C.J.C. goza de buena salud," *Insula* 279 (February 1970): 6.

15. See Janet Díaz, "Techniques of Alienation in Recent Spanish Novels," *Journal of Spanish Studies: Twentieth Century* 3 (Spring 1974): 5–16 (including *San Camilo* among four novels analyzed).

16. See Vicente Cabrera, *Juan Benet* (Boston: Twayne, 1983). Benet wrote much of his work after 1983, but the essentials did not change.

17. Camilo José Cela, interview by José Méndez Ferrín, *Triunfo,* November 1972.

18. The most wrenching is the death of Tránsito, or "Toisha," his girl-friend and lover, blown apart by a mortar shell before his eyes (related in *Memorias*). Catherine R. Perricone, in "Camilo José Cela and His Poetry of Civil Strife," *Antípodas* 4, no. 2 (December 1992): 91–99, reminds readers that *Pisando la dudosa luz del día* was composed largely between 1 November 1936 (the day of Toisha's death) and 11 November.

19. Cela's exploitation of the potential for sacrilege is clearly deliberate.

20. For more on the relationship between history and fiction, see Janet Pérez, "Historical Circumstance and Thematic Motifs in *San Camilo, 1936,*" *Review of Contemporary Fiction* 4, no. 3 (Fall 1984): 67–80.

21. Leo Hickey, *Realidad y experiencia de la novela* (Madrid: Editorial CUPSA, 1978), 240; hereafter cited in text. Hickey cites the prologue to *Los españoles pintados por sí mismos* (Madrid: Banco Ibérico, 1971). Cela's view of the civil war as freeing Spaniards to indulge their pent-up hatred and aggression suggests a counterbalancing role for the message of Uncle Jerónimo, spokesman for free love—untrammeled eroticism.

22. Antonio Iglesias Laguna, *Treinta años de novela española, 1938–1968* (Madrid: Prensa Española, 1969), 3. Many sections refer to Cela, but see especially 223–31.

23. For example, see Gareth Thomas, "Irrationalism and Anti-historicism in the Later Novels of the Civil War (1967–1975)," in *The Novel of the Spanish Civil War (1936–1975)* (New York: Cambridge University Press, 1990), 207–19.

24. Edmundo Vandencammen, "Cinco ejemplos del ímpetu narrativo de Camilo José Cela," *Cuadernos Hispanoamericanos* 387–88 (1978): 81–89.

25. Diane Wilder Cornwell, "Language as Expression of Consciousness in Cela's *San Camilo 1936,*" in *Camilo José Cela: Homage to a Nobel Prize,* ed. Joaquín Roy (Coral Gables, Fla.: University of Miami Press, 1991), 63; hereafter cited in text.

26. Camilo José Cela, preface to *La colmena,* 4th ed. (Madrid: Castalia, 1984), 111.

27. See J. H. R. Polt, "Cela's *San Camilo 1936* as Anti-History," *Anales de la Literatura Española* 6 (1988): 444; hereafter cited in text.

28. See Stephen Greenblatt, introduction to *The Power of Forms in the English Renaissance,* ed. Stephen Greenblatt (Norman, Okla.: Pilgrim Books, 1982). Greenblatt analyzes works in relation to the author's life and characteristics of his society and epoch (ideas relevant, and perhaps even indispensable, to the understanding of Cela's writings).

29. Supplementary information on this tendency appears in Fredric Jameson, *Narrative as a Socially Symbolic Act* (Ithaca, N.Y.: Cornell University Press, 1981); and Brian Stock, *Listening for the Text: On the Uses of the Past* (Baltimore, Md.: Johns Hopkins University Press, 1990).

30. See Gemma Roberts, "La culpa y la búsqueda de la autenticidad en *San Camilo 1936,*" in *Novelistas españoles de postguerra,* ed. Rodolfo Cardona (Madrid: Taurus, 1976). 205–18.

31. Roland Barthes, "Historical Discourse," in *Introduction to Structuralism,* ed. Michael Lane (New York: Basic Books, 1970), 145–55.

32. A judicious exposition appears in David Henn, "Endemic Violence and Political Balance in Cela's *San Camilo, 1936,*" *Romance Studies* 3 (Winter 1983–1984): 31–46.

Chapter Five

1. The original edition (Barcelona: Editorial Noguer, 1973) contained the number 5 as part of the shortened title, *Oficio de tinieblas, 5.* Cela explained that upon submitting the manuscript for publication, he had encountered four prior uses of the title; when preparing a note for the cover, he had found three more, making it "Oficio de tinieblas, 8." Despairing of ever locating all prior uses, he deleted the number thereafter. I quote from the sixth edition (1974); all translations mine. Hereafter cited in text as *Oficio.*

2. Robert Saladrigas, review of *Oficio de tinieblas,* by José Camilo Cela, *Destino,* 27 December 1973.

3. Gonzalo Navajas, "Cela y el nuevo debate en torno a la modernidad," *El Extramundi* 12 (Winter 1997): 122; hereafter cited in text. (Navajas did not direct these remarks specifically to *Oficio,* but they could well apply.)

4. Rafael Conte, "Cela en busca de la novela perdida," *El Extramundi* 12 (Winter 1997): 43–70; hereafter cited in text. (Conte's article, an overview of Cela's work, reveals the perplexity still generated by *Oficio* for a major critic a quarter century after the work's publication.)

5. Knut Ahnlund, "*Mazurca para dos muertos* observado desde el Norte," *El Extramundi* 12 (Winter 1997): 245–273; hereafter cited in text.

6. Quoted in José María Martínez Cachero, *La novela española entre 1936 y 1970: Historia de una aventura* (Madrid: Castalia, 1985), 347; hereafter cited in text.

7. Gonzalo Torrente Ballester, *Nuevos cuadernos de La Romana* (Barcelona: Destino, 1976), 232; hereafter cited in text.

8. Quoted in Carol Wasserman, *Camilo José Cela y su trayectoria literaria* (Madrid: Playor, 1990), 155; hereafter cited in text. The book is a revised version of Wasserman's dissertation, emphasizing *Oficio*.

9. In Charlebois, *Oficio de tinieblas* is studied in chapter 6 (64–73). Gottfried Wilhelm Leibniz (1646–1716), a German philosopher, mathematician, and precursor of atomic theory, first developed the concept of the monad as the smallest particle of matter.

10. See Gonzalo Sobejano, "El Surrealismo en la España de postguerra: Camilo José Cela," in *Surrealismo/Surrealismos,* ed. Peter G. Earle and Germán Gullón (Philadelphia: University of Pennsylvania, 1976), 138; hereafter cited in text as Sobejano 1976.

11. Max Ernst, "¿Qué es el Surrealismo?" *Boletín Informativo Fundación Juan March* 158 (April 1986): 24–28; hereafter cited in text.

12. Pere Gimferrer, "*Oficio de tinieblas, 5* de Camilo José Cela," *Destino,* 4 May 1974, literary page "La semana literaria."

13. Phonic values are lost in translation: "Los guerreros creucobolos montaban grandes pájaros ahítos de mariposas quemadas grandes pájaros con yerba vivaz verbena mostaza cáñamo en lugar de plumas."

14. Alonso Zamora Vicente, *Camilo José Cela: Acercamiento a un escritor.* (Madrid: Editorial Gredos, 1962), 248. This premier critical interpreter is a long-time personal friend of Cela.

15. See chapter 2 in this volume for a discussion of Lejeune.

Chapter Six

1. Camilo José Cela, *Mazurca para dos muertos* (Barcelona: Seix Barral, 1983), 11; hereafter cited in text as *Mazurca;* all translations mine. (However, I recently saw an English version, *Mazurka for Two Dead Men,* trans. Patricia Haugaard [New York: New Directions Books, 1992].)

2. Charlebois affirms that "*Mazurka* is about what don Camilo finds out concerning what happened to his family in Galicia during his years of absence. . . . Since his relatives are the primary source of information, the narrative discourse is deeply rooted in Galicia's oral/aural tradition" (76). She cites an interview that "speaks of a vengeance similar to that of the Carroupo-Guxindes [feud in *Mazurca*] which his relatives carried out against a Falangist from Carballino for having killed a family member" (148 n. 3).

3. Another example appears in "El bonito crimen del carabinero."

4. Juan Antonio Masoliver Ródenas, "*Mazurca para dos muertos* Seen through Its Characters," *Review of Contemporary Fiction* 4, no. 3 (Fall 1984): 84; hereafter cited in text. Presumably the reference to biographical and autobiographical content concerns Gallego "relatives" of the Cela clan appearing in the novel; some autobiographical "resonances" are unrelated to Galicia.

5. Given the revival of regional languages and cultures and newly autonomous regions in the post-Franco era, questions of Cela's use of Galician language in *Mazurca* received considerable critical attention. See Carlos Casares, "Cela, Galicia, y galleguismos," *Insula* 518–19 (February–March 1990): 15–16; Basilio Losada, "Cela, escritor gallego," *Insula* 518–19 (February–March 1990): 48–49; and Irene Andrés-Suárez, "El bilinguismo en la obra de C. J. Cela," in *Literatura y bilinguismo: Homenaje a Pere Ramírez,* ed. Elvezio Canonica and Ernst Rudin (Kassel: Reichenberger, 1993), 223–39.

6. The Galician variant of a vampire is a "fat sucker" *(sacaúntos),* not a bloodsucker, preferring children and adolescents. Emilia Pardo Bazán has a chilling gothic novelette on this motif, "El sacaúntos."

7. Cela initially used this dedication for his first book of poetry, *Pisando la dudosa luz del día,* a surrealist work written largely during the bombardment of Madrid in the Spanish civil war but not published until 1945. He used the words of the dedication again with minimal modification in *San Camilo, 1936* and cites them almost verbatim (with further commentary) in *Memorias.* Such unusual emphasis on these words indicates his desire to make absolutely clear his sympathy with young Spaniards of both sides who were sacrificed in the civil war, while distancing himself ideologically from the contending parties and denouncing the "foreign adventurers" of all political hues who intervened in Spain's "funeral." The title ("Treading Doubtful Daylight"), borrowed from the baroque poet Góngora, alludes to initial aesthetics of poets of the Generation of 1927 (including Vicente Aleixandre, García Lorca, Rafael Alberti, et al., early Spanish practitioners of surrealism) but also evokes the wartime atmosphere of Madrid under siege.

8. Nancy L. Dinneen, "Setting in *San Camilo, 1936* and *Mazurka para dos muertos,*" in *Camilo José Cela: Homage to a Nobel Prize,* ed. Joaquin Roy (Coral Gables: University of Miami Press, 1991), 74; hereafter cited in text.

9. See David Herzberger, "Small Narrations: Localizing the Civil War in Cela's *Mazurca,*" *Revista de Estudios Hispánicos* 29, no. 1 (January 1995): 107–19. For an alternative view, see Sara M. Saz, "*Mazurca para dos muertos,* ¿Obra de creación literaria, cachondeo, escarceo u otro meneo?" in *Actas del X Congreso de AIH,* vol. 3, ed. A. Vilanova (Barcelona: Promociones y Publicaciones Universitarias, 1992), 265–79.

10. More on the demythologization of Francoist historiography appears in David Herzberger, *Rewriting the Past: Fiction and Historiography in Postwar Spain* (Durham, N.C.: Duke University Press, 1995).

11. For example, see Ilie; others, however, were similarly indignant.

12. An analysis of *Mazurca* as based on personal experience appears in Dieudonné Mendogo Mensongui, "Lo autobiográfico en *Mazurca . . .* de CJC," in *Scripta Philologica en Memoriam, Manuel Taboada Cid,* ed. M. Casado Velarde et al. (La Coruña: Universidade da Cruña, 1996), 569–78; including linguistic and dialectal considerations.

13. Cela clarifies personal linkages as Robin and the "artilleryman Camilo" discuss the latter's brief military service, wound, and hospitalization in Logroño.

14. A pervasive aspect of Celtic mythology, the legends of lakes with buried cities beneath their waters are widespread in Galicia and have been explained as a variant of the Atlantis myth.

15. Further developed in Janet Pérez, "*Mazurca para dos muertos:* Demythologization of the Civil War, History, and Narrative Reliability," *Anales de la Literatura Española Contemporánea* 13, nos. 1–2 (1988): 83–104.

16. Narratorial fallibility, significant in *San Camilo,* achieves heightened visibility in *Cristo versus Arizona, El asesinato del perdedor, La cruz de San Andrés,* and *Memorias,* complementing the demythologization of history and echoing deconstructionist attitudes toward "truth."

Chapter Seven

1. Cela explains that *versus* is used in its original Latin connotation, motion in the direction of (Arizona) (indicating not conflict but something like "[Moving] Christ toward Arizona"). Quoted by Luis Blanco Vila, *Para leer a Camilo José Cela* (Madrid: Palas Atenea, 1991), 194 (from an article by Cela in *El País,* 14 February 1988). I quote from the original edition of *Cristo versus Arizona* (Barcelona: Seix Barral, 1988); hereafter cited in text as *Cristo;* all translations mine.

2. *Mrs. Caldwell habla con su hijo* includes the narrator-protagonist's memories or fantasies of extra-Peninsular events and places, but she blends and (con)fuses characters, events, and settings of the Iberian Peninsula with those elsewhere. External locales are merely evoked (existing largely in her mind).

3. Pedro Sorela, "Cela escribe *Cristo versus Arizona,* una novela con un solo punto," *El País,* 24 February 1988.

4. This information on the dust jacket is never stated within the text, and the dubious protagonist-narrator repeatedly "unwrites," questioning, contradicting, doubting, and subverting his own prior affirmations.

5. A general discussion of the New Historicism appears in chapter 2 of this volume.

6. For Stephen Miller's examination of Native American myths in this novel, see his "Civilización, barbarie y Eros en *Cristo versus Arizona,*" *Antípodas* 4, no. 2 (December 1992): 80–81; hereafter cited in text.

7. Castellet's comment first appeared in a postpublication review, republished decades later (suggesting belief that time had shown his judgment to be correct). See José María Castellet, "El libro de la semana: *La Catira,*" *Revista* (Barcelona), 7 April 1955; reprinted in *Prólogo* 5 (October–December 1989): 34.

8. See Juan Antonio Masoliver-Ródenas, "Cela a las puertas del deleite obsceno," review of *Cristo versus Arizona,* by Camilo José Cela, *La Vanguardia* (Barcelona), 18 February 1988. The observation concerning the absence of plot applies to characters invented by Cela, since he respects "historical" background," or extant versions of the shoot-out at the OK Corral.

9. Charlebois devotes a chapter to this novel.

10. See Pilar Rotella, "La serpiente como símbolo y estructura en *Cristo versus Arizona,*" in *Estudios en homenaje a Enrique Ruiz Fornells,* by Juan Fernández Jiménez et al. (Erie, Pa.: ALDEEUU, 1990), 585–92.

11. Gonzalo Torrente Ballester, "*La colmena,* cuarta novela de C.J.C.," originally published in *Cuadernos Hispanoamericanos* 22 (July–August 1951); reprinted in *El "Quijote" como juego y otros trabajos críticos* (Barcelona: Destino, 1984), 36.

12. Further developed in Janet Pérez, "Motivos constantes y estructuras líricas en *Cristo versus Arizona,*" in *Camilo José Cela: Homage to a Nobel Prize,* ed. Joaquín Roy (Coral Gables Fla.: University of Miami Press/Ideas 92, 1991), 26–32.

13. The account in Alexandrine verse incorporates implied dialogue between Méndez as narrator and Cela. See Miguel Méndez, "De cuando Camilo José Cela visitó Tucsón, Arizona, entre el 12 y 25 de febrero de 1987," *El Extramundi* 4 (1995): 95–113.

Chapter Eight

1. Camilo José Cela, *El asesinato del perdedor* (Barcelona: Seix Barral, 1994), 129; hereafter cited in text as *El asesinato;* all translations mine.

2. Ana María Platas Tasende and Luis Iglesias Feijoo, "Unidad y sentido en *El Asesinato del perdedor* de Camilo José Cela," in *Scripta Philológica in Memoriam Manuel Taboada Cid,* vol. 2 (La Coruña: Ediciones Universidade da Coruña, 1996), 606; hereafter cited in text as Platas and Iglesias.

3. Ana María Platas Tasende, "*El asesinato del perdedor,*" *Revista Galega do Ensino* 5 (November 1994): 205.

4. Charlebois devotes chapter 9 (101–15) to *El asesinato.*

5. Federico García Lorca experimented with having human actors play the roles of puppets, as in *Los títeres de Cachiporra,* or combining marionettes and human actors (e.g., in *Tragicomedia de Don Perlimplín con Belisa en su jardín*).

6. Camilo José Cela, *La insólita y gloriosa hazaña del Cipote de Archidona* (Barcelona: Tusquets, 1997). This trivial little tome appeared in the erotica series "La sonrisa vertical." *Cipote,* essentially untranslatable, has several meanings, the most relevant alluding to exceptionally large genitalia. For examination of Cela's treatments of the lewd and obscene with specific focus on *El Cipote,* see Janet Pérez, "Euphemism, Euphuism, Euchologue: Cela and the Poetics of Polite Obscenity," *Antípodas* 4, Special Number on Three Hispanic Nobels, ed. Stephen Miller (December 1992): 59–75.

7. Camilo José Cela, *Izas, rabizas, y colipoterras: Drama con acompaña-miento de cachondeo y dolor de corazón* (Barcelona: Lumen, 1964). The three initial words of the title, highly colloquial, are degrading terms for prostitutes, roughly "Bawds, Slatterns, and Whores."

8. See David W. Foster, "Cela and Spanish Marginal Culture," *Review of Contemporary Fiction* 4, no. 3 (Fall 1984): 55–59. Foster posits Cela's assumption of a "metaphoric" link between academic philology and censorship, suggesting a "philological inquisition" by Cela that defies "the cultural imperatives of a dictatorial regime" (56).

9. Javier Gómez de Liaño, "La justicia en la obra de Camilo José Cela," *El Extramundi* 12 (Winter 1997): 357–401; hereafter cited in text.

10. Camilo José Cela, *A vueltas con España* (Madrid: Seminarios y Ediciones, 1973), 151.

11. Miguel García-Posada, "Entre Quevedo y el surrealismo," *El País,* 4 April 1994, 10–11.

12. Conte notes echoes of "treatises of Thomas Bernhard" in *El asesinato* and *La cruz* (70).

13. From an article by Cela entitled "Malos tiempos," published 18 March 1993, and cited by Gómez de Liaño, 377.

14. Gareth Thomas, *The Novel of the Spanish Civil War (1936–1975)* (New York: Cambridge University Press, 1990), 14. Thomas's study includes sociopolitical context for several of Cela's novels.

15. Jo Labanyi, *Myth and History in the Contemporary Spanish Novel* (New York: Cambridge University Press, 1989), 179; see also "Fiction as Release" (178–246), which treats *San Camilo, 1936.*

16. See Janet Pérez, "Text, Context, and Subtext of the Unreliable Narrative: Cela's *El asesinato del perdedor,*" *Anales de la Literatura Española Contemporánea* 21 (1996): 85–100.

Chapter Nine

1. Cela alluded sardonically to the polemics in "El premio Planeta," *ABC,* 23 October 1994, 21.

2. The primary focus of Iglesias Feijoo's excellent study concerns the narrator(s)' identity.

3. *El asesinato* was apparently begun before 1980, when a fragment comprising several folios was published. *La cruz* may have begun later, but certainly before Cela completed *El asesinato.*

4. Camilo José Cela, *La cruz de San Andrés* (Barcelona: Planeta, 1994), 1; hereafter cited in text as *La cruz;* all translations mine. The word used in this quote, *derrumbamiento,* denotes a structure's collapse or a landslide.

5. This "Nota a la segunda edición" (1952), first published in *Papeles de Son Armadans,* appeared prefacing this novel in the truncated 1960 *Obra completa.*

6. In the definitive edition of *Mrs. Caldwell* prepared for inclusion (1969) in Cela's *Obra Completa* (Barcelona: Destino, 1969), 198.

7. Mikhail Bakhtin, in "From the Prehistory of Novelistic Discourse," in *The Dialogic Imagination: Four Essays* (Austin: University of Texas Press, 1981), underscores postmodern tendencies to subvert, ridicule, and eventually destroy "monoglossic," or single-voiced, structures of official genres.

8. Jean François Lyotard, translated to Spanish as *La cuestión postmoderna: Informe sobre el saber* (The postmodern question: Report on knowledge) (Madrid: Cátedra, 1984). Lyotard defines postmodernism as the state of culture after transformations changing "the rules of the game" for science, literature, and the arts in the twentieth century.

9. Gonzalo Torrente Ballester, in *El "Quijote" como juego* (Madrid: Guadarrama, 1975), analyzed how the Cervantine "found manuscript" device (often used by Cela) functions in the self-conscious novel, complicating levels of reality as the author distances himself from the text by inventing other intermediaries or transmitters. Ontological bases of the text shift when the author inserts himself into the text as author, as a character, or both (as Cela does in several novels).

10. Legend has it that St. Andrew the apostle (brother of Simon Peter and fisherman of Bethsaida) was crucified on an X-shaped cross. The narrator insinuates that he was crucified head down and naked, the same fate supposedly awaiting her husband and herself (never shown). La Coruña (the site of the novel) has a downtown street named Calle de San Andrés, but no connections are established.

11. For characteristics of the postmodern, see Douwe Fokkema, *Literary History, Modernism, and Post-Modernism* (Amsterdam: John Benjamins, 1984); and Brian McHale, *Post-modern Fiction* (New York: Methuen, 1987), hereafter cited in text. McHale stresses that the world projected by postmodern fiction is destabilized, paradoxical, and contradictory. Its landscape, plural and anarchical, is permeated by "secondary realities" (37).

12. Gonzalo Torrente Ballester, *Fragmentos de apocalipsis* (Barcelona: Destino, 1977). This extraordinary exercise of postmodern literary theory demonstrates that the novelistic edifice is only a construct of words that can be erased at the stroke of a pen.

13. Iglesias cites F. Torres Yagues, *Medio siglo entre escritores* (Madrid: Gráficas Yagues, 1972), 38, as the first to publish Cela's authorship of this biography of St. John of the Cross. Elsewhere, Cela's essays mention his interest in St. Teresa. Matilde's attribution of these interests to her "mother," another cross-gender switch, further muddies Cela's literary parenthood.

14. See also Janet Pérez, "Lo experimental, constante y post-moderno en *La cruz de San Andrés,* de Cela," *Confluencia* 11, no. 2 (Spring 1996): 27–38.

Chapter Ten

1. Camilo José Cela, *La rueda de los ocios* (Barcelona: Mateu, 1957), 18.

Selected Bibliography

Primary Works

Novels and English Translations

La familia de Pascual Duarte. Burgos: Aldecoa, 1942. As *Pascual Duarte's Family,* London: Eyre and Spottiswoode, 1946. As *The Family of Pascual Duarte,* Boston: Little, Brown, 1964. As *Pascual Duarte and His Family,* New York: Las Américas, 1965.

Pabellón de reposo. Madrid: Afrodisio Aguado, 1943. As *Rest Home,* New York: Las Américas, 1961.

Nuevas andanzas y desventuras de Lazarillo de Tormes. Madrid: La Nave, 1944.

La colmena. Buenos Aires: Emecé, 1951; Barcelona: Noguera, 1955. As *The Hive,* New York: Farrar, Straus, and Young, 1953; London: Gollancz, 1953.

Mrs. Caldwell habla con su hijo. Barcelona: Destino, 1953. As *Mrs. Caldwell Speaks to her Son,* Ithaca, N.Y.: Cornell University Press, 1968.

Tobogán de hambrientos. Barcelona: Noguer, 1962.

San Camilo, 1936: vísperas, festividad, y octava de San Camilo del año 1936 en Madrid. Madrid: Alfaguara, 1969. As San Camilo, 1936; *The Eve, Feast, and Octave of St. Camillus of the Year 1936 in Madrid,* Durham, N.C.: Duke University Press, 1992.

Oficio de tinieblas, 5, o novela de tesis escrita para ser cantada por un coro de enfermos. Barcelona: Noguer, 1973.

Mazurca para dos muertos. Barcelona: Seix Barral, 1983. As *Mazurka for Two Dead Men,* New York: New Directions, 1992.

Cristo versus Arizona. Barcelona: Seix Barral, 1988.

El asesinato del perdedor. Barcelona: Seix Barral, 1994.

La cruz de San Andrés. Barcelona: Planeta, 1994.

Obra completa. 14 vols. Barcelona: Destino, 1962–1983.

Obras completas. 25 vols. Barcelona: Planeta-Agostini, 1989–1990.

Madera de boj. Madrid: Espasa-Calpe, 1999.

Selected Nonfiction

Mesa revuelta. Madrid: Sagitario, 1945; enlarged ed., Madrid: Taurus, 1957. Essays.

Pisando la dudosa luz del día. Barcelona: Zodíaco, 1945; revised and enlarged ed., Palma de Mallorca: Papeles de Son Armadans, 1963. Poems.

San Juan de la Cruz (as Matilde Verdú). Madrid: Hernando, 1948. Biographical essay.

Ensueños y figuraciones. Barcelona: G.P., 1954. Essays.

Mis páginas preferidas. Madrid: Gredos, 1956. Anthology.

La rueda de los ocios. Barcelona: Mateu, 1957. Essays.

La obra literaria del pintor Solana. Palma de Mallorca: Papeles de Son Armadans, 1957. Critical essay.

Recuerdo de don Pío Baroja. Mexico City: De Andrea, 1958. Critical essay.

La rosa. La cucaña, vol. 1. Barcelona: Destino, 1959; Barcelona: Destino, 1979. Memoirs.

Al servicio de algo. Madrid: Alfaguara, 1969. Essays.

Diccionario secreto. 2 vols. Madrid: Alfaguara, 1968–1972. Erudition on obscenity.

A vueltas con España. Madrid: Seminarios y Ediciones, 1973. Essays.

Enciclopedia del erotismo. Madrid: Sedmay, 1977; 3 vols., Barcelona: Destino, 1982–1986; as *Diccionario del erotismo,* rev. ed., 2 vols., Barcelona: Grijalbo, 1988.

Crónica del Cipote de Archidona. Madrid: Gisa, 1977. Burlesque erotica.

Vuelta de hoja. Barcelona: Destino, 1981. Essays.

Los vasos comunicantes. Barcelona: Bruguera, 1981; Barcelona: Plaza y Janés, 1989. Essays.

El juego de los tres madroños. Barcelona: Destino, 1983. Essays.

El asno de Buridán. Madrid: El País, 1986. Articles.

Conversaciones españolas. Barcelona: Plaza y Janés, 1987.

Elogio a la fábula (Eulogy to the Fable). Stockholm: Nobel Foundation, 1989. Nobel lecture.

Páginas escogidas. Ed. Darío Villanueva. Madrid: Espasa-Calpe, 1991. Anthology.

Memorias, entendimientos y voluntades. Barcelona: Plaza y Janés, 1993.

El huevo del juicio. Barcelona: Seix Barral, 1994. Essays.

¡A bote pronto! Barcelona: Seix Barral, 1998. Essays, articles, and miniessays.

Secondary Works

Critical Works

Antípodas 4 (December 1992). *Three Hispanic Nobels* (Cela, Gabriel García Márquez, Octavio Paz). Includes interview with Cela and six articles on Cela's fiction and poetry.

Blanco Vila, Luis. *Para leer a Camilo José Cela.* Madrid: Palas Atenea, 1991. Overview of life and works, including materials from a summer seminar on Cela's latest novels (ending with *Cristo versus Arizona*). Also contains an interview with Cela concerning how his works should be read.

Camilo José Cela: Nuevos enfoques críticos. Madrid, 1991. Collected essays by various writers presenting new perspectives on Cela's best-known works, *Pascual Duarte* and *La colmena,* with some studies of his brief fiction.

Cela, Camilo José. *Páginas escogidas.* Ed. with "Estudio preliminar" (9–65) by Darío Villanueva. Madrid: Espasa-Calpe, 1991. Good one-volume introduction to Cela's style and themes in extracts representing multiple aspects of the writer, plus a developmental perspective of a half century of Cela's work from the 1940s to his receipt of the Nobel. Critical overview by one of the authorities on Cela.

Cela Conde, Camilo José. *Cela, mi padre.* Madrid: Ediciones Temas de Hoy, 1989. An intimate look at the novelist and life in his family from the loyal perspective of the only son of the famous writer. Especially revealing of the lighter side of Cela.

Charlebois, Lucile. *Understanding Camilo José Cela.* Columbia: University of South Carolina Press, 1998. Studies 10 of Cela's novels, devoting a chapter to each (omitting only the *"Nuevo Lazarillo," La Catira,* and *Tobogán de hambrientos*). Highly recommended overview; only work in English covering all of the "later novels."

Cuadernos Hispanoamericanos 337–38 (1978). Special "homenaje" issue devoted to Cela with linguistic and bibliographical studies; examination of poetics, travel books, works of social conscience, and theater; retrospectives.

El Extramundi 9 (Spring 1997). Special issue of quarterly published by the Camilo José Cela Foundation. Important overview by Alonso Zamora Vicente; significant articles by Francisco Umbral, Darío Villanueva, and Víctor García de la Concha, among others, with studies of *Cristo versus Arizona* by Gonzalo Sobejano, and *La cruz de San Andrés* by Luis Iglesias Feijoo.

El Extramundi 12 (Winter 1997). Second major monographic issue devoted to Cela. Important overviews by Rafael Conte and Gonzalo Navajas, and thematic studies by Fernando Cabo Aseguinolaza, José María Martínez Cachero, Javier Gómez de Liaño, plus analyses of *Mazurca* by Knut Ahnlund and of *San Camilo, 1936* by Maryse Bertrand de Múñoz.

Foster, David W. *Forms of the Novel in the Work of Camilo José Cela.* Columbia: University of Missouri Press, 1967. Studies narrative structure in the first six novels, with observations of continuing validity that illuminate aspects of the more experimental later novels.

Giménez Frontín, José Luis. *Camilo José Cela: Texto y contexto.* Barcelona: Montesinos, 1985. Contains six essays on the postwar novel, emphasizing *La colmena, San Camilo, 1936,* and *Mazurca.*

Ilie, Paul. *La novelística de Camilo José Cela.* Madrid: Gredos, 1971. Studies Cela's first six novels, analyzing themes, existential elements, presence of surrealism, and more, with scholarly rigor and many valid insights.

Insula 518–19 (February–March 1990). Post-Nobel homage to Cela, with eight-page pullout bibliography section by Pedro Abad Contreras; interview with Cela; and articles by some 50 contributors, including many members of Real Academia Española de la Lengua and experts on the contemporary Spanish novel such as Andrés Amorós, Maryse Bertrand de Muñoz, Carlos Casares, Dru Dougherty, David W. Foster, Víctor García de la Concha, Domingo García-Sabell, José L. Giménez Frontín, David Henn, Luis Iglesias Feijoo, Paul Ilie, Robert Kirsner, John Kronik, José M. Martínez Cachero, Juan Antonio Masoliver, Eugenio de Nora, Randolph Pope, Ricardo Senabre, Gonzalo Sobejano, Antonio Vilanova, Darío Villanueva, Francisco Yndurain, and more.

Kirsner, Robert. *The Novels and Travels of Camilo José Cela.* Chapel Hill: University of North Carolina Press, 1963; Madrid: Gráficas P y Punto, 1986. Book-length study of Cela's first-period novels, story collections, and other creative work through 1959. Thematic exegesis with study of repetitive motifs and symbols.

Labanyi, Jo. *Myth and History in the Contemporary Spanish Novel.* New York: Cambridge University Press, 1989. Includes chapter (178–246) on *San Camilo, 1936,* Goytisolo's *Reivindicación del Conde don Julián,* and Torrente Ballester's *La saga/fuga de J.B.;* provides essential literary context for Cela's work and comparisons with other postwar and post-Franco novels.

Mazurca para Camilo José Cela. Ed. Francisco López. Madrid: Gráficas P y Punto, 1986. Essay collection honoring the writer's 70th birthday, with varied tributes, anecdotes, survey articles, portraits, and some literary exegesis.

McPheeters, D. W. *Camilo José Cela.* New York: Twayne Publishers, 1969. Classic bio-bibliographic overview and analysis in English of Cela's first quarter century, studying the novels through *Tobogán de hambrientos.*

Review of Contemporary Fiction 4, no. 3 (1984). Number devoted to Cela, with translations of selected extracts, interview, and essays by the writer plus scholarly articles by David W. Foster, Robert Kirsner, John Kronik, Janet Pérez, and more.

Roy, Joaquín, ed. *Camilo José Cela: Homage to a Nobel Prize.* Coral Gables, Fla.: University of Miami Press, 1991. Contains 17 studies on Cela's poetry, travels, journalism, and novels, with sections devoted to *Pascual Duarte, La colmena,* and *San Camilo, 1936.*

Thomas, Gareth. *The Novel of the Spanish Civil War, 1936–1975.* New York: Cambridge University Press, 1990. Helpful historical background for the wartime and postwar novels treating Spain's civil conflict. Distinguishes four periods, situating and contextualizing Cela's *San Camilo, 1936* and providing sociopolitical data.

Wasserman, Carol. *Camilo José Cela y su trayectoria literaria.* Madrid: Playor, 1990. Reworked version of her 1981 dissertation, which emphasized *Oficio de tinieblas.* Focus on stylistic aspects, especially "aphoristic" discourse (comparisons with Gracián). Discusses short fiction, plus some later novels, with emphasis on *San Camilo, 1936, Oficio,* and *Mazurca para dos muertos.*

Zamora Vicente, Alonso. *Camilo José Cela*. Madrid: Gredos, 1962. The first and still one of the best studies of Cela's early period by a lifelong friend and distinguished critic. Free of critical jargon; integrates Cela's themes with sociohistorical circumstances, life experience, and larger literary context, providing interpretation and insights into symbols, themes, and techniques, which are basic to most subsequent exegesis.

Bibliographies of Cela Criticism

Abad Contreras, Pedro. "Bibliografía de Camilo José Cela." *Insula* 518–19 (February–March 1990). Pullout section of an issue honoring Cela following the Nobel Prize. "Monographic" section lists 45 entries, 10 special issues of periodicals, plus books, mostly by single authors. "Selected Studies" contains 170 titles, no pre-1962 entries (given prior bibliographic work in 1962). Criteria of selection and exclusion inconsistently applied (many significant essays missing, especially by U.S. Hispanists). Coverage better for Cela than the critical works, as more than five of eight pages are devoted to Cela, including foreign editions, translations, critical editions, and so forth. Coverage of the secondary literature is uneven, with Spain and Europe apparently better represented than the United States. Nothing indicates that MLA on-line bibliography or other electronic databases were used; some articles contained in Festschrifts or other collections are listed; other times only the collection. Now 10 years out of date.

Asún, Raquel. Introduction to *La colmena*, by Camilo José Cela. Madrid: Castalia, 1984. This critical edition of the novel's text contains a useful introduction and bibliography dealing primarily with *La colmena*, with 46 entries for this novel, including several missed by Abad Contreras.

Huarte Morton, Fernando. "Bibliografía de Camilo José Cela." *Revista Hispánica Moderna* 28 (1962; published 1963). Cites some 165 studies while allegedly omitting newspaper reviews and interviews (however, includes many entries from popular press and mentions in literary histories, panoramic studies of the Spanish contemporary novel, and other general works). (Abad Contreras's coverage begins where this bibliography ends.) Huarte Morton also has compiled a bibliophile's primary bibliography on the first quarter century of *Pascual Duarte:* "Ensayo de una bibliografía de *La familia de Pascual Duarte*," *Papeles de Son Armadans* 142 (1968), subsequently updated and published as a separate volume on the novel's 40th anniversary.

Martínez Carazo, Cristina. "La crítica frente a camilo José Cela." *Explicación de textos literarios* (1991–1992). Twenty-three-page bibliography of secondary literature, approximately contemporaneous with compilation of Abad Contreras; more accurately reflects dimensions of the critical corpus while making no claims to exhaustive inclusiveness.

Index

ABC (newspaper), 12, 24, 74
adulthood, young, 3–6
Ahnlund, Knut, 103
aire de un crimen, El (Benet), 140
Alberti, Rafael, 4, 168n. 7
Album de taller (Cela), 17
Aldecoa, Ignacio, 109
Aleixandre, Vicente, 4, 168n. 7
Alfaguara, 15
Alfaro, José María, 74
Alfonso X (Castile), 87
Alonso, Dámaso, 5
Andrés Bello Medal, x
Andrew, Saint, 172
antinovel, 47–50, 71–73
Antolín Rato, Mariano, 55, 74–75, 81
Apuntes carpetovetónicos (Cela), 13, 48
árbol de la ciencia, El (Baroja), 62
Argentino, El (newspaper), 4
Arozamena, Joaquín, 161n. 7
Arturo Ui (Brecht), 16
Aseguinolaza, Cabo, 42
asesinato del perdedor, El (Cela), 18, 123,
    171n. 3; auto-dialogues, 25; chronology,
    · 133–34; and Civil Code, 4; and *costum-
    brismo,* 41; "criminal justice," 123–25;
    and *cruz de San Andrés, La,* 140, 142,
    143, 144, 145, 147, 149, 151; environ-
    ment, 158; and *familia de Pascual Duarte,
    La,* 39; interpretation, 156; and
    Mazurca para dos muertos, 100; narratorial
    fallibility, 169n. 16; and neo-*costum-
    brismo,* 42; and *Oficio de tinieblas, 5,* 70,
    72, 77, 81, 82; and other works,
    126–29; and *San Camilo, 1936,* 67, 68;
    sociocultural context, 129–32; structur-
    ing devices, unwriting, and unreliable
    narrator, 134–39; themes, 157
authorial attitude, *Cristo versus Arizona,*
    121–22
"autobiográfico en *Mazurca . . . de CJC"*
    168n. 12
autobiography: genre, 20–22; and *Oficio de
    tinieblas, 5,* 84–85
Ayala, Francisco, 156

Azcoaga, Enrique, 27
Azorín, 24

Bakhtin, Mikhail, 57, 143, 146, 172n. 7
Balada del vagabundo sin suerte (Cela), 16
bandada de Palomas, La (Cela), 16
Barcelona (Cela), 16
Baroja, Pío, 24, 25, 34, 50, 62, 75, 113,
    159
Barthes, Roland, 67
Bazán, Emilia Pardo, 87, 168n. 6
Benet, Juan, 57, 69, 70, 140, 165n. 16
Bernanos, Georges, 5
Bernstein, J. S., 44
Bertrand de Múñoz, Maryse, 52, 55
Beyle, Marie-Henri. *See* Stendhal
Blanco Vila, Luis, 84, 169n. 1
bola del mundo, La: Escenas cotidianas (Cela),
    16
Boletín del Colegio de Huérfanos de Ferroviarios
    (periodical), 9
Bosch, Hieronymus, 38
Brecht, Bertolt, 16
Bretón, André, 81–82
Buckley, Ramón, 41
Burroghs, William, 75
Buscón, El (Quevedo), 42
Butor, Michael, 55

Cabrera, Vicente, 165n. 16
Cachero, Martínez, 75
Cadalso, José de, 41
Cajón de sastre (Cela), 12
Camilo José Cela (Gómez Santos), 161n. 7
Camilo José Cela (Machicao), 161n. 7
Camilo José Cela (McPheeters), ix
"Camilo José Cela and His Poetry of Civil
    Strife" (Perricone), 165n. 18
Camilo José Cela Foundation, 17, 18, 31, 32
Camilo José Cela y su trayectoria literaria
    (Wasserman), 167n. 8
Camus, Albert, 38
Capote, Truman, 21
carro de heno o el inventor de la guillatina, El
    (Cela), 15, 38

Cartas marruecas (Cadalso), 41
Castellet, José María, 81, 111, 169n. 7
Castro, Américo, 4
Catholicism, 2, 77, 80, 85, 150, 151, 155
Catira, La (Cela), ix, 12, 45–46; and *Cristo versus Arizona*, 104, 111; and genre, 50; and *Mrs. Caldwell habla con su hijo*, 45; reception of, 16; repetition, 164n. 7; and *San Camilo, 1936*, 54; setting, 41
Cela (Arozamena), 161n. 7
Cela, Camilo José, ix–xi, 1; adulthood, young, 3–6; character of, 35–36; and Conde, Cela, 31–34; family and youth, 1–3; postwar years, early, 9–12; second period, 15–18; success and recognition, 12–15; war years, 6–9

WORKS
Album de taller, 17
Apuntes carpetovetónicos, 13, 48
asesinato del perdedor, El, 18, 123, 171n. 3; auto-dialogues, 25; chronology, 133–34; and Civil Code, 4; and *costumbrismo*, 41; "criminal justice," 123–25; and *cruz de San Andrés, La*, 140, 142, 143, 144, 145, 147, 149, 151; environment, 158; and *familia de Pascual Duarte, La*, 39; interpretation, 156; and *Mazurca para dos muertos*, 100; narratorial fallibility, 169n. 16; and neo-*costumbrismo*, 42; and *Oficio de tinieblas*, 70, 72, 77, 81, 82; and other works, 126–29; and *San Camilo, 1936*, 67, 68; sociocultural context, 129–32; structuring devices, unwriting, and unreliable narrator, 134–39; themes, 157
Balada del vagabundo sin suerte, 16
bandada de Palomas, La, 16
Barcelona, 16
bola del mundo, La: Escenas cotidianas, 16
Cajón de sastre, 12
carro de heno o el inventor de la guillatina, El, 15, 38
Catira, La, ix, 12, 45–46; and *Cristo versus Arizona*, 104, 111; and genre, 50; and *Mrs. Caldwell habla con su hijo*, 45; reception of, 16; repetition, 164n. 7; and *San Camilo, 1936*, 54; setting, 41
Celestina, La, 16
Cinco glosas a otras tantas verdades de la silueta que un hombre trazó a sí mismo, 16

ciudadano Iscariote Reclús, El, 14
colmena, La, 42–44; and *asesinato del perdedor, El*, 129, 130, 139; and *Catira, La*, 46; composition of, 11, 18, 31; and *costumbrismo*, 41; and *Cristo versus Arizona*, 109, 112, 117, 118, 120; and *cruz de San Andrés, La*, 141; English translation, 12; and experimentation, 154; and *Mazurca para dos muertos*, 86, 89, 93, 96, 98; and *Oficio de tinieblas, 5*, 71; and *San Camilo, 1936*, 53, 56, 57, 58, 61, 64, 67; and *Tobogán de hambrientos*, 50; and Vanguard years, 5; and *viejos amigos, Los*, 13; and war, 7, 26, 30
companies convenientes, Las, 14
Cristo versus Arizona, 104–5, 169n. 1; and *asesinato del perdedor, El*, 123, 124, 127, 128, 129, 130, 132, 137, 138; and *Catira, La*, 46; and *colmena, La*, 42, 43, 44; and *cruz de San Andrés, La*, 141, 143, 144–45, 147, 149, 150, 151, 152; and experimentation, 156; and *Mazurca para dos muertos*, 86, 98, 102; narrative devices and antecedents, 109–14, 169n. 16; and *Oficio de tinieblas, 5*, 72, 77, 78, 81; and other works, 116–19; picaresque elements, 41; plot, absence of, 170n. 8; "reality" and fiction, 119–20; and *San Camilo, 1936*, 57, 59, 66; and second period, 17; spatiotemporal parameters, 105–7; subtexts and authorial attitude, 121–22; title, 163n. 6; and *Tobogán de hambrientos*, 48, 50; truth, memory, and unreliable narrator, 107–8; Wendell's life, 114–16
cruz de San Andrés, La, 1, 140–41, 171nn. 3, 4; antecedents for structure and form, 141–44; and *asesinato del perdedor, El*, 123, 128, 132, 135; characters and events, 149–51; chronicle and history, 151–53; and *colmena, La*, 43; and *Cristo versus Arizona*, 120; and experimentation, 156–57; and Galicia, 161n. 2; and *Mazurca para dos muertos*, 87, 100, 103; and *Mrs. Caldwell habla con su hijo*, 45; narrator, 144–49; narratorial fallibility, 169n. 16; and *Oficio de tinieblas, 5*, 72, 77, 82; picaresque elements, 41; and *San Camilo, 1936*, 67; and second period, 18; setting, 158; and *Tobogán de hambrientos*, 48

Cucaña, La, 19, 26
Cuentos para leer después del baño, 17
Del Miño al Bidasoa, 11, 87
Diccionario secreto, 15, 16, 131, 132
"Don Anselmo," 10
"Elogio de la fábula," 36, 159
Enciclopedia del erotismo, 17, 132
Esas nubes que pasan, 10
familia del héroe, La, 14
familia de Pascual Duarte, La, 37–39; and
    asesinato del perdedor, El, 126, 127, 128,
    138; and *colmena, La,* 43; and *Cristo ver-
    sus Arizona,* 104, 107, 110, 112; and
    experimentation, 154; picaresque ele-
    ments, 40, 41, 42; postwar years, 9, 10;
    and *San Camilo, 1936,* 60; and second
    period, 15; success of, 15; and *Tobogán de
    hambrientos,* 50; and war, 7, 8, 19, 30, 31
gallego y su cuadrilla y otros carpetovetónicos, El,
    11, 87
Garito de hospicianos, 14
Gavilla de fábulas sin amor, 13–14
Historias de España: Los ciegos, los tontos, 12, 13
huevo del juicio, El, 17–18
*insólita y gloriosa hazaña del Cipote de Archi-
    dona, La,* 131, 132, 170n. 6
Izas, rabizas y colipoterras, 14, 44, 46, 131,
    171n. 7
Judíos, moros y cristanos, 12
"lagarto del miedo, El," 28
Lenny dialogues, 16
Madera de boj, xi; and *asesinato del perdedor,
    El,* 123, 138; and *cruz de San Andrés, La,*
    143; Galicia, 161n. 2; and *Mazurca para
    dos muertos,* 87; and second period, 17, 18
Mancha en el corazón y en los ojos, La, 16
"Marcelo Brito," 10
María Sabina, 15, 16, 34, 48
Mazurca para dos muertos, 1, 86–87, 168n.
    12; and *asesinato del perdedor, El,* 123,
    126, 127, 129, 132, 136, 137, 138,
    139; clan structure and related subplots,
    97–99, 167n. 4; and *colmena, La,* 43,
    44; and *Cristo versus Arizona,* 108,
    110–11, 113, 114, 118; and *cruz de San
    Andrés, La,* 140, 141, 142, 143, 144,
    152; and earlier works, 89–92; and
    experimentation, 155–56; Galicia,
    87–89, 92–94, 161n. 2, 167n. 2, 168n.
    5; narrative elements, 94–97; and *Oficio
    de tinieblas, 5,* 72, 78, 79, 84; picaresque

elements, 41, 42; poetic structure and
    fugal structure, 99–103; and *San
    Camilo, 1936,* 53, 56, 57, 61, 68; and
    second period, 17; and *Tobogán de ham-
    brientos,* 48, 50; and war, 7, 8, 28
Memorias, entendimientos y voluntades, 19,
    21–22; adulthood, young, 4, 6; dedica-
    tion, 168n. 7; family and youth, 2–3,
    22–27; and history, 157; and *Mazurca
    para dos muertos,* 93–94, 97; narrative
    fallibility, 169n. 16; postwar years, 9,
    10; and *San Camilo, 1936,* 52, 58; sec-
    ond period, 17, 18; war years, 7–9,
    27–31
"Memory of La Coruña," 28, 94
Mesa revuelta, 10
"moneda al aire, La," 28
Mrs. Caldwell habla con su hijo, 44–45; and
    asesinato del perdedor, El, 128; and *Catira,
    La,* 46; and *colmena, La,* 43; and *Cristo
    versus Arizona,* 110, 116; and *cruz de San
    Andrés, La,* 142; and experimentation,
    13, 154; and *Mazurca para dos muertos,*
    94; memories, 169n. 2; and *Obra Com-
    pleta,* 172n. 6; and *Oficio de tinieblas, 5,*
    71; postwar years, 11–12; and *San
    Camilo, 1936,* 56–57, 58; and second
    period, 16, 18; and surrealism, 5; and
    Tobogán de hambrientos, 50
"Nota a la segunda edición," 171n. 5
*Nuevas andanzas y desventuras de Lazarillo de
    Tormes,* 10, 41
Nuevas escenas matritenses, 14, 43, 46
Obras completas, 11, 171n. 5, 172n. 6
Oficio de tinieblas, 5, 166nn. 1–4; and anti-
    novel, 71–73; and *asesinato del perdedor,
    El,* 128, 130, 132, 136; autobiographi-
    cal substrata, 84–85; classifications of,
    74–75; and *Cristo versus Arizona,* 110,
    120; and *cruz de San Andrés, La,* 142,
    143, 150; and experimentation, 154,
    155; ideas in, 75–81; and Leibniz, Got-
    tfried Wilhelm, 167n. 9; and *Mazurca
    para dos muertos,* 86, 94, 95, 102, 103;
    and *Mrs. Caldwell habla con su hijo,* 45;
    and New Narrative, 69–71; and *San
    Camilo, 1936,* 54, 56, 59, 64; and sec-
    ond period, 16; surrealist aspects, 5,
    81–83; and *Tobogán de hambrientos,* 48,
    50; and Villanueva, Darío, 162n. 8; and
    Wasserman, Carol, 167n. 8

Once cuentos de fútbol, 14, 46
Pabellón de reposo, 39–40; and *Cristo versus Arizona,* 111; and *cruz de San Andrés, La,* 142; and experimentation, 154; genesis of, 3, 25; and *Mazurca para dos muertos,* 94; postwar years, 10; and *San Camilo, 1936,* 56, 58
Páginas de geografía errabunda, 14
pata de palo, A la, 14
"Photographs of Countess {Emilia} Pardo Bazán," 9–10
Pisando la dudosa luz del día, 4–5; composition of, 165n. 18; dedication, 168n. 7; and *Mazurca para dos muertos,* 90; and *Mrs. Caldwell habla con su hijo,* 45; and *San Camilo, 1936,* 58; and war, 7, 27
"premio Planeta, El," 171n. 1
Primer viaje andaluz, 13
Rol de cornudos, 17
rosa, La, 3, 13, 19, 22, 98
rueda de los ocios, La, 12
San Camilo, 1936, 51–52; and Alfaguara, 15; and *asesinato del perdedor, El,* 132, 136, 137, 139; and Charlebois, Lucile, 164n. 3; and childhood years, 22–23, 25; and *colmena, La,* 43, 44; composition of, 33; and *Cristo versus Arizona,* 108, 109, 118; and *cruz de San Andrés, La,* 141, 142, 150, 151–52; dedication, 168n. 7; and experimentation, 157, 158; historical and cultural contexts, 58–64, 154–55; language and rhetoric, 64–65; literary contexts, 53–58; and *Mazurca para dos muertos,* 86, 89, 90, 91, 92, 94–95, 98, 102, 103; narratorial fallibility, 169n. 16; and national identity, 159; New Historicism, 66–68; and *Oficio de tinieblas, 5,* 69–71, 77, 78, 79, 84; picaresque elements, 42; and Press Law, ix–x; and second period, 16; and surrealism, 5; title, 164n. 9; and *Tobogán de hambrientos,* 50; and war, 6, 7, 19, 26, 28, 29, 154–55
servicio de algo, Al, 16
Solitario y los sueños de Quesada de Rafael Zabaleta, 14, 45, 46, 58
sueños vanos, los ángeles curiosos, 17
tacatá oxidado, El, 16
Tobogán de hambrientos, ix, 47–50; and *Catira, La,* 46; and *costumbrismo,* 33; and *Cristo versus Arizona,* 110; and experi-

mentation, 13; and *Mazurca para dos muertos,* 94, 96; and *Mrs. Caldwell habla con su hijo,* 45; and *Oficio de tinieblas, 5,* 69, 71, 72; picaresque elements, 41; and *San Camilo, 1936,* 58; and second period, 16; and war, 7
Toreo de salon, 14
"Torremejía," 30
vasos comunicantes, Los, 17, 82
Viaje a la Alcarria, 10–11
Viaje al Pirineo de Lérida, 14
Viaje a USA, 14
viejos amigos, Los, 13, 43
Vuelta de hoja, 17, 35, 123, 132
vueltas con España, A, 16

Cela, Jorge, 3
Cela, mi padre (Conde), 5–6
Cela, Ricardo, 84
"Cela a las puertas del deleite obsceno" (Masoliver Ródenas), 170n. 8
"Cela and Spanish Marginal Culture" (Foster), 171n. 8
"Cela en busca de la novella perdida" (Conte), 166n. 4
Cela en Mallorca (Ferret and González), 161n. 7
"Cela y el Nuevo debate en torno a la modernidad" (Navajas), 166n. 3
Cela y Fernández, Camilo, 2
Celestina, La (Cela), 16
censorship, ix–x
Cervantes, Miguel de, 142
Cervantes Prize, x–xi, 18
Charlebois, Lucile, 161n. 7; and *asesinato del perdedor, El,* 128, 134; and childhood, 2, 3; and *Cristo versus Arizona,* 113, 119; and *cruz de San Andrés, La,* 141, 143; and *Mazurca para dos muertos,* 167n. 2; and *Oficio de tinieblas, 5,* 77, 81, 82, 84, 167n. 9; and postwar years, 10; and *San Camilo, 1936,* 63, 164n. 3; and war years, 8, 161–62n. 9
Chicharro, 31
childhood, 1–3, 22–27
Cinco glosas a otras tantas verdades de la silueta que un hombre trazó a sí mismo (Cela), 16
ciudadano Iscariote Reclús, El (Cela), 14
"Civilización, barbarie y Eros en *Cristo versus Arizona*" (Miller), 169

civil war. *See* Spanish Civil War
CJC y la medicina (Tejerino), 161n. 7
clan structure, *Mazurca para dos muertos,* 97–99
classifications, of, *Oficio de tinieblas, 5,* 74–75
colmena, La (Cela), 42–44; and *asesinato del perdedor, El,* 129, 130, 139; and *Catira, La,* 46; composition of, 11, 18, 31; and *costumbrismo,* 41; and *Cristo versus Arizona,* 109, 112, 117, 118, 120; and *cruz de San Andrés, La,* 141; English translation, 12; and experimentation, 154; and *Mazurca para dos muertos,* 86, 89, 93, 96, 98; and *Oficio de tinieblas, 5,* 71; and *San Camilo, 1936,* 53, 56, 57, 58, 61, 64, 67; and *Tobogán de hambrientos,* 50; and Vanguard years, 5; and *viejos amigos, Los,* 13; and war, 7, 26, 30
Colombine, 78
Como se escribe una novela (Unamuno), 66
compañías convenientes, Las (Cela), 14
Conde, Cela, 31–34, 161n. 7; and adulthood, young, 5–6; and Alfaguara, 15; and childhood years, 3; and *Memorias, entendimientos y voluntades,* 21, 22, 26–27; and second period, 17; and success, 13, 15
Conte, Rafael, 73, 74, 75, 135, 151, 166n. 4
Cornwell, Diane Wilder, 65
Costa, Joaquín, 54
costumbrismo, 33, 40–41, 48
"criminal justice," 123–25
Cristo versus Arizona (Cela), 104–5, 169n. 1; and *asesinato del perdedor, El,* 123, 124, 127, 128, 129, 130, 132, 137, 138; and *Catira, La,* 46; and *colmena, La,* 42, 43, 44; and *cruz de San Andrés, La,* 141, 143, 144–45, 147, 149, 150, 151, 152; and experimentation, 156; and *Mazurca para dos muertos,* 86, 98, 102; narrative devices and antecedents, 109–14, 169n. 16; and *Oficio de tinieblas, 5,* 72, 77, 78, 81; and other works, 116–19; picaresque elements, 41; plot, absence of, 170n. 8; "reality" and fiction, 119–20; and *San Camilo, 1936,* 57, 59, 66; and second period, 17; spatiotemporal parameters, 105–7; subtexts and authorial attitude, 121–22; title, 163n. 6; and *Tobogán de hambrientos,* 48, 50;

truth, memory, and unreliable narrator, 107–8; Wendell's life, 114–16
cruz de San Andrés, La (Cela), 1, 140–41, 171nn. 3, 4; antecedents for structure and form, 141–44; and *asesinato del perdedor, El,* 123, 128, 132, 135; characters and events, 149–51; chronicle and history, 151–53; and *colmena, La,* 43; and *Cristo versus Arizona,* 120; and experimentation, 156–57; and Galicia, 161n. 2; and *Mazurca para dos muertos,* 87, 100, 103; and *Mrs. Caldwell habla con su hijo,* 45; narrator, 144–49; narratorial fallibility, 169n. 16; and *Oficio de tinieblas, 5,* 72, 77, 82; picaresque elements, 41; and *San Camilo, 1936,* 67; and second period, 18; setting, 158; and *Tobogán de hambrientos,* 48
Cucaña, La (Cela), 19, 26
Cuentos para leer después del baño (Cela), 17
cuestión postmoderna, La: Informe sobre el saber (Lyotard), 172n. 8
cultural context, *San Camilo, 1936,* 58–64

Dalí, Salvador, 3
Decameron (Boccaccio), 47
"De cuando Camilo José Cela visitó Tucsón, Arizona, entre el 12 y 25 de febrero de 1987" (Méndez), 170n. 13
Delibes, Miguel, 111, 155
Del Miño al Bidasoa (Cela), 11, 87
Destino (magazine), 83
Dialogic Imagination, The: Four Essays (Bakhtin), 172n. 7
Díaz, Janet, 162n. 6
Diccionario secreto (Cela), 15, 16, 131, 132
Dickens, Charles, 25
Dinneen, Nancy L., 90, 97, 101
Domingo, José, 52, 74
Doña Bárbara (Gallegos), 45
"Don Anselmo" (Cela), 10
Don Quixote (Cervantes), 142
Dos Passos, John, 5, 42, 55
Dostoyevsky, Fyodor, 25

Earp, Wyatt, 105
Eliot, T. S., 141
"Elogio de la fábula" (Cela), 36, 159
Enciclopedia del erotismo (Cela), 17, 132
Eoff, Sherman, 41
Epoca, La (newspaper), 24

Ernst, Max, 83
Esas nubes que pasan (Cela), 10
esperpentos, 38
"Euphemism, Euphuism, Euchologue: Cela
   and the Poetics of Polite Obscenity"
   (Pérez), 170n. 6
exoticism, geographic, 45–46
Extramundi, El (literary quarterly), 18, 166n. 4

familia del héroe, La (Cela), 14
familia de Pascual Duarte, La (Cela), 37–39;
   and *asesinato del perdedor, El,* 126, 127,
   128, 138; and *colmena, La,* 43; and *Cristo
   versus Arizona,* 104, 107, 110, 112; and
   experimentation, 154; picaresque ele-
   ments, 40, 41, 42; postwar years, 9, 10;
   and *San Camilo, 1936,* 60; and second
   period, 15; success of, 15; and *Tobogán de
   hambrientos,* 50; and war, 7, 8, 19, 30, 31
family, 1–3
Fantasía (magazine), 31
Farmacia Nueva (periodical), 9
Faulkner, William, 5, 55
Fernández, Juan Jacobo, 2, 20
Ferres, Antonio, 11
Ferret, Gabriel, 161n. 7
Fokkema, Douwe, 172n. 11
Fontán, 34
Forster, E. M., 75
Foster, David William, 41, 131, 171n. 8
Fowler, Roger, 21
Fragmentos de apocalipsis (Torrente Ballester),
   146, 172n. 12
"From the Prehistory of Novelistic Dis-
   course" (Bakhtin), 172n. 7
Franco, Francisco, 7, 8, 19, 27, 51, 55, 57,
   79, 93, 152
Fuentes, Carlos, 55
fugal structure, *Mazurca para dos muertos,*
   99–103

Galdós, Pérez, 24
Galiano, Antonio Alcalá, 20
Galicia, 1, 2, 7, 8, 9, 17, 28, 32; and Celtic
   mythology, 169n. 14; and *cruz de San
   Andrés, La,* 1, 141, 143, 148, 161n. 2;
   and *Madera de boj,* 161n. 2; and *Mazurca
   para dos muertos,* 86, 87–89, 92–94, 96,
   99, 100, 101, 161n. 2, 168nn. 5, 6
Gallegos, Rómulo, 45

gallego y su cuadrilla y otros carpetovetónicos, El
   (Cela), 11, 87
Galván, Enrique Tierno, 25
Ganivet, Angel, 54, 159
García de la Concha, Víctor, 31
García Lorca, Federico, 4, 35, 168n. 7,
   170n. 5; and *asesinato del perdedor, El,*
   130; and *Cristo versus Arizona,* 109; and
   Oficio de tinieblas, 5, 83; and *San Camilo,
   1936,* 51
García Márquez, Gabriel, 100
García Morente, Manuel, 4, 61
Garito de hospicianos (Cela), 14
Gavilla de fábulas sin amor (Cela), 13–14
Generation of 1898, 24, 159
Genette, Gerard, 148
geographic exoticism, 45–46
Gibson, Ian, 60
Gide, André-Paul-Guillaume, 5
Gimferrer, Pere, 83
Gómez de la Serna, Ramón, 3
Gómez de Liaño, Javier, 132, 134
Gómez Santos, Marino, 161n. 7
Góngora, 168n. 7
González, Fernando, 161n. 7
Goya, Francisco José de, 38
Goytisolo, Juan, 11, 20, 159
Greenblatt, Stephen, 66, 166n. 28
Guereña, Jacinto Luis, 161n. 7

Heraclitus, 55
Hernández, Miguel, 4, 27, 79
Herzberger, David, 168n. 10
heteroglossia, 143
Hickey, Leo, 61, 62, 64, 67, 165n. 21
historical context, *San Camilo, 1936,* 58–64
Historia clínica del niño CJC Trulock (Tejerino),
   161n. 7
Historias de España: Los ciegos, los tontos (Cela),
   12, 13
Hita, Archbishop of, 40
Hive, The. See *colmena, La* (Cela)
homo absurdus, 70
huevo del juicio, El (Cela), 17–18
Hurtado de Mendoza, Diego, 10

ideas, in *Oficio de tinieblas, 5,* 75–81
Iglesias Feijoo, Luis, 171n. 2; and *asesinato
   del perdedor, El,* 134, 135; and *cruz de San
   Andrés, La,* 140, 145, 146, 149

Ilie, Paul, 52, 164n. 4
In Cold Blood (Capote), 21
Informaciones de las Artes y las Letras (magazine), 74
insólita y gloriosa hazaña del Cipote de Archidona, La (Cela), 131, 132, 170n. 6
intrahistoria (Unamuno), 53, 54, 66, 155
Izas, rabizas y colipoterras (Cela), 14, 44, 46, 131, 171n. 7

jitanjáfora, 83
John of the Cross, Saint, 172n. 13
Joyce, James, 5, 55, 57, 71, 83
Juan Benet (Cabrera), 165n. 16
Juan Carlos I (Spain), x, 16
Judíos, moros y cristanos (Cela), 12

Labanyi, Jo, 52, 59, 62
"lagarto del miedo, El" (Cela), 28
Laguna, Antonio Iglesias, 64
Landeira, Ricardo, 162n. 6
language, *San Camilo, 1936,* 64–65
Larra, Mariano José de, 40
Lautréamont, 83
Lawrence, D. H., 105
Lebozán, Robin, 90
Leibniz, Gottfried, 77, 167n. 9
Lejeune, Philip, 20, 84
Lenny dialogues (Cela), 16
León, Fray Luis de, 49
Lera, Angel María de, 79
Lettres persanes (Montesquieu), 41
Libro de buen amor (Archbishop of Hita), 40
"libro de la semana, El: *La Catira*" (Castellet), 169n. 7
literary contexts, *San Camilo, 1936,* 53–58
Literary History, Modernism, and Post-Modernism (Fokkema), 172n. 11
López-Salinas, Armando, 11
Lukacs, György, 67
Lyotard, Jean François, 144, 172n. 8

Machado, Antonio, 54, 77
Machicao, Porfirio Díaz, 161n. 7
Madera de boj, xi; and *asesinato del perdedor, El* (Cela), 123, 138; and *cruz de San Andrés, La,* 143; Galicia, 161n. 2; and *Mazurca para dos muertos,* 87; and second period, 17, 18

Mairena, Juan de, 77
Malaparte, Curzio, 11
Mancha en el corazón y en los ojos, La (Cela), 16
Manhattan Transfer (Dos Passos), 42, 55
"Marcelo Brito" (Cela), 10
Marías, Julián, 4, 30, 61
María Sabina (Cela), 15, 16, 34, 48
Maritain, Jacques, 5
Martín, Abel, 77
Martín, Santos, Luis, 69
Martínez Ruiz, José. *See* Azorín
Masoliver Ródenas, Juan Antonio: and *Cristo versus Arizona,* 112, 170n. 8; and *Mazurca para dos muertos,* 87–88, 89, 98, 167n. 4
Matute, Ana María, 79
Mauriac, François, 5
Mazurca para dos muertos (Cela), 1, 86–87, 168n. 12; and *asesinato del perdedor, El,* 123, 126, 127, 129, 132, 136, 137, 138, 139; clan structure and related subplots, 97–99, 167n. 4; and *colmena, La,* 43, 44; and *Cristo versus Arizona,* 108, 110–11, 113, 114, 118; and *cruz de San Andrés, La,* 140, 141, 142, 143, 144, 152; and earlier works, 89–92; and experimentation, 155–56; Galicia, 87–89, 92–94, 161n. 2, 167n. 2, 168n. 5; narrative elements, 94–97; and *Oficio de tinieblas,* 72, 78, 79, 84; picaresque elements, 41, 42; poetic structure and fugal structure, 99–103; and *San Camilo, 1936,* 53, 56, 57, 61, 68; and second period, 17; and *Tobogán de hambrientos,* 48, 50; and war, 7, 8, 28
"*Mazurca para dos muertos* Seen through Its Characters" (Masoliver Ródenas), 167n. 4
McHale, Brian, 148–49, 172n. 11
McPheeters, D. W., ix, 161n. 7; and adulthood, young, 4; and childhood, 2, 3; and *familia de Pascual Duarte, La,* 38; and *Oficio de tinieblas, 5,* 71; and postwar years, 9, 10, 11; and success, 12, 13, 14; and *Tobogán de hambrientos,* 47, 48; and war years, 7
Medina (weekly), 10
Medio siglo entre escritores (Yagues), 172n. 13
memoirs, 20–21

Memorias, entendimientos y voluntades (Cela), 19, 21–22; adulthood, young, 4, 6; dedication, 168n. 7; family and youth, 2–3, 22–27; and history, 157; and *Mazurca para dos muertos,* 93–94, 97; narrative fallibility, 169n. 16; postwar years, 9, 10; and *San Camilo, 1936,* 52, 58; second period, 17, 18; war years, 7–9, 27–31

memory, *Cristo versus Arizona,* 107–8

"Memory of La Coruña" (Cela), 28, 94

Méndez, Miguel, 119, 170n. 13

Mendogo Mensongui, Dieudonné, 168

Menéndez Pidal, Ramón, 4, 12

mensajero del Corazón de Jesús, El (periodical), 9

Mesa revuelta (Cela), 10

metalepsis, 148

Miller, Stephen, 56, 108, 113, 116, 169n. 6

Miró, Joan, 12

modification, La, 55

"moneda al aire, La" (Cela), 28

Montes, Gregorio, 61

Montesinos, José, 4

Montesquieu, 41

Mrs. Caldwell habla con su hijo (Cela), 44–45; and *asesinato del perdedor, El,* 128; and *Catira, La,* 46; and *colmena, La,* 43; and *Cristo versus Arizona,* 110, 116; and *cruz de San Andrés, La,* 142; and experimentation, 13, 154; and *Mazurca para dos muertos,* 94; memories, 169n. 2; and *Obra Completa,* 172n. 6; and *Oficio de tinieblas, 5,* 71; postwar years, 11–12; and *San Camilo, 1936,* 56–57, 58; and second period, 16, 18; and surrealism, 5; and *Tobogán de hambrientos,* 50

muerte de Artemio Cruz, La, 55

Muñoz, Bertrand de, 154

Muñoz de la Peña, Arsenio, 161n. 7

Naked Lunch (Burroughs), 75

Napoleon Bonaparte, 20

narration: *Cristo versus Arizona,* 109–14; *Mazurca para dos muertos,* 94–97; *Oficio de tinieblas, 5,* 71

narrator: *asesinato del perdedor, El,* 134–39; *Cristo versus Arizona,* 107–8; *cruz de San Andrés, La,* 144–49

National Prize for Literature, x, 17, 87

Navajas, Gonzalo, 72, 85, 166n. 3

neo-*costumbrismo,* 41, 42, 48, 71

Neruda, Pablo, 9

New Historicism, 20, 66–68, 107–8, 169n. 5

New Narrative, 57–58, 69–71

New Novel, x, 74, 140

Niebla (Unamuno), 147

Nieva, Francisco, 31

Nobel Prize for literature, x, 17, 36, 42, 139

noche en que mataron a Calvo Sotelo, La (Gibson), 60

"Nota a la segunda edición" (Cela), 171n. 5

Novela española actual (Zamora Vicente), 167n. 14

"Novelist as Poet, The: A Key to the Literary Evolution of Camilo José Cela" (Díaz and Landeira), 162n. 6

Novel of the Spanish Civil War (1936–1975), The (Thomas), 162n. 1

Nuevas andanzas y desventuras de Lazarillo de Tormes (Cela), 10, 41

Nuevas escenas matritenses (Cela), 14, 43, 46

Nuevos ensayos sobre CJC y la medicina (Tejerino), 161n. 7

objective biography, 21

Obras completas (Cela), 11, 171n. 5, 172n. 6

Oficio de tinieblas, 5 (Cela), 166nn. 1–4; and antinovel, 71–73; and *asesinato del perdedor, El,* 128, 130, 132, 136; autobiographical substrata, 84–85; classifications of, 74–75; and *Cristo versus Arizona,* 110, 120; and *cruz de San Andrés, La,* 142, 143, 150; and experimentation, 154, 155; ideas in, 75–81; and Leibniz, Gottfried Wilhelm, 167n. 9; and *Mazurca para dos muertos,* 86, 94, 95, 102, 103; and *Mrs. Caldwell habla con su hijo,* 45; and New Narrative, 69–71; and *San Camilo, 1936,* 54, 56, 59, 64; and second period, 16; surrealist aspects, 5, 81–83; and *Tobogán de hambrientos,* 48, 50; and Villanueva, Darío, 162n. 8; and Wasserman, Carol, 167n. 8

OK Corral, 105, 106

Olney, Richard, 20

Once cuentos de fútbol (Cela), 14, 46

Ortega y Gasset, José, 4, 20, 25, 54, 159

Ory, Carlos Edmundo de, 31
"Our Glorious National Crusade," 55. *See also* Spanish Civil War

Pabellón de reposo (Cela), 39 – 40; and *Cristo versus Arizona*, 111; and *cruz de San Andrés, La*, 142; and experimentation, 154; genesis of, 3, 25; and *Mazurca para dos muertos*, 94; postwar years, 10; and *San Camilo, 1936*, 56, 58
Páginas de geografía errabunda (Cela), 14
País, El (newspaper), 42, 74
Pampín, Papiano Grillo, 93
Papaeles de Son Armadans (literary monthly), 12, 14
Para leer a Camilo José Cela (Vila), 169n. 1
pata de palo, A la (Cela), 14
Paz en la Guerra (Unamuno), 30, 54
Pérez, Genaro, 56, 62
Pérez, Janet, 170n. 6
Perricone, Catherine R., 165n. 18
"Photographs of Countess {Emilia} Pardo Bazán" (Cela), 9 –10
picaresque, 40 – 42
Picaresque Narrative, Picaresque Fictions: A Theory and Research Guide (Wick), 42
Picasso, Pablo, 12, 13, 14, 84
Pierrot, 78
Pisando la dudosa luz del día (Cela), 4 – 5; composition of, 165n. 18; dedication, 168n. 7; and *Mazurca para dos muertos*, 90; and *Mrs. Caldwell habla con su hijo*, 45; and *San Camilo, 1936*, 58; and war, 7, 27
Pius XI (pope), 2, 98
Pi y Margall, Francisco, 61
Plaja, Serrano, 27
Planeta Prize, 18, 140
Platas Tasende, Ana María, 128, 134, 135
poetic structure, *Mazurca para dos muertos*, 99 –103
"Politics of Obscenity in *San Camilo, 1936*" (Ilie), 164n. 4
Polt, John H. R., 51, 66, 67
Portrait of the Artist as a Young Man (Joyce), 5
Postista poets, 31
Post-modern Fiction (McHale), 172n. 11
Power of Forms in the English Renaissance, The (Greenblatt), 166n. 28

"premio Planeta, El" (Cela), 171n. 1
Press Law, ix–x, 52
Primer viaje andaluz (Cela), 13
Prince of Asturias Literary Prize, x, 17
Prjevalinsky, Olga, 164n. 7
Project for a Revolution in New York (Robbe-Grillet), 75
Proust, Marcel, 5
Pueblo (newspaper), 11

Quevedo, Francisco Gómez de, 38, 42
"*Quixote, El*," *como juego* (Torrente Ballester), 172

racial diversity, 109, 122
Realidad y experiencia de la novella (Hickey), 165n. 21
Rest Home. See *Pabellón de reposo* (Cela)
Retrato de Camilo José Cela (Guereña), 161n. 7
Rewriting the Past: Fiction and Historiography in Postwar Spain (Herzberger), 168n. 10
rhetoric, *San Camilo, 1936*, 64 – 65
Rivera, Primo de, 66
Robbe-Grillet, Alain, 75
Roberts, Gemma, 67
Roig, Antonio, 17
Rol de cornudos (Cela), 17
rosa, La (Cela), 3, 13, 19, 22, 98
Rosario Conde Picavea, María del ("Charo"), 10
Royal Academy of the Spanish Language, 12–13, 21, 23
Royal Galician Academy, x, 88
rueda de los ocios, La (Cela), 12

Saladrigas, Robert, 72
Salinas, Pedro, 4
San Camilo, 1936 (Cela), 51–52; and Alfaguara, 15; and *asesinato del perdedor, El*, 132, 136, 137, 139; and Charlebois, Lucile, 164n. 3; and childhood years, 22–23, 25; and *colmena, La*, 43, 44; composition of, 33; and *Cristo versus Arizona*, 108, 109, 118; and *cruz de San Andrés, La*, 141, 142, 150, 151–52; dedication, 168n. 7; and experimentation, 157, 158; historical and cultural contexts, 58 – 64, 154–55; language and rhetoric, 64 – 65; literary contexts,

San Camilo (continued)
   53–58; and *Mazurca para dos muertos,*
   86, 89, 90, 91, 92, 94–95, 98, 102,
   103; narratorial fallibility, 169n. 16; and
   national identity, 159; New Historicism,
   66–68; and *Oficio de tinieblas, 5,* 69–71,
   77, 78, 79, 84; picaresque elements, 42;
   and Press Law, ix–x; title, 164n. 9; and
   second period, 16; and surrealism, 5;
   and *Tobogán de hambrientos,* 50; and war,
   6, 7, 19, 26, 28, 29, 154–55
Sánchez Barbudo, Antonio, 27
San Juan de la Cruz (Verdú), 146–47
Sanz Villanueva, Santos, 55, 62
second period, 15–18
servicio de algo, Al (Cela), 16
sí/no dialectic, 54
sistema estético de Camilo José Cela, El: Estruc-
   tura y expresividad (Prjevalinsky), 164n. 7
Sobejano, Gonzalo, 41, 45, 50, 71, 80, 81,
   101–2, 109, 120
social literature, 15–16, 48, 69, 109
sociocultural context, *El asesinato del perdedor,*
   129–32
Sol, El (newspaper), 24
Solana, 12, 38
Soldevila, Ignacio, 41
Solitario y los sueños de Quesada de Rafael
   Zabaleta, El (Cela), 14, 45, 46, 58
Spanish Civil War, 6–9, 19, 24, 154; and
   asesinato del perdedor, El, 137; and *col-*
   mena, La, 43; and *Mazurca para dos muer-*
   tos, 17, 91, 92–94. See also *San Camilo,*
   1936 (Cela)
spatiotemporal parameters, 105–7
Stendhal, 25, 74
Stranger, The (Camus), 38
structuring devices, *El asesinato del perdedor,*
   134–39
subplots, *Mazurca para dos muertos,* 97–99
subtexts, *Cristo versus Arizona,* 121–22
Sueños, Los (Quevedo), 42
sueños vanos, los ángeles curiosos, Los (Cela), 17
surrealism, 4–5, 13, 31, 35, 81–83

tacatá oxidado, El (Cela), 16
Tejerino, José María R., 161n. 7
Tell, William, 124
Thomas, Gareth, 162n. 1
378-A, Madera de hérve, 155

Tiempo de silencio (Martín Santos), 69
Títeres de Cachiporra, Los (García Lorca),
   170n. 5
Tobogán de hambrientos (Cela), ix, 47–50; and
   Catira, La, 46; and *costumbrismo,* 33; and
   Cristo versus Arizona, 110; and experi-
   mentation, 13; and *Mazurca para dos*
   muertos, 94, 96; and *Mrs. Caldwell habla*
   con su hijo, 45; and *Oficio de tinieblas, 5,*
   69, 71, 72; picaresque elements, 41; and
   San Camilo, 1936, 58; and second
   period, 16; and war, 7
Tolstoy, Leo, 154
Toreo de salon (Cela), 14
Torre, Guillermo de, 49
"Torremejía" (Cela), 30
Torrente Ballester, Gonzalo, 74, 87, 117,
   146, 172nn. 9, 12
Torres Yagues, F., 172n. 13
Tragicomedia de Don Perlimplín con Belisa en su
   jardín (García Lorca), 170n. 5
tremendista, 162n. 4
triunfalismo, 29
Trives, Eduardo, 161n. 7
Trulock, John, 22
truth, *Cristo versus Arizona,* 107–8
Tzara, Tristan, 26

Ulysses (Joyce), 5, 55
Umbral, Francisco, 23
Unamuno, Miguel de, 24, 30, 34, 35, 37,
   50, 53, 54, 64, 147, 159
Una semana con CJC (Trives), 161n. 7
Understanding Camilo José Cela (Charlebois),
   164n. 3
unreliable narrator: *asesinato del perdedor, El,*
   134–39; *Cristo versus Arizona,* 107–8
unwriting, *El asesinato del perdedor,* 134–39
usurpadores, Los (Ayala), 156

Valéry, Paul, 5
Valle-Inclán, Ramón del, 3, 24, 25, 38, 42,
   81, 87, 88, 159
Vandencammen, Edmundo, 65
Vanguardism, 5, 26, 35, 74, 83
Vargas, "Toisha," 7
vases communicants, Les (Bretón), 82
vasos comunicantes, Los (Cela), 17, 82
Verdú, Matilde, 146
Viaje a la Alcarria (Cela), 10–11

Viaje al Pirineo de Lérida (Cela), 14
Viaje a USA (Cela), 14
viajes de CJC por Extremadura (Muñoz de la
  Peña), 161n. 7
vida de Lazarillo de Tormes, La (Hurtado de
  Mendoza), 10, 40
Vida del Buscón (Quevedo), 38
viejos amigos, Los (Cela), 13, 43
Villanueva, Darío, 14, 31–32, 162n. 8
*Vísperas, festividad y octava de San Camilo del
  año 1936 en Madrid.* See *San Camilo,
  1936* (Cela)
Volverás a Región (Benet), 69
Vuelta de hoja (Cela), 17, 35, 123, 132

vueltas con España, A (Cela), 16

war. See Spanish Civil War
War and Peace (Tolstoy), 154
Wasserman, Carol, 77, 167n. 8
Wick, Ulrich, 42

youth, 1–3, 22–27

Zambrano, María, 4, 9, 81
Zamora Vicente, Alonso, 5, 26, 48, 49, 61,
  83, 167n. 14
Zayas, María de, 47
Zubiri, Xavier, 4

The Author

Janet Pérez earned the M.A. and Ph.D. in romance languages from Duke University and has taught at Duke, Trinity College (Catholic University of America), Queens College (City University of New York), the University of North Carolina at Chapel Hill, and Texas Tech University, where she is Paul Whitfield Horn Professor of Spanish and associate dean of the Graduate School. She has published more than 200 scholarly articles and chapters in books and has presented some 150 papers at scholarly meetings, primarily treating twentieth-century Spanish novels, poetry, theater, and essays. Books in print include *The Major Themes of Existentialism in the Works of Ortega y Gasset* and, in the Twayne World Authors Series, *Ana María Matute, Miguel Delibes, Gonzalo Torrente Ballester, Contemporary Women Writers of Spain,* and *Modern and Contemporary Spanish Women Poets* (the latter also published on CD-ROM). She has written or edited several other scholarly and reference works and has in press *The Feminist Encyclopedia of Spanish Literature* (coedited with Maureen Ihrie). Pérez is currently preparing *Post-Franco Women Poets.*